THINK
Before You Leap

Strategic Leadership in a World of Chaos

Douglas M. Sweeny

ISBN: 1-4392-2590-7
ISBN-13: 9781439225905
LCCN: 2009900776

Visit www.booksurge.com to order additional copies.

CONTENTS

PROLOGUE

*The best CEOs I know are teachers, and at the core
of what they teach is strategy.*
– Michael Porter

*Perception is strong and sight weak. In strategy it is important
to see distant things as if they were close and to take
a distanced view of close things.*
– Miyamoto Musashi

This book is intended for leaders or those aspiring to be leaders at every level of an organization. It provides a framework and
scores of practical ideas to help you create winning strategies and
successful businesses. And it does so against a global economic
backdrop that can be described only as utter chaos: complex, unpredictable, and extremely tumultuous. During thirty-five years,
I was fortunate to be deeply engaged in some of the most critical and strategic decisions IBM had ever faced—launching the e-
Business revolution, the epic shift into services, and initiating new
ventures like Life Sciences and Pervasive Computing, businesses
that are now producing over $65 billion in new annual revenues
for IBM. In the process, I interacted with many of the world's best-
known strategic thinkers, transformational business leaders, and
entrepreneurs pioneering their way into the new digital network
economy. The books these world-class strategists authored are the
business classics of the past two decades and the most practical in
the field of business strategy. Of course, no one has the complete

answer. Each of these experts looks at the complex facets of strategy through the prism of his or her area of expertise, reflecting a specific theory of business. They leave it to the enterprise to be the point of interpretation, integration, and application. The challenge is that there are literally thousands of strategic tools, models, and theories advanced by academics and strategy consultants. In fact, if you Google "business strategy," fifty million references are returned. It's up to the individual enterprise and its leaders to sort through them, assess their value, and apply them to develop winning strategies.

This book presents a blueprint of the best, proven strategy concepts and new emerging techniques assembled into an integrated strategy management system that my colleagues and I created during the transition to the new millennium. It's in the blending of these creative and complementary ideas that even more value is created and we realize the benefits of a "brilliant collection of minds." After weaving a dozen different concepts together into a dynamic framework, we successfully applied it inside IBM and elsewhere. For IBM, the primary delivery vehicle was the Strategic Leadership Forum, which we conducted nearly two dozen times at the Harvard Business School over a four-year period for the senior teams of 150 businesses and 2,500 executives. It is this integrating framework, remarkably understandable and durable, that serves as the underlying structure of this book. It views strategy as a closed-looped process, structured enough to reduce complexity and avoid confusion, but pliable enough to embrace continuous creativity and change. It facilitates the creation of agile, customer-focused, and technology-enabled strategies.

That model and this book reinforce three fundamental themes: *adaptability*, *synergy*, and *reality*, which we will explore in depth in the pages that follow. Unlike the static strategy approaches of the past, a dynamic strategy process is now required to address the ever-changing market. As business leaders, we need to stretch our thinking to longer-term opportunities while successfully managing the current business. That creates a natural tension of striving to be boldly innovative and revolutionary, while maintaining the stability and discipline of an incumbent market player. We need to make our organizations *ambidextrous*, driving both evolutionary and revolutionary change at the same time, competing today and tomorrow. No simple task.

The strategy forums we conducted reconfirmed for me the need for future business leaders to develop a much better grasp of *strategic leadership* and for enterprises to enhance their *strategic competence*. A firm's strategy charts the course for the future, focuses the collective effort, defines and leverages the uniqueness of an organization, and provides motivational pull. As leaders, we must answer several questions: How can we better understand the big picture and discern the most critical shifts in the marketplace? How can we ensure that we are responsive to customer needs and wants at every point in the firm? How can we lead by inspiring and crafting uniquely competitive strategies? How can we leverage technology, information, and the Internet to create a digitally-enhanced strategy? How can we boldly change the performance vectors our companies are on and transform to become more innovative and successful? How can we enlist and empower every employee in this quest? And finally, how do we pull all the pieces together—market insights, innovation, skills, culture, and structure—to create a winning, executable strategy and an enduring enterprise?

When I finally was able to see how to integrate the various pieces, I was amazed at how many of the ideas reinforced others and how easily the concepts applied across the spectrum of businesses inside our firm, from component technology through high-level consulting services. After my IBM career, I helped create a boutique consulting firm and developed strategies for nonprofit foundations, some smaller businesses, a multiline Wall Street firm, a multibillion-dollar automation company, and a large agency of the federal government. Again, I saw how these fundamental techniques could be transferred to other organizations across the spectrum of company size, type, industry, and complexity.

We are in a unique moment in economic history, one that is more globally connected, dynamic, unpredictable, and competitive than we have ever seen before. In an era of increasing distributed leadership and empowerment, overall company strategy is no longer just the purview of the CEO. In the new economy, it's a topic every business leader and every employee must understand, embrace, and advance. Those who genuinely understand and can apply *strategic leadership*—the integrating of strategy and execution to deliver market results—will play a critical and valuable role in getting their companies to outperform their peers. And that's my primary reason for writing this book: to help future business leaders and organizations achieve more enduring success by increasing their strategic competence. In the process, I strive to de-complicate, teach, and promote the subject of business strategy.

So, whether you're a current or future business leader, an owner of a small business, a corporate business strategist, the director of a nonprofit, a public sector executive, an MBA student, or a valued employee in the field of business, I sincerely hope and believe this book will propel you and your organization to a higher level of strategic innovation and performance.

Douglas Sweeny

SECTION I:

The Urgent Need for Strategic Leadership

CHAPTER 1:

The New Economy: A World of Chaos

*We stand on the threshold of a new age – the age of revolution,
an age of upheaval, of tumult, of fortunes made and unmade
at head-snapping speed. In the twenty-first century, change
is discontinuous, abrupt, seditious. And in this new age,
a company that is evolving slowly is already
on its way to extinction.*
– Gary Hamel

*We must take change by the hand or,
rest assuredly, it will take us by the throat.*
– Winston Churchill

This book's focus is on how enterprises and leaders can develop strategic competence. Although the focus is on a well-defined process of strategic leadership, the continuing and accelerating global economic turmoil is a context that we cannot ignore. Global economic shocks are now commonplace. Markets are emerging and disappearing overnight. Competition is smarter, faster, and coming from any industry, any part of the globe. New digital e-businesses like Google and Amazon are outperforming industrial age leaders like GM and Chrysler. And in the midst of this turbulence, an unprecedented global financial meltdown has destabilized the old order. The credit markets, the growth engine that powers the American and global economy, have unraveled, leading to the collapse of major banks such as Washington Mutual and Lehman Brothers. Iconic corporations such as Merrill Lynch and Bear Stearns have failed, as others teeter at the brink. And since we are all interconnected and interdependent, our world systems are functioning as a single, integrated living creature. The uncertainty and disruptive change of today's chaotic world is what makes *dynamic strategy* an absolute necessity. So, before beginning the discussion of strategic capability, we need to understand the context of this new economy and the concept of chaos.

A critical element of strategy is to see the big picture, focusing on the entire system holistically, not the individual elements. *Chaos theory* helps us understand complex and dynamic processes like the global economy. When viewing a waterfall, each single drop of water behaves chaotically, but by stepping back and looking more broadly, we see that the overall flow of water can demonstrate a clear pattern. Unfortunately, the entire world is moving constantly toward more chaos and disarray, or what scientists call *entropy*. Of course, this isn't new news. It's the second law of thermodynamics, a nineteenth-century concept. All processes and objects are moving in the direction of rising entropy and increasing chaos.

Chaos (Χάος) or Khaos in Greek mythology was the original state of existence, the dark void of space, from which the first gods appeared. Comprised of a mixture of the four elements of earth, air, water, and fire, Chaos meant "primal emptiness, a gaping void, or chasm." The ancient Greeks saw chaos as a bottomless gulf where anything fell endlessly and in every direction, a place without any possible orientation. More modernly, chaos *has come to mean "complete disorder" or "unpredictability."*

Mathematicians define chaos as "the irregular, unpredictable behavior of deterministic, non-linear dynamical systems." What seems contradictory is that chaotic systems look random but some aren't. They're deterministic systems, predictable if we have enough information and are governed by physical laws. But, they remain very difficult to predict accurately. Global climate change and weather forecasting are classic examples.

In business, chaos theory, and the related complexity theory and complex adaptive systems, are projected to be the new science of organizations someday. Even though we have massive amounts of available information, it is still too difficult to formulate a viable survival strategy for enterprises based on deterministic modeling and math. That's the future promise of artificial intelligence. In the interim, the focus will remain on enabling organizations to adapt quickly to the increasing chaos in the environment.

With chaos as the backdrop, one of the best appraisals of our changing world appears in *Global Trends 2025: A Transformed World*, published in November 2008 by the National Intelligence Council (NIC). It concludes, "The International system will be almost unrecognizable by 2025 owing to the rise of emerging powers, a globalizing economy, an historic transfer of wealth from West to East and the growing influence of non-state actors." These actors include large businesses, religious groups, criminal networks, high-seas pirates, and major Ponzi schemers like Madoff and Stanford. Added to the list of uncertainties and disruptive forces are growing energy, food, and water concerns; climate change; and the aging population of the developed world, all limiting future growth and prosperity. The NIC sees the next twenty years as fraught with risk with strategic rivalries revolving around trade, investment, and technology innovation. Formulating a sound business strategy against that backdrop is a daunting task.

The World's CEOs See Accelerating Change

During mid-2008 before the financial collapse, IBM published the results of its third biennial CEO study, the largest ever conducted using face-to-face interviews. The survey sampled 1,130 global CEOs whose firms collectively produced over $2.2 trillion in revenue. In the previous survey, in 2006, the IBM consulting team was surprised to learn that over two-thirds of the surveyed CEOs said their organizations were facing substantial change over the next three years. In 2008, their perceptions of change went even higher with over 80 percent of the top executives seeing their organizations facing substantial change, even before the global financial crisis. The three forces causing major change included external market factors, people skills, and technological advances.

The rising challenge is that these same CEOs rated their ability to manage that change at 22 percent lower than their expected need for it, leaving a *change gap* that's three times what it was two years ago. As Jack Welch once remarked, "When the rate of change in the marketplace exceeds the rate of change in the orga-

> *Success in business used to be determined by scale, scope, and market dominance. But, in this new economy, value intrinsically arises from new areas: modularity, integrated solutions, speed, adaptability, and innovation.*

nization, the end is in sight." There's no question that a highly dynamic environment demands an adaptive strategy for survival and a keen understanding of the sources of value. Success in business used to be determined by scale, scope, and market dominance. But, in this new economy, value intrinsically arises from new areas. Value now lies in modularity, having well-defined modules of processes, capabilities, or offerings that we can connect together.

Value lies in integrating and orchestrating various components into fully integrated multifirm solutions through value nets of business partners working together. Value lies in speed and rapid adaptability, reconfiguring core competencies and networks of partners to respond to new market opportunities or new threats. And most important, value lies in innovation.

The New Economy

It's impossible to pinpoint when the new economy arrived. Like successive waves crashing on the shore, who can tell precisely when high tide arrives? The new economy is even less predictable than the tides. It's a tectonic transformation of our world's basic systems, far more disruptive than different companies and industries just changing places in their Fortune rankings. It's a new economic order with multiple causes, some conflicting, some reinforcing, presenting distinct opportunities, challenges, and new rules. Those who understand chaos and play by the new rules will succeed; those who don't will surely fail. We are seeing only the beginning of the loss and gain, the anxiety and exhilaration, that companies and individuals are experiencing as we shift to this new world order.

The new economy has at least six distinguishing characteristics: it was enabled at first by services, technology, and information; it is massively interlinked; it is digital; it is global; it is decentralized and empowering; and it is constantly and exponentially changing, an unpredictable chaos. Together these attributes produce a new type of market and society, one based on information, relationships, and democratization, the participation of the entire world's population. Let's look at each of these six factors.

Signs of a New Era Led by Services, Technology, and Information

Reflecting back, it was in the mid-fifties of the previous century that economists first noticed that "white collar" workers were surpassing "blue collars" as a share of the total U.S. workforce. As the industrial age waned, the economy was overtaken by businesses that were more services driven and by work that was more knowledge based, performed by workers with "intellectual capital."

Peter Drucker, the iconic management thinker of the last century, was clairvoyant in seeing the end of the age of continuity, the metamorphosis of the world political order, and the emergence of the employee society. In *Managing in Turbulent Times*, he introduced the notion of converting these threats of destabilizing change into strategic opportunities. However, not everyone saw these economic shifts as turbulence. When the transition first started, some experts were more conservative. Lester Thurow, the MIT economist, termed it the "third industrial wave," following the first two waves of steam-driven and assembly line manufacturing. Other trend spotters simply punted and called it the "post-industrial era." In the 1970s, the "information age" emerged as the new label, as computers and telecom increased in their enabling power and information was perceived to be "the wealth-creating asset of the future." That sounded pretty progressive with intangible "information" as the fuel for a new age, a clean, renewable source of energy! As an aside, we now estimate that four exabytes (four times ten to the nineteenth power) of unique information will be created this year, more than the last five thousand years combined!

While the information age label stuck for at least a decade, some market researchers began calling the new economy the "knowledge age." The rationale was that data, even if digitized, is merely a discrete set of facts, but when relevance and meaning are added, it becomes more valuable as information. Even further, when information is framed and used in context, it becomes applied knowledge, a much more valuable asset.

During the mid-eighties, I became deeply involved in developing a comprehensive "Knowledge Management" strategy for IBM. It included an enterprise framework, tools, a new consulting practice, and the Knowledge Management (KM) Institute as we attempted to seize thought leadership in the new era. Larry Prusak, head of our KM Institute, defined knowledge as "...*a fluid mix of framed experiences, values, contextual information and expert insight that provides a framework for evaluating and incorporating new experiences and information,*" a definition that demonstrates how unwieldy and complex the concept was. Academics, inherently and heavily invested in the field of knowledge, applauded the efforts. Unfortunately, the "knowledge age" just didn't resonate with pragmatic CEOs. It was too vague and abstract, in their view, not the overarching theme or driving force of the new economy.

In 1995, *Newsweek* coined the phrase "new economy" and painted it in glowing terms. They projected a future service-based global economy, a state of permanent growth, with immunity to boom and bust cycles, accelerated productivity, and the obsolescence of industrial age practices, all largely attributed to the delayed benefits of the computer age. Just five years later, as we transitioned from one millennium to another, it seemed like the new economy had finally arrived. Business-

> *Only once or twice before in human history has such a profound transition occurred so rapidly.*

es, governments, and individuals were overwhelmed with seismic change, a radically new and rapidly changing landscape affecting every dimension of life: communications, commerce, entertainment, social relationships, politics, everything. Only once or twice before in human history has such a profound transition occurred so rapidly. In industry after industry, disruptive change became the norm as new asset-less start-ups overtook industry leaders. For the fast-moving challengers, it was an era of promise, for the traditional incumbents, an era of peril. But the spark that ignited the new economy wasn't services. It was the worldwide adoption of the Internet, which some called "the most significant human development since the invention of fire!"

The Network of Networks

Networks have existed in every economy. What's different now is that networks are turbocharged by technology, multiplying range and reach. They've already penetrated our lives so deeply through social directories such as buddy lists, Facebook, and e-mail distributions that the "network" has now become the organizing metaphor for our lives, our businesses, and our economy. Unless we understand the logic of networks, we can't profit from the economic transformation under way.

Bob Metcalfe, the inventor of Ethernet, first observed a network's tendency to explode in value exponentially. He concluded that the value of a network correlates to the square of the number of users connected and that networks need to achieve critical mass to make them worthwhile. From a pure economics perspective, the new networked economy was best described by Brian Arthur of the Santa Fe Institute in the July '96 *Harvard Business Review* in what he termed "increasing return economics." Arthur translated the old Billie Holiday lyrics "Them that's got shall get, them that's not shall lose," into economic terms. The key concept Arthur advanced was that traditional manufacturing industries exhibit diminishing returns as the most successful companies run into limitations and reach a predictable equilibrium of price and market share. By contrast, knowledge-based, networked industries can benefit from scale in which those who get ahead have a tendency to get even further ahead, because of network effects. Winners win big; losers lose big. Value increases when it's shared with others, so once a particular architecture, product, or service has achieved the status of the "de facto standard," it attracts widespread acceptance. Think of the Windows Operating System and the economic power Bill Gates has accrued, or the popularity of eBay, Google, or craigslist. In the mid-nineties, the Internet and seeds of the "network age" took hold as nearly every company created a Web site and networks became robust and reliable enough to support inter-enterprise connections and basic e-commerce. "Network-centric computing" emerged as a new buzzword, with the future promise of ubiquitous, or "pervasive computing," enabled by nanotechnology.

Pervasive Computing

Networks have two fundamental components: nodes and connections. In the broadest sense, the size of the nodes is shrinking while the quantity and quality of the connections are expanding. Recall that it was Moore's Law that predicted that the number of transistors, the building blocks of electronics, on an integrated chip will double every two years. As the chips shrink, a single silicon transistor can be seen only through a microscope, and soon an entire chip will be that size. As the size of chips shrinks to the microscopic, their costs shrink as well. A transistor that cost five dollars in 1950 cost one-tenth of a cent in 1975, and costs less than a nanocent today, one ten-millionth of a cent. Chips are becoming tiny enough and cheap enough to embed into *every object we make* with the promise of the connectivity of everything—people, devices, appliances, cars, clothing, even digestible computers.

One technology in IBM Research converts a person into a "personal area network" using the salinity of the body as an electrical conductor, creating a walking living computer. Eventually, every can or box of food will have a chip in it, as will every light switch, every book, every shirt, and even wallpaper. There are ten trillion objects manufactured in the world each year, and soon all will become legitimate nodes of the global Internet. To enable this fully connected world, a new Internet Protocol (Version 6) expands Internet addressing from the measly 4.2 billion today to an inexhaustible 340 trillion, trillion, trillion addresses!

As exciting as *pervasive computing* is, one could argue that the new age is not about the network or computing, but about what rides on it or through it or what the global network enables. The sea change is about "e-commerce," or even more broadly, "e-business."

The Network Economy and e-Business

The number of Internet users has grown exponentially in three decades from one hundred to one and a half billion people, over 20 percent of the world's population. Heralded as the electronic meeting place and marketplace of the future, the Web is now in its fourth stage of development.

> *Networks are now supplanting the industrial age hierarchies as the dominant organizational form and competitive entity of the new marketplace.*

Networks are now supplanting the industrial age hierarchies as the dominant organizational form and competitive entity of the new marketplace. It began humbly as an experimental network in 1969 funded by the U.S. Department of Defense

Advanced Research Projects Agency (DARPA), to connect university computing centers. In the early 1980s, the research-driven stage began. The National Science Foundation (NSF) established more than three thousand institutional nodes in a new network called NSFnet, funded and managed by IBM, MCI, and the State of Michigan, and it soon attracted over ten thousand users. The third stage began in 1990 as the World Wide Web technologies became available to enable ease of access to any Internet server in the world. In this organization-driven stage, Internet use swelled to ten million users. Now in its fourth stage, the Internet is a commercially driven phenomenon with well over one billion users. And the mobile, dispersed, connected, empowered workforce is ultimately the new democracy.

Figure 1.

Exponential Growth of Internet Users

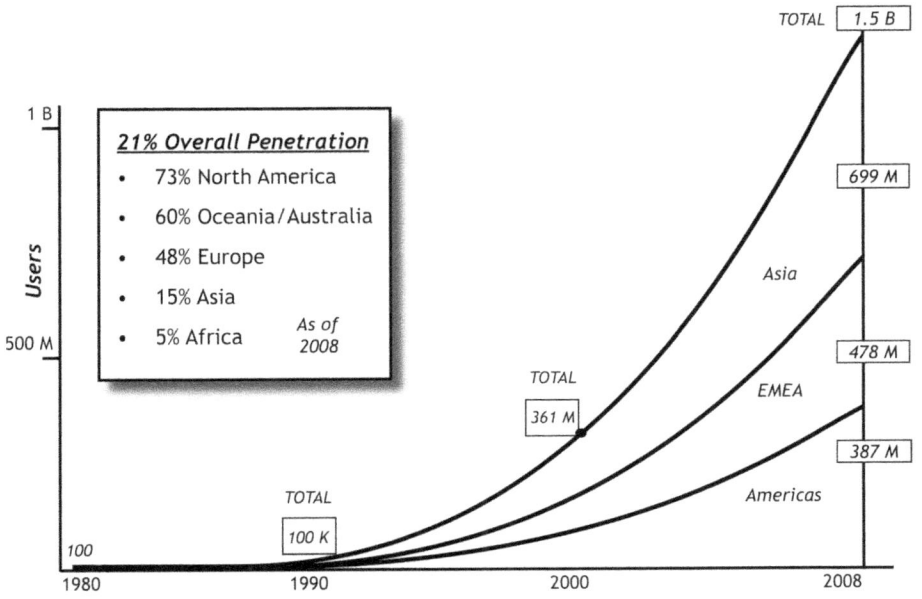

SOURCE: IDC, INTERNET WORLD STATISTICS, IBM

It's the first time in history that information technology is being used as a primary medium for human communications, as a billion people are now connected around the globe. They're e-mailing, texting, instant messaging, YouTubing and Twittering to each other, connected through MySpace, Facebook, Jigsaw, or LinkedIn communities. And beyond just communicating, people are shopping online. Less than a decade ago, consumers expressed concern with ID theft, privacy, and credit card fraud as barriers to shopping online. With additional safeguards and experience, consumer comfort has increased, convenience has triumphed over security concerns, and consumers are driving e-commerce at extraordinary growth rates. In the United States, over $230 billion is now being spent online for travel, books, gifts, and services; that's over $3,500 per online household! E-commerce is now 16 percent of all U.S. retail. In the new economy, business-to-consumer e-commerce has soared to nearly $1 trillion and business-to-business growth exploded to $10 trillion a year!

Of course, many marketing experts believe the best route to market is not online e-commerce alone, but a hybrid model that utilizes a physical store, the Web, and the phone in combination to provide the best quality customer service and flexibility.

Figure 2.
Global e-Business: $12.4 Trillion by 2012

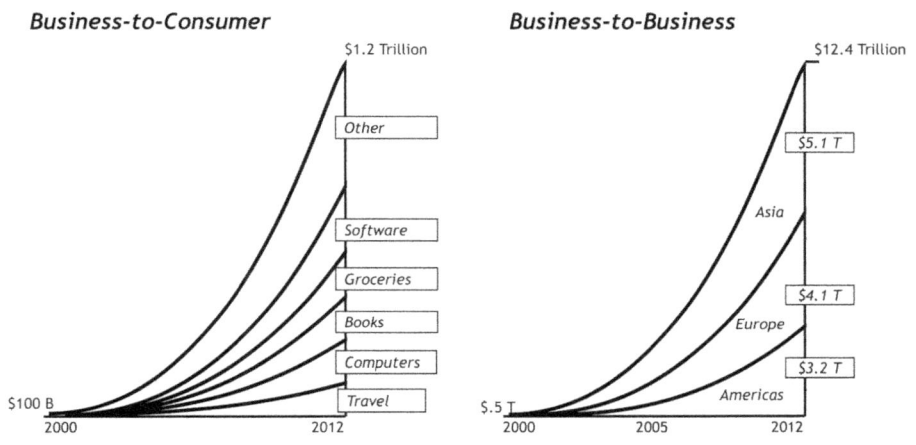

SOURCE: IDC 2008

Being Digital

In the new economy, every form of information becomes digital: letters, numbers, graphs, photos, videos—all can be created, compressed, integrated, and transported via "bits" at the speed of light, at much higher quality than analog, and with the added opportunity for interactivity. For example, those of us who now get our news online, can also watch a short video clip, see a variety of pictures, and respond to an instant poll, in addition to just reading text. In this "digital age," the signal is digital instead of analog; communications can be either synchronous or asynchronous; the end-user devices or information appliances are intelligent; and, most important, the media has the potential to be interactive or two-way. That means the consumer transforms from being a passive observer or listener to an active participant and a creator or editor of content: a *prosumer*.

Two devices that symbolize this new digital media era are Internet Protocol TV (IPTV) and the digital e-book, as evidenced by Amazon's Kindle. The Kindle, launched at the end of '07, is an *electronic-paper* display that provides a sharp, high-resolution screen that looks and reads like real paper. Wireless connectivity enables us to shop the Kindle Store directly from our Kindle where we can buy any of 260,000 books and have them delivered wirelessly in less than a minute. Download and read the first chapters free before we buy. Or, we can download newspapers like the *New York Times, Wall Street Journal,* and *Washington Post,* or top magazines like *TIME, Atlantic Monthly,* and *Forbes* and more than 1,100 blogs. Lighter and thinner than a typical paperback, it weighs only ten ounces and holds over two hundred titles. The latest version, Kindle 2, can even read the book to us, and we get to pick a voice of our choice!

IPTV differs from regular TV in that it has a return path for interactivity. In a typical broadcast TV or satellite network, all the content flows downstream to each customer, and the customer switches the content at the set-top box. A switched IP network works differently. Content remains in the network, and only the content the customer selects is sent into the user's home. That frees up bandwidth, and the customer's choice is less restricted by the size of the "pipe" into the home.

IPTV also allows significant opportunities to make the TV viewing experience more interactive and personalized. An interactive program guide can allow viewers to search for content by title or actor's name, or a picture-in-picture feature can allow them to "channel surf" without leaving the program they're watching. Viewers may be able to look up a player's stats while watching a sports game or control the camera angle. They also may be able to access photos or music from their PC on their television, use a wireless phone to schedule a recording of their favorite show, or adjust parental controls so their child can watch a documentary while they're away from home.

Nicholas Negroponte, founder of the MIT Media Lab, touted the advantages of digital components (bits) over physical ones (atoms) in his classic *Being Digital*. For example, digitized data compression allows for the delivery of huge quantities of information such as digital video at high speeds and low cost by using less channel capacity. Yet digitization is about more than simply reducing costs and increasing speed. It's also about a change in the distribution of intelligence and the transposition of one medium to another so that information "can be consumed differently by different people at different times." And, in a digital world, essentially every physical thing can become virtual and reside in "cyberspace," resulting in a virtual enterprise, virtual store, virtual market, virtual village, virtual school, and, of course, virtual reality. One side effect of the digital revolution is that the technologies and sectors involving computing, communications, consumer electronics, and information content all converge as they become digital and increasingly based on open standards. Another is that global commerce will become increasingly decentralized.

While the new digital age promises much to be optimistic about, it will also provide us with many challenges: intellectual property abuse, invasion of privacy, digital vandalism, software piracy, and competition with the rest of the world for "digital-based" labor, which leads to the next attribute of the new economy.

Globalization

Although we didn't need such a cataclysmic reminder, the global financial crisis of 2008 accentuated the extent to which the world is now fully interconnected. Business and knowledge know no boundaries, and we're witnessing the decline of nation states as regional and global economic unions strengthen. The world has instantly become smaller because of globalization. Thomas Friedman, a Pulitzer Prize winner and one of IBM's strategy advisers, wrote a trilogy of best sellers on the theme. He says the simple definition of globalization is "the interweaving of markets, technology, information systems and telecommunications systems in a way that is shrinking the world from a size medium to a size small, and enabling each of us to reach around the world farther, faster, deeper, and cheaper than ever before." It has its own rules, logic, pressures, and incentives that will affect every country, every company, and every community.

Globalization is driven by technology and is characterized by one overarching feature: integration. In this new system, all our threats and opportunities increasingly flow from whom we're connected to. The central logic of globalization exactly mirrors the logic of the Internet. We're all increasingly connected, but nobody's in charge. One consequence of this global connected world is that the time between a firm achieving the pinnacle of success to the depths of failure can be shortened to a single economic cycle.

Fareed Zakaria, the editor of *Newsweek International*, takes an even longer view of economic history. In his book *The Post-American World*, he explains how we're living through the third great power shift in modern history. The first was the *rise of the Western world* in the fifteenth through the eighteenth centuries that produced the foundations of Western thought and culture, as we know it today. The second shift took place near the end of the nineteenth century, the *rise of the United States*. And once the United States industrialized, it became the most powerful nation in the world, and has remained so for decades. During this "Pax Americana," as he calls it, the global economy has accelerated dramatically, and that expansion is the driver behind the third great power shift, *the rise of the rest*. Along nearly every dimension—industrial, financial, social, cultural—the distribution of power is shifting, moving away from American dominance. In parallel, there's a general diffusion of power from states to empowered groups and individuals, as hierarchy, centralization, and control become things of the past.

For the first time ever, most countries around the world are practicing sensible economics; currencies are floating; and global economic growth, until recently, has been soaring. And it's not just because of China and India's rapid development, nor is it centered there, even though they've added 2.5 billion consumers into the mainstream global economy. The growth is much more broad based with 124 countries growing more than 4 percent in the 2006–07 period, including 30 in Africa alone. The global economy has more than doubled in size over the last fifteen years and is now approaching $54 trillion! Global trade has grown by 133 percent in the same period, aided by the reach and reliability of high-performance networks. The expansion of the global economic pie has been so great, with so many countries participating, that it has become the dominating feature of the current era.

Zakaria's solution for the United States in this period of global power diffusion calls for America to leverage its greatest strength: openness. Like an adaptive enterprise, the United States must pursue an open, collaborative, flexible strategy, responding quickly and effectively to the world's challenges. It must push the boundaries of individual freedom and realize that innovation is not about the ingenuity of central government, or corporate headquarters, but about the vigor of society, the ideas and inventiveness of the people and culture. The parallels with business are astounding.

Dispersion, Empowerment, and Prosumption

As the worlds of business, government, communications, and entertainment become more networked, we see information and power become more dispersed to the end points. This is evidenced by the growth trend toward small and medium-sized enterprises and an overarching dispersion of power to individuals within a business, a *democratization* that parallels the distribution of power among consumers. Armed with the power of the Internet, consumers and employees can increasingly find the information they need anywhere in the world and connect directly with their counterparts to make things happen. They are no longer reliant on the hierarchy or intermediaries. There's a clear shift away from multilevel hierarchies and an elimination of anything or anyone who stands between producers and consumers including dealers, agents, distributors, and middle managers. At the same time, human collaboration enabled by networking and digitalization blurs the line between the consumer and the producer of offerings, especially in the areas of software and information products. Futurist Alvin Toffler coined the concept of "prosumer," a contraction of *proactive producer* and *consumer*, the new entity enabled by a digital interactive world.

The impact of the Internet seemed like enough disruptive change for our lifetimes, but futurists say we haven't seen anything yet. The tip of a new iceberg is just appearing, Web 2.0, viewed widely as *the next big thing*. Introduced in 2007, the "2.0" label carries enough buzz to power a small city and has been applied so indiscriminately that it's been rendered virtually meaningless. However, underlying this overexposed 2.0 term is a set of valuable collaborative tools that leading companies are using to make an impact today, while building the workplace and products of tomorrow. Web 2.0 provides rich social networking applications to enhance creativity, share information, and collaborate.

Web 2.0 is about embracing the Web as a powerful platform, exploiting the unique and magical powers of the Internet, and leveraging the strengths of a global audience. It really doesn't involve new technology as the name implies; it combines the features that have been available since the Web's inception. The key essence of Web 2.0 is the harnessing of collective intelligence by way of user participation. At its core are a rich user experience, dynamic content, scalability, openness, and freedom. Collectively, these features have led to the rapid development of Web-based communities or social networking. One concept that illustrates the power of Web 2.0 is *wiki*, the Hawaiian word for "quick." Don Tapscott, author of *Wikinomics*, calls wikis "Weapons of Mass Collaboration." By definition, wikis are about openness, peering, sharing, and acting globally. Perhaps the best-known example is Wikipedia, the largest encyclopedia in the world. It's free, created and updated entirely by volunteers on an open platform, and as this is being written, has four million articles in over two hundred languages. As social networking and e-communities soar, another new term, *crowdsourcing*, has emerged, with its mantra: "a million minds are better than one."

> *The key essence of Web 2.0 is the harnessing of collective intelligence by way of user participation. At its core are a rich user experience, dynamic content, scalability, openness, and freedom.*

The architecture of participation creates network effects and fosters innovation by pulling together features from independent developers. The leading firms of Web 2.0 appeal to early adopters and include new online ventures such as Wikipedia, eBay, craigslist, Skype, AdSense, and TripAdvisor. The essence of the idea is that there is reciprocity between the user and the provider and with the freedom to share and reuse information, there's an increase in the economic value of the Web.

Students of the Web 2.0 social networking trend see it affecting nearly every industry, every function. Recruitment 2.0 is the future for talent acquisition, Manufacturing 2.0 for multi-enterprise collaborative manufacturing, and Buildings 2.0 for defining a new way to design and build buildings. Banking 2.0 is about person-to-person lending sites, with names like Prosper.com, Zopa, Lending Club, and GlobeFunder. They use social networking tools to simplify the borrowing and lending of capital among family, friends, and even strangers. In a post-Madoff world, Banking 2.0 may appear risky, but for some entrepreneurs, it offers an alternative source for much-needed capital. For lenders, the fast-growing sites offer competitive rates of return and the opportunity to easily participate in the cornerstone activity of capitalism.

Exponential, Unpredictable, Chaotic Change

One thing is certain: the network economy is not the end of history, and given the accelerating rate of change, it may not endure more than a generation in its current form. The critical point is that the change is not linear, but exponential. The classic example is world population growth. It took thousands of years for the earth's population to grow to a billion people by 1850. It then added a billion more in just eighty years (1930), another billion in twenty-six years (1956), grew to four billion in nineteen years (1975), five billion in just thirteen years (1988), and hit six billion in eleven more (1999). Exponential growth means more change occurred during the hundred years from 1900 to 2000 than occurred during the previous millennium. And going forward, exponential growth implies that we will see more change during this decade, from 2000 to 2010, than during the last century, and more change in the single year of 2011 than occurred during this decade.

Looking backward, the rapid adoption of new technologies seems to illustrate the point. In just one century, we saw the introduction and worldwide proliferation of automobiles, telephones, electricity, airplanes, TVs, and computers. But in just the last decade, the Internet, cell phones, iPods, online e-commerce, Twittering and Googling have instantly become part of everyday life. The accompanying information explosion has resulted in more information, and disinformation, being created in one year than in the previous five thousand! Now try to imagine the impact of exponential change on more intangible dimensions such as world politics, religion, health, culture, and the environment.

Tom Friedman points to a convergence of powerful forces as the drivers of this new era we're heading into. "The operative word is *new*. We need to stop thinking of ourselves as post something—post-colonial, post-cold war, post-anything. Those eras are meaningless today, wash them out of your mind." He says we're pre-something new, at one of those bright moments in history when things could change in so many ways that we can hardly imagine, and across a broad number of areas simultaneously. His shorthand for it: the energy-climate era, driven by the earth becoming hot, flat, and crowded all at once. It's exponential population growth combining with the development of the U.S. quality of life.

In technology, once networks and nanocomputers have "pervaded" every space in our lives, an entirely new paradigm may well take hold. IBM Research, looking ten to twenty years out, sees a world of smart traffic systems, intelligent energy grids, smart healthcare with embedded personal monitors, smart traceable food distribution systems and smart water management systems. All of these concepts are already in prototype with innovative clients. Projecting longer term, futurists like Raymond Kurzweil extend Moore's Law to describe exponential growth. In his essay "The Law of Accelerating Returns," he says:

> An analysis of the history of technology shows that technological change is exponential. So we won't experience 100 years of progress in the 21st century, it will be more like 20,000 years of progress. There's even exponential growth

> *in the rate of exponential growth. Within a few decades, machine intelligence will surpass human intelligence, leading to technological change so rapid and profound it represents a rupture in the fabric of human history. The implications include the merger of biological and non-biological intelligence, immortal software-based humans, and ultra-high levels of intelligence that expand outward in the universe at the speed of light.*

Kurzweil believes that, between now and 2050, technology will become so advanced that new medical techniques will allow us to extend our life spans while improving quality of life. The aging process may at first be slowed, then halted and reversed as breakthrough medical nanotechnology arrives. Imagine microscopic machines traveling through our bodies to repair damage at the cellular level. According to Kurzweil, a new global paradigm will likely appear by 2050 as these futuristic technologies take hold.

Of course, with change accelerating, beyond Web 2.0 there will come the inevitable next wave of Internet innovation, dubbed Web 3.0. Driven by dramatic increases in Internet connection speeds, modular applications, and advances in computer graphics, the first phase will likely be the emergence of "the data Web." As all structured data records are published to the Web, it will become a giant integrated database, a "Google on steroids." The next phase may be the "semantic Web," in which computers perform more of the tedious work involved in finding, sharing, and combining information on the Web through "intelligent agents." Ultimately, this is a path to artificial intelligence, reasoning in a quasi-human fashion, research projects IBM and Google are intensely pursuing. One thing for sure is immediacy. The new real-time economy is occurring at the speed of light, not the speed of the post office, and it is accelerating as industrial age product and marketing cycles collapse.

The Strategic Response by Enterprises

In this seismic shift to the new dynamic economy, every dimension of business seems to be changing at once. Industry structure is changing from vertically integrated firms and oligopolies to multi-firm value nets, virtual corporations, and dynamic affiliations. Local and regional "mass markets" are being replaced with global markets at one end of the spectrum and micro-markets down to a "market of one" at the other. Well-established market channels with human intermediaries are quickly being replaced with interactive electronic channels, eliminating the go-betweens of old. Hybrid marketing and mixed-and-matched digital and physical distribution and sales channels now exist under the banner of "clicks and mortar." Market entry that had been restricted with high barriers has become increasingly open and deregulated. And commodity products with standard features and pricing are being replaced with a much wider choice of offerings, custom tailoring, and differentiated pricing.

Figure 3.
A Global Industry Transformation

	From Industrial Era	To Digital Network Economy
Industry Structure	Vertical integration Oligopolies Few Established Partners	Virtual corporations Multi-firm value nets Dynamic value nets
Market Entry	Restricted, regulated High barriers	Open, deregulated Low barriers
Markets	Mass market Local, regional Homogeneous	Micro markets Global Diverse segments
Channels	Established A few dominant Human intermediaries Static value chain	New, dynamic, multiple Direct electronic channels Disintermediation, new intermediaries Dynamic value net for each micro market
Products	Standard commodity Narrow product choice Relatively uniform pricing	Personally tailored Broad product choice Differential pricing
Consumers	Little product knowledge, passive, weak	Highly informed, active prosumers, powerful
Sources of Differentiation	Scale and scope	Knowledge and innovation, digital, network connections

SOURCE: IBM GLOBAL MARKET TRENDS

As the digital network economy grows and the pace quickens, more demands and challenges are placed on every management team. On the one hand, the company can now focus on its core operations and outsource the extraneous processes to others, especially since the cost of coordination has dropped so significantly. But the complex web of interfirm linkages that results can be difficult to manage. Standards and the central "shaper" position in the value net wield enormous power, and, as Metcalfe's law reminds us, the value of a network equals the square of the number of nodes. As eBay, Amazon, Google, and Facebook have demonstrated, size does matter!

There are three overarching strategic responses required: perceptive market insight, agility, and innovation. Innovation and creativity replace scale and scope as the primary drivers of economic and business success, and they apply beyond products to processes, marketing, management, strategies, and business models. In addition, to capitalizing on the new economy, businesses must forge links for better collaboration with suppliers, partners, employees, and customers; digitize business processes for better efficiency, flexibility, and cross-functional teamwork; accelerate time to develop and market; collapse the old business cycles and lead times; focus on core strengths; and outsource everything else to specialty firms wherever they're located in the world.

The dot-com survivors like Amazon and Google have produced valuable lessons for the rest of us during this early phase of the new economy. These "net-generation" businesses are inherently network based, designed to exploit attributes of the network economy, leveraging digital rather than physical assets. They had an advantage of new start-up cultures and had no risk of having to cannibalize existing revenue streams. But entrepreneurism is the purest form of meritocracy in which successful risk takers are generously rewarded. Amazon is the preeminent pioneer in creating personalized, database-driven e-commerce. It knows as much about the preferences of its base of twenty million customers as the local general store used to know about its customer base of a few hundred.

As Adrian Slywotsky and David Morrison wrote in *How Digital Is Your Business*, "*Becoming a digital business is not about having a great website, setting up separate e-businesses, having next generation software, or wiring your work force. It is about using digital technology to become unique... to create and capture profits in new ways.*"

Summary

So, a combination of powerful underlying forces has been at work for some time driving the universal law of entropy and the new economy. They include:

- The shift to services enabled by information ubiquity and innovative technology;
- Worldwide telecommunications deregulation and the advent of reliable broadband and mobile networks via the Internet;
- The digitization of everything, enabled by the growth of open technology standards;
- The globalization of capital, production, and marketing, including the previous outliers of China, India, and nations of the former Soviet Union;
- The rise of decentralization, empowerment, buyer power and prosumers; and
- The success of innovative "e-business" designs in nearly every industry.

It's an era of continuous and accelerating change that requires agility and leverage of the network and interactive digital media, both inside and outside the enterprise. It's an era in which customers operating in social networks around the world are fully connected and armed with powerful information, with the youngest "millennial generation" driving the most interactivity and buying power. As the IBM CEO study concluded, those firms that pursue the boldest plays—the most global, collaborative, innovative, and adaptive business models—will likely outperform the peers in their industry. The questions are: How do we develop the most innovative, unique, and adaptive business strategies for this environment? How do we align all the critical key pieces of execution to ensure their success? And how do we tap the reality of the marketplace to assess our progress and continuously adapt to meet customer needs? We will discuss the answers in the chapters ahead.

CHAPTER 2:

Adopting New Guiding Principles

The truth is that our finest moments are most likely to occur when we are feeling deeply uncomfortable, unhappy, or unfulfilled. For it is only in such moments, propelled by our discomfort, that we are likely to step out of our ruts and start searching for different ways or truer answers.
– M. Scott Peck

Successful business strategy is about actively shaping the game you play, not playing the game you find.
– Adam Brandenburger and Barry Nalebuff

CEO Challenges

One of the best indicators of the challenges facing today's leaders and their strategic responses is the biennial IBM CEO study, which I referenced in the last chapter. The 2008 study of global CEOs came to five overarching conclusions:

1. Organizations are bombarded by change, and companies are really struggling to keep up. In fact, the gap between the amount of expected change and the company's ability to manage it has tripled in the last three years.

2. CEOs view more demanding customers, not as a threat, but as an opportunity to differentiate their firms and offerings. And they're spending more to attract and retain increasingly prosperous and informed customers.

3. Nearly all CEOs are focused on adapting their business models, making those models more innovative and more collaborative with their partners and customers.

4. CEOs are moving to more effective *global* business designs, having moved beyond the superficial clichés of globalism to real organizational design and strategic partnerships to accomplish it.

5. The most "outperforming companies," measured by a track record of above-average growth and profits in their industry, are making bolder plays, becoming more global, anticipating change earlier, and partnering more extensively.

Those same themes of discontinuous change and the need for customer centricity, adaptability, global integration, bold disruptive plays, and competing through business designs are reinforced over and over throughout this book. Many of them came to light in the '80s and '90s as the Internet, services, and digital media began to change the world in unexpected ways. These themes are even more relevant today.

The Current Dilemma: Tyranny of the Status Quo

While CEOs can collectively see and articulate these challenges and opportunities, getting their organizations to adapt is an overwhelming challenge. As Laurence Peter astutely observed in *The Peter Principle*, "Bureaucracy defends the status quo long past the time when the quo has lost its status." Of course, organizational inertia preceded the arrival of the new economy, but it is clearly amplified as market pace quickens and innovation rules. For established companies, the litany of problems is all too familiar. Many firms tend to focus on short-term cost cutting versus strategic investment for growth. They often have slow, uninspired, "me too" development instead of new market creation based on bold visionary leadership. Their response to market issues is reactionary and event driven, not thoughtfully prepared or anticipated. Established companies and their operational managers often have their plates full and stay "heads down," executing against current products and programs in their current markets. To use Michael Tushman and Charles O'Reilly's term, firms are not sufficiently *ambidextrous* to maintain current success through evolutionary change, while at the same time establishing the foundations for revolutionary future growth. We must compete for today and tomorrow!

Harvard's Michael Porter believes that the problem is that too many leaders are caught up in pursuing operational effectiveness. It's seductive because it's immediate, concrete, and actionable. CEOs are under constant pressure to deliver immediate results, and the need to have a strategy appears less urgent and less critical. And yet, that's the essence of a general manager's role. The core of his or her leader responsibility is strategy: defining and communicating the company's

> *Strategy is about making explicit choices and tradeoffs, more difficult and riskier than making incremental improvements to the current business.*

unique position, making explicit strategic choices, and deciding which customer segments to serve and, as important, which customers *not* to serve.

Too often, these and other common business problems are simple laments, perhaps voiced by frustrated employees or customers, but not sufficiently described or analyzed in a way that helps them to be solved. Or they are vaguely expressed as leadership issues, without specific accountability. Clearly, a specific strategic diagnosis and root cause analysis is warranted for each and every firm. But in the meantime, see how many of these symptoms you can spot in your company. Check off five or more and it may mean you're on a course for extinction!

1. Customer- and market-based firms in slogan only: Despite claims of putting the customer first, being market oriented or customer centric, many firms continue to relegate marketing and customer interface to something that the sales and marketing departments do, and only after the product or service is developed. Market intelligence is not highly valued, is too analytical, and doesn't produce real market understanding. Our current approach for gathering market insights is antiquated and focused on existing served markets and customers, not future prospects or emerging markets. For example, a large retailer client we work with conducts a frequent and detailed survey of customers who shop at their stores, not those who don't. Our customer-based processes like customer satisfaction, loyalty, and incentive systems are not mature and can be manipulated by line management.

<u>Consequences</u>: Existing customers are poised to switch to other vendors who better understand their real needs. We are overreliant on outside firms to provide market research and firsthand customer contact. We are exposed to market shifts and will likely respond later than our competitors who first sense the change, or even cause the change to occur. We maintain a false sense of security by talking mainly to our best and most loyal customers, who may also be motivated to maintain the status quo.

2. Preoccupied with current served markets and offerings: As Clayton Christensen observed in *The Innovator's Dilemma,* "Great companies fail because they are wedded to current high profit technologies or products and their best high profit customers." We ride the old maturity curves too long, like keeping the pitcher in the game two innings after he's peaked. The shared vision of the company is often just an extrapolation to a larger and better-performing version of what it is today. Instead of fostering *creative destruction*, little sun setting of products or programs occurs, regardless of how unprofitable or ineffective they may be. We may add more new stuff, but it just dilutes our focus.

Consequences: We have an overreliance on our mature businesses and have missed a large percentage of emerging business opportunities. We are repeatedly attacked from areas outside our core customer set and traditional buyers, a market that continues to shrink, and we're left exposed to disruptive business models from fresh, powerful, and exciting new competitors.

3. Short-term tactical thinking: Management systems reward execution that produces short-term results and provides no encouragement or incentive for strategic business building. You can be fired for missing your monthly, quarterly, or annual objectives, but may not even be criticized if you fail to identify or pursue new growth opportunities. In some firms, the tenure, and hence the horizon, of the senior executives is only three or four years, too short to really change the vector of a firm's business. The erroneous perception is that *real* leaders are tactical, action oriented, tough, and focused on cost cutting and sales to meet immediate goals. Employees *can't be trusted* to work hard on their own, so weekly conference calls are required to make sure they're working as hard as they can. Work harder, not smarter! Execute flawlessly! Keep a maniacal focus on today's issues!

Consequences: We remain narrowly focused on existing operations and are slow to recognize and address emerging opportunities. Micromanagement and the lack of empowerment stifle employee creativity and foster an underlying feeling of resentment. Our entrepreneurial skills are weak since they are not practiced, encouraged, or rewarded. New internal ventures start out overburdened with the metrics, disciplines, and processes appropriate for mature businesses. We recognize and reward short-term leadership and those who produce current-year results, even if the strategic foundation for those results was established years before.

4. Financials as the primary or only measurement: Since public firms are constantly evaluated on their quarterly revenues and profits, our measurement system reinforces financial measures, sustained profit, and EPS over strategic actions to drive higher price-earnings ratios. Despite the popularity of "balanced scorecard" measurements, which include customer, employee, and partner perspectives, financials are the only trusted, verifiable, and auditable metrics. Wall Street analysts, often less interested in long-term strategies, reinforce this short-term financial focus. Many enterprises have a one-year financial plan and only extrapolate to years two through five for board meetings or the annual report. Upper management attention to current-year performance reinforces that *that's what's most important.*

Consequences: Because we don't value customer, employee, and other *leading* measures of performance, we're looking backward, steering by our wake. We participate very weakly in our industry's new wealth creation and remain vulnerable to new disruptive business models. With the focus on short-term financials, we inadvertently encourage inappropriate ways to defer expenses and accelerate revenues to prop up near-term profits. We undervalue the creative role that customers and employees play in long-term success.

5. No explicit innovation process: Innovation is a desirable attribute for any company or employee, but it's a vague, immeasurable behavior. We may have promoted innovation through posters, memos to employees, slogans, or speeches, but it's addressed superficially at a high level with no effective support. There's no specific process for identifying, selecting, investing in, experimenting with, or terminating new growth offerings or businesses. So there's no comprehensive innovation system, and we are not even explicit about whose responsibility it is. If every horizontal or pervasive process like this gets kicked upstairs to the busy CEO, nothing gets done.

Consequences: We remain glued to our traditional core business, which receives the lion's share of our funding and attention. We lack an adequate portfolio of exploratory activities that give us options on emerging growth opportunities. We do not reserve any funding for initiating and nurturing internal start-ups. Other policies restrict our flexibility for minority ownership, asset swaps, and creative partnering with other companies. As our business slowly matures and declines, it becomes increasingly difficult to attract new investment, excitement, and talented employees.

6. Lack of bold strategic choices: Many seemingly strategic decisions are merely incremental when viewed long term or in the context of industry positioning. Evolutionary innovations rarely change the business domain or center of gravity of a firm, or create quantum leaps in growth, profit, or market value. Instead of swinging for the fences, we try to bunt around the bases. When Jack Welch reflected back on his career as GE's legendary CEO, he said the one thing he'd do over is "I should have been *bolder.*" Toyota explicitly decided to dominate every major automotive market it entered. When IBM decided to enter the services business, they did it *boldly,* planning a 150,000-person unit growing at two to three times market growth rates. Too often, disciplines to evaluate major strategic alternatives are inadequate and we make no explicit choice, procrastinate, and wait for clearer market signals—until it's too late.

<u>Consequences</u>: We develop an enterprise-wide fear of bold moves, become overly tentative, and prefer the safety of incremental improvements. We fail to invest to lead or play in new growth markets and fail to exit seriously declining ones. This makes us increasingly irrelevant in the industry. We are not attracting positive press, the best talent, or higher market value that bold exciting actions produce, and as the firm matures, it slips into irrelevancy. Very simply, we are trapped by inertia.

7. Unrealistic view of core competencies: Too many firms tend to inflate their own capabilities and diminish those of their top competitors. We don't spend enough time benchmarking our best competitors in the way they do things, the skills they attract and develop, or the cost structure they maintain. We spend so much time explaining to customers how good we are and why we're better that it infects our bias. As the adage goes, "we smoke our own exhaust!" This in turn leads to setting unrealistic goals, like "Be the market leader in three years." But how do we accomplish that from a standing start or from a fourth-place market position? Our major measurement systems are not market based. We fail to assess the critical success factors involved in entering new markets.

<u>Consequences</u>: Many of our new programs fail in execution. We may have the quantity of skills but not the quality to be competitive. We say our employees are our most valuable assets, but we don't invest to increase that value. We set unrealistic market objectives, and when we fall short prematurely, we terminate the projects or lose heart and reduce investment. We don't do in-market experiments to test new concepts or businesses in a limited or protected market. Without *leading indicator* metrics, we're constantly assessing past failures, attempting to assign blame for chronically poor performance.

8. Vague or undefined business models: In an age when competitive warfare is all about business models, our business designs are vague, unaligned, or not even articulated. We lack a common definition of a business model across the enterprise, one that all employees can understand, and one that is more than a financial expression, such as "our model is to grow 10 percent per year and improve margins to 20 percent." Anecdotal evidence and prevailing myths about new markets go undisputed. For example, "Services are growing rapidly, but are just not that profitable."

Consequences: Without a common model, we work against each other because employees or departments develop their own interpretations of the business strategy, based on scant evidence found in CEO speeches or the like. Our employees can't easily make decisions on their own because there are no guidelines, priorities, or general direction established. It's like playing in the Super Bowl without a game plan, a coach, or even a quarterback. Our actions often work at cross-purposes against each other; we spend a lot of time fighting internal battles versus external rivals.

9. No development of "horizontal" strategic leaders: Subspecialties increasingly keep people focused in narrow silos. The traditional vertical structure lives on, making it difficult to see how each employee's deliverable fits into the overall context and workflow. Downsized and stressed with productivity goals, most employees are too busy to see big trends impacting the overall business. Only the CEO has a good vantage point. So our operational leaders lack both the time and the distance to contribute to strategy. We also develop bad habits like information hoarding for power purposes versus information sharing, collaboration, and empowerment. Our personal development plans don't explicitly include building strategic competencies, since it's not perceived to be part of mainstream operational management.

<u>Consequences</u>: There's little optimization of the firm as a whole. The valuable insights that each employee develops in his or her daily interaction with customers or product development are not effectively shared or used to advantage the firm's competitive position. The collective creativity of the workforce is not being mined and exploited. Marketing and development cycles are unnecessarily long as legacy steps remain. Collaboration among departments, business units, or companies is significantly underdeveloped. The "strategic quotient" (SQ) of leaders is not developed at lower levels and remains low for everyone but the CEO.

10. Shackled by our traditional culture: Perhaps the most insidious and difficult thing to pin down is the intangible attribute of corporate culture. We attract, cultivate, and reward people who look and behave just like us, and then we assign them to preside over *existing* product lines, *current* customer sets, or *rigid* business processes. Collectively, that keeps firms confined, bound by a noncompetitive culture and inertia. The issue is exacerbated by the lack of an objective perspective of the quality of our leader team and our company's core competencies. The problem gets highlighted when we attempt to collaborate with strategic partners, acquire new firms with radically different cultures, hire new resources into our existing culture base, or pursue a new business strategy.

<u>Consequences</u>: Our operational culture skews efforts toward efficient core products. Our culture is generally risk averse, and if we do consider a big bold move, we often abdicate those business decisions to legal, finance, procurement, or business practice specialists who counsel against taking any undo business risk, so we do nothing. We celebrate, reward, and promote individuals who reflect our existing norms and behaviors. We become inbred, insular, and generally resistant to new approaches.

A Classic Dilbertism on Strategy

> *Pointy-haired boss: Here's the company vision and business plan.*
>
> *Dilbert: "Vision: Empowered employees working toward a common plan"...Sounds good, but the business plan is blank!*
> *Boss: It's confidential.*
> *Dilbert: How am I supposed to know what to do?*
> *Boss: I'll yell at you if you do the wrong thing.*
> *Dilbert: I thought I was empowered?*
> *Boss: Don't be so literal.*
> *Dilbert: I'll keep doing what I was doing.*
> *Boss: NO, YOU FOOL!*
> *Dilbert: We're doomed, aren't we?*
> *Boss: I don't know. I haven't seen the plan.*

Scott Adams

Adopting New Guiding Principles

To address the issues listed above, close the CEO change gap, and capitalize on the new economy, we clearly need new guiding principles. These strategic principles are the underpinnings of the leadership model that tie the themes of this book together. We usually think of principles as being solid and immutable, but in the world of chaos, we need to be adaptive. As Groucho Marx once

> *For long-term success, the one attribute companies should strive to master above all others is strategic competence.*

wryly remarked, "*These are my principles, and if you don't like them... well, I have others.*"

1. Become a strategic enterprise: Firms earn a reputation that reflects their deepest and most fundamental strength. Some are known for their great engineering or innovation prowess, others for their extraordinary customer service, and others for their high efficiency on a global basis. Firms can also be known for their strong pervasive values, being extremely paternalistic, socially responsible, quality driven, or tough and disciplined.

This book makes the case that for long-term success, the one attribute companies should strive to master above all others is *strategic competence.* As a leader, you should help make your company ambidextrous, competing successfully in both the short term and the long term. In a strategy-focused firm, every employee should invest time and energy to achieve future success. Importantly, the core skill that needs to be embedded throughout the enterprise is strategic *thinking,* not strategic *planning,* and the difference is more than subtle. Traditional strategic planning is analytical and static, part of a dreaded, bureaucratic periodic exercise that produces important-looking, thick binders loaded with financial projections that are rarely read. Dilbert, the corporate cynic, suggested stacking them on your chair to get a better view over the cubicle walls! The thicker the document, the better, since there's no other way to ascertain its value.

By contrast, a living strategy is a dynamic, continuous, and useful process—the game plan for the business. It's better if it's short, digital, and used by the entire team. By allocating time to review, adapt, and discuss it during every meeting or so, strategic leaders instill a sense of strategic purpose in the whole team. "We know where we're going and how we're going to get there." In the slower industrial age, we had more time to plan and methodically grow the core business with top-down focus; with the chaos of the new economy, we need to exercise a broad-based strategic capability, enter new markets quickly as windows open, experiment, and adapt.

2. Lead by inspiration: Almost every leadership expert suggests that the most important role that a leader must play is to inspire his or her followers, create a climate that develops and reinforces the shared beliefs and values of the firm, and provide a sense of purpose and direction. Ironically, it remains the one key leadership skill that typically falls short, according to leadership professors Jim Kouzes and Barry Posner. Whether we call it strategic intent, vision and mission, the shared values and beliefs, or the overarching strategic theme, the core issue is how we can create work environments that inspire individuals to give their very best. In today's creative economy, empowered workers desire not only autonomy, latitude, and general direction, but also a noble purpose for the firm beyond making profits. This is especially true for the young millennial generation, and especially important for an enterprise striving to be highly dynamic and adaptive to market forces. What is it that the firm's leaders and employees feel truly passionate about, passionate enough to take initiative and work to the best of their human ability? Whether you're the overall leader of the firm, a business unit, a work team, or a subgroup, you need to articulate a shared inspirational vision and then go about demonstrating it and reinforcing it in everyday behaviors.

3. Innovate or die! At its core, strategy is about innovation, creativity, and causing change. It's about finding new and better ways to create and deliver customer value. It's about evolutionary continuous improvement *and* bold revolutionary change that establishes a new basis for the firm to compete. Effective strategy envisions a future state radically different than today's. It attempts to lay out major steps for how to get from "out there" back to here, as opposed to extrapolating today's current trends from here into the future. A firmwide commitment to innovation requires a lot more than an occasional motivational speech on the need to innovate. It demands a comprehensive system of broad-based buy-in, explicit processes, investment, follow-up, incentives, and measurements. The most innovative companies empower everyone to play a role and encourage dissenting voices. The key question is: how can we create new products, faster processes, new businesses, and new markets, instead of just competing in existing ones? One effective way to stimulate more creativity is to engage more voices that are diverse in the strategy creation process from those less invested in the present course. Engage new-to-the-firm employees, all levels of management, future leaders, key strategic partners, dissenters, a cross section of business function representatives, remote business units far from headquarters, industry observers...even your most vocal and critical customers and prospective new ones in this critical process.

4. Make the market drive the strategy: The business landscape is littered with companies that failed to perceive critical shifts in customer value, new buying trends, major market changes, industry profit shifts, or competitor strategies. Power has now shifted to the customer. Since the ultimate purpose of any business is to create customer value, no external insight is more critical than understanding what the customer perceives as important. In fact, insightful customer analysis can determine patterns and the unarticulated needs well in advance of the customers realizing it themselves.

Continuous scanning and feedback processes are necessary to monitor subtle market shifts, and if you sense them before competitors do, you can respond first or even preempt them. The marketplace has the wisdom to reveal the profit patterns that can yield tremendous success. Understand where profits are migrating in the industry in general and where both traditional competitors and new entrants are planning their next moves. In all areas of external market trends, you must demand fact-based analyses so that business logic trumps emotional response to a single customer anecdote. As we enter the next age of "customer experience," this factor will grow even more important. To succeed in this fast-paced dynamic environment, firms must be agile, continuously adapt to market feedback, be ambidextrous, and be able to maintain the traditional business while innovating in promising new areas. Where to put the market probes and how frequently to sample and adjust them are some of the critical decisions.

5. Compete with innovative business design: Business models are the new competitive battleground, replacing narrower product or services differentiation, the warfare of the past. *Business design* is not a vague or abstract concept. Cohesive business design specifically articulates which customers or market sets are being selected to be served, what the unique value proposition we provide to them is, what the scope of our business is, which activities we will do, how we will capture profit and then sustain that profit over time, and what organizational design is most appropriate given all the above. And in a digital networked world, an explicit strategy for how our model will leverage technology and information is also warranted. When all the elements are designed together, coherently and congruently, a well-reinforced business model is difficult to defeat or imitate. And, as we discussed above, in a highly dynamic business climate, a living strategy is required that constantly explores and tests alternative business designs in a portion of the market. You must be prepared to change the business design as new market learnings come to light.

6. Execute with intensity, urgency, and synergy: Execution must be intrinsically tied to strategy, not a separate event, and we must avoid the polarizing and fruitless debate that a company's ills are the fault of *either* poor strategy *or* poor execution. Company employees always seem to be busy, but what they're working on may be completely disconnected from the CEO's strategic priorities. The starting point for strategic execution is identifying the few most critical strategic tasks to be performed, with clarity, clear accountability, and firm deadlines, even as we experiment in the market. A sense of urgency and competitive intensity distinguishes the market leaders. As important, you must be particularly perceptive about your organization's capabilities, skills, culture, and current structural design, sensing its weaknesses and taking action to close the gaps. The key to successful execution is developing all these components synergistically. Markets and competitors move very quickly in this networked age, and so market timing is also critical. An innovative strategy may fail because it is too complicated for a firm to execute or is too late because the market is already defined and controlled by a well-entrenched competitor.

7. Lead from strength: Skilled and motivated people make things happen, especially in empowered firms and in a hyperdynamic world in which adaptability is critical to success. This is another one of the softer and yet critical elements of strategy. We need to develop and deploy the best skills possible, empower those who possess them, and lead from that strong skill base. Successful strategy correlates directly with a firm's recognized strength, but a realistic assessment of the core competencies as perceived by customers is required. We tend to overestimate our own capabilities and underestimate those of competitors. Customer feedback and an independent core competence assessment can provide a valid perspective on our strengths. Obviously, some firms have changed their competitive position by explicitly developing or acquiring new skills. But it can take years to assimilate a new company and its culture, and strategic risks may well increase. Boldly moving into a new attractive domain can make good strategic sense, but we must ensure we acquire the talent, skills, and processes to be successful.

8. Shape a high-performance culture: A firm's culture is its most powerful secret ingredient, its hidden DNA. The deep values, the widely practiced business behaviors, the informal communications network, the way power is distributed, the way we deal with each other—these are all components of an organization's unique culture or character. Long-established firms develop deeply ingrained habits and inculcate those in others in the way they hire, develop, and lead their employees. Company culture often remains invisible until one of two things happens: we acquire another firm with distinctly different work cultures than our own and we need to assimilate the two; or we discover that our deeply ingrained culture is no longer competitive in today's market and for a new required business strategy. A high-performance culture leverages the firm's empowered workforce and distributed leadership to become more innovative, collaborative, adaptive, and successful.

9. Leverage structure for competitive advantage: Structure encompasses a lot more than the organization chart. It entails the processes, linkages across functions and companies, the management system, rewards, and the informal organization. In a world of highly interconnected businesses, the speed and adaptability of the entire value net becomes crucial. In this networked world, the cost of coordination among different firms has dropped dramatically. Businesses around the world are increasingly connected through reliable broadband networks and standard software, which makes global outsourcing a reality. The business model defines in its scope which activities we plan to do ourselves for clear competitive advantage. The key element of the model's organizational design is the multifirm network of partners, working together to provide customer value and support a brand. The most valuable position for a firm is to be the "shaper" of a value net, establishing the standards and controlling the brand. But an active participant in one or more value nets defined by others can also be effective and profitable. Increasingly, competition is among rival value nets supporting one standard over another.

10. Measure success by market reality: In a free market economy, there is no more accurate or brutal way to measure success than by market performance. It is reality. For public firms, quarterly revenue growth and profitability are often all that Wall Street cares about. But strategically, market share growth is more indicative of long-term progress. And to be balanced, primary measures should include customer satisfaction and shareholder value, our two most important constituents. We can start embedding market-based thinking by establishing a realistic baseline of where we are, where we have been, and where we intend to go. An overall market map can show how we compare to market leaders in revenue or profit shares. Then, setting realistic stretch goals in market share is a good start. And if employees really are our most valued assets, we should monitor trends in their satisfaction, productivity, and competence as well. And finally, we need to set and monitor long-term strategic goals, addressing what we call the *opportunity gaps*.

Figure 4.

New Guiding Principles

The Overarching Themes: Adaptability, Synergy, Reality

1. Become a Strategic Enterprise
2. Lead by Inspiration
3. Innovate or Die!
4. Make the Market Drive the Strategy
5. Compete with Innovative Business Design
6. Execute with Intensity, Urgency and Synergy
7. Lead from Strength
8. Shape a High Performance Culture
9. Leverage Structure for Competitive Advantage
10. Measure Success by Market Reality

Summary

Embedded in this list of new guiding principles are the three recurring themes of this book: the need for adaptability, synergy, and reality. *Adaptability* applies especially to the strategy formulation stage as we continually sense new market insights and surface new innovation opportunities and then adapt the business model and execution elements to reflect those opportunities or threats. *Synergy* applies especially to the execution stage as we pursue critical tasks employing the best structure, the correct skills, and the strongest culture appropriate for the strategy. *Reality* refers to the need for ongoing measurement of short-term and long-term performance gauged by the truth of market results, especially those relating to customer value. In the next chapter, you'll see how these principles interrelate and form the foundation of a strategic, market-based leadership model.

CHAPTER 3:

Strategic Thinking and the New Leadership Model

Great leaders always seem to embody two seemingly disparate qualities.
They are both highly visionary and highly practical.
— **John Maxwell**

Leaders are paid to be dreamers. The higher you go in leadership, the
more your work is about the future.
— **Hans Finzel**

Seeing the Big Picture and Systems Thinking

Over the several decades I've spent in the business world, I've noticed that really good strategic leaders approach business problems differently than good operational managers or tacticians. Of course, excellent leaders are ambidextrous, good at strategy and operations. But strong strategists seem to have a natural or instinctive way to approach the solving of complex problems. They use whole-brain thinking. They blend analysis with intuition and creativity and ultimately return to a pragmatic set of actions to be pursued. They employ more creative *strategic thinking* than analytical *strategic planning*, a distinction we'll soon explore, and maintain a high level of adaptability. They also find ways to balance both long-term and short-term focus. I firmly believe this intuitive sense of strategic thinking or strategic competence can be described and taught to others.

So what is it exactly that good strategists do? As a starting point, they broaden the perspective by blending both insight and foresight. And beyond that, they develop a capability for what David Gerlenter, A Yale computer science professor calls *topsight.* In his book, *Mirror Worlds* (1992), Gerlenter says topsight provides a "far-overhead vantage point, ...a bird's eye view that reveals the whole—the big picture" and how all the component parts fit together. He believes it's "the most precious intellectual commodity known to man." This right-brain creativity enables us to visualize the harmonious whole and complex multivariate concepts, put them into an understandable context, and then convey the mental models to others and ourselves. After all, a common definition of *strategy* is that it is both the *art and science* of deploying resources toward an objective. Academics and consultants have developed an arsenal of tools, diagrams, and frameworks to help companies understand their strategic positioning and create successful strategies. One's even called a "strategic canvas," emphasizing the strategy-as-art metaphor. A 3M research study concluded that people process images sixty thousand times faster than words alone, and 80 percent of the population need to see pictures when making a decision. Obviously visual thinking is very valuable.

The second thing strategic leaders do is more analytical and gets at the *process* of strategic thinking. They take the multiple market and internal events that are presented, view them through different lenses, and dissect them into component parts. The parts are essential, but what's more important is the interrelationship among the parts as they work together to fulfill the purpose of the whole system of value creation. It's the interwoven context that's key. In doing

> *Strategic thinking in top leaders is a rare and critically important skill. And the lack of it can be disastrous.*

that, they apply the concept of "systems thinking," what Peter Senge viewed as the most critical discipline of the learning organization in his classic *The Fifth Discipline.* They see the linkages within the business ecosystem and identify the major causes and effects, both short and long term. Strategists analytically and intuitively view the current system from multiple perspectives and then challenge it. They consider a variety of better alternatives and then reassemble the pieces in a way that best advantages their own firms. Throughout, they also demonstrate a high level of adaptability and are willing to test the hypotheses and adjust to changing conditions and market realities. Strategic thinking in top leaders is a rare and critically important skill. And the lack of it can be disastrous. Failure to grasp the essence of a complex issue, to define a problem and its root causes and the ultimate consequences of a decision, can cause great frustration and long-term failure.

Once you develop this "strategic thinking" capability—seeing the big picture, distinguishing the key pieces from the whole, understanding linkages and long-term causes and effects, viewing from various vantage points, challenging the status quo—you'll use it as a framework in everyday analyses of political news, economic events, energy policies, or weather patterns. It helps you to gain a better understanding of almost any complex topic. I remember turning many lunch hours with my strategy staff into miniworkshops, filling napkins with drawings, arrows, and ideas for new charts, new feedback systems, and new mental models. It drove the team crazy, in part because I tended to scribble illegibly, and because I converted the lunch break into one more work session. Someone once said, "Can't you just explain what you mean without drawing another complex picture?" "No," I said flatly. It was just part of teaching *systems thinking.*

The word *strategy* derives from the Greek word *stratēgia,* meaning "generalship." And although strategic planning and strategic thinking both share this root word and are often used interchangeably, they are distinctly different. Strategic planning is a process designed for another era when change was slower, functions were more clearly defined, and there were more rigid boundaries separating companies and industries. Planning was focused on achieving incremental productivity gains, usually in manufacturing. The plans were often too detailed, too long, and too financial, and too few people used them. The thicker the document, the less likely it would be read or used. By contrast, the focus in this book is on *strategic thinking*, a more creative, adaptive, and innovative process. The effective executives I have most admired were strategic thinkers, men and women who could communicate the vision and values to everyone from the most junior employee to the highest executive.

Figure 5.
An Important Distinction

	Strategic Planning	Strategic Thinking
Vision of the Future	Predictable, Specific, Financial Extrapolation	Imaginative, Motivational, Sense of Direction, Discovery, Purpose
Strategy Formulation and Execution	Two distinctly different functions and processes. Periodic calendar event	Strategy and Execution are integrated. Part of Value Creation Ecosystem, Continuous and adaptive process
Management and Employee Roles	Senior executives create a plan, get needed info from lower level managers and employees	Empowered employees, customers, partners ... all have voices and contribute to the strategy process
Control Mechanism	Tight measurement systems, clearly defined specialty roles/ accountability	Strategic intent and purpose embedded as general guidelines throughout the enterprise
Core Disciplines	Left Brain, rigorous analysis, discipline, "form filling," data-driven, highly financial	Whole Brain, innovative, intuitive, synthesis, adaptive. Challenging existing assumptions, alternative new ideas, new learnings

In developing or evaluating a company's business strategy, there are several pictures I always look for or attempt to build:

1. A two-dimensional *market map*, a landscape or profile of the industry that highlights the most attractive business domains and depicts the factors that affect competition among players.

Once the landscape is drawn, it provides a clear way to depict value migration trends, major competitor profiles and vectors, and the company's own presence, strengths, and direction.

2. A *strategy map*, a pictorial depiction of the company strategy laying out explicit staged initiatives from one step to another. If industry competition is analogous to warfare, this is the battle plan. Where do we launch a frontal assault, outflank the competition, partner with or acquire another firm to enter new domains, and create new customer value?

3. A *portfolio view* of the relative size and success vectors of each of the various businesses or product lines to better understand the current and future contribution of core businesses and new growth businesses. A two-dimensional growth/profit matrix and bubble chart is useful here.

4. A comprehensive *system view of the strategy process* itself, showing all the interrelated elements and linkages and important market feedback loops to enable dynamic change.

It's this fourth picture of the system that I'd like to zero in on; it's the framework for this book and envisions strategy as an organic closed-loop ecosystem. It embraces the three attributes of adaptability, synergy, and reality, and in my opinion, it's the best way to transfer and teach that intuitive strategic thinking sense to others.

The Forerunner: The 7-S Model

In the early '80s, Tom Peters and Robert Waterman of McKinsey & Co. introduced the first comprehensive framework for strategy that I had seen. As published in the article "Structure Is Not Organization" and later in *In Search of Excellence* (1982), the 7-S model was based on the premise that an organization is not just structure, but consists of seven interrelated elements. Their theory was that the most successful firms achieve fit or synergy among these elements. They depicted the 7-S model as a network surrounding the core of shared values that included:

1. Structure (degree of specialization and coordination)
2. Skills (distinctive competencies)
3. Style (organizational culture and management style)
4. Staff (number of people of different types, development processes)
5. Strategy itself
6. Systems (formal and informal processes)
7. Shared values or "superordinant goals" (guiding concepts, basic beliefs, and strategic intent)

Peters and Waterman went on to make a distinction between the hard elements of structure, strategy, and systems, which are very tangible and easy to identify in a firm, and the soft elements, which are more difficult to describe and are continuously developing and changing. These softer elements of style, skills, staff, and shared values lie below the surface and tend to be determined by the people who work in the firm. Peters and Waterman observed in their research that too many firms focus their change management efforts on the hard S's, with less emphasis on the soft S's. And yet, it's these soft factors that can make or break a successful change process, especially since new structures and strategies are difficult to build on inappropriate cultures and values. We'll come back to this critical point later.

For all the value of the 7-S model in introducing synergy, the model missed several important elements including the pivotal role of the customer and marketplace, innovation, adaptability, execution, and business design. To correct this, several people later attempted to add on other factors, but finding appropriate "S" words wasn't easy, and the whole model, based on the perfection of the number 7, lost its balance.

An Integrated Strategy Management System

In the midnineties, as we struggled to describe the ideal way that strategy should be developed, linked to actions, and adapted, my team came across some work done by Dr. Robert Burgleman of Stanford University along with Andy Grove of Intel called "strategic dissonance." Burgleman and Grove pointed out that conflicting voices emerge within an organization when a firm's competencies suddenly diverge from its basis of competition or when a company's stated strategy differs dramatically from what it actually does. That's the dissonance. Their model portrayed business strategy as a function of five major activities that when integrated together and properly aligned could produce sustained business success. The model and its linkages appear below.

Figure 6.
Strategic Dissonance

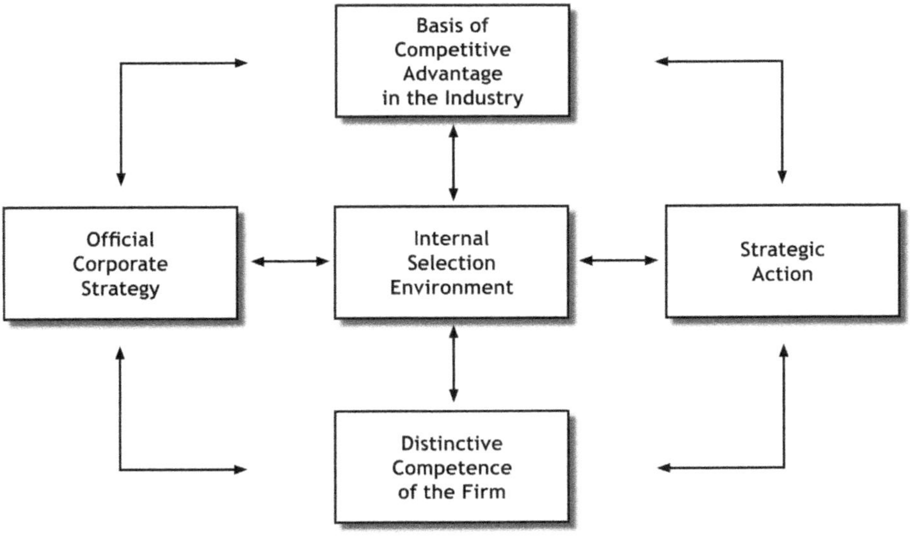

SOURCE: R. BURGELMAN, A. GROVE

A starting point for strategy formulation begins with a clear understanding of the basis for competitive advantage in the marketplace, in essence the Michael Porter five-force perspective of strategy. (Porter concluded that five key forces determine the competitive intensity and therefore the attractiveness of a market: the power of suppliers and customers, the threat of new entrants and substituters, and the rivalry among competitor firms). What factors combine to make our served markets attractive, including the forces of consumer power, competitor strength, entry barriers, and substitution? And considering marketplace discontinuities, what's our shared view of the future looking out five years; which specific markets are most attractive, and what do buyers in those markets value most?

Looking internally, Burgleman suggests we need to realistically assess our distinctive competencies. What strong capabilities do we have today; where do they reside in the company; and as market dynamics change, which competencies need to be protected, strengthened, acquired, or shed?

Next, understanding the market and our own strengths, we can formulate the official corporate strategy, encompassing the definition of the business core, the basis for uniqueness, the customer value proposition, and strategic intent. Ideally, from this strategy will flow the strategic actions including the specific businesses, products, channels, and alliances to realize the goals.

And finally, linking all these activities is the internal selection environment or investment allocation process that commits resources. When all five of these processes are in alignment, a company can achieve a high level of strategic harmony, as IBM did from the 1950s through the 1970s. By contrast, when one or more of these is out of sync, *strategic dissonance* results, IBM's dilemma in the mideighties and afterward.

The Burgleman model provided a good start at systems thinking and synergy, but didn't explicitly encompass or emphasize all the key pieces. So, during the next year, my team and I created the strategic management system. One key motivation was to clearly move away from the bureaucratic strategic planning processes we had been following for decades and transition to a more *continuous* organic ecosystem.

Figure 7.
Strategic Management System

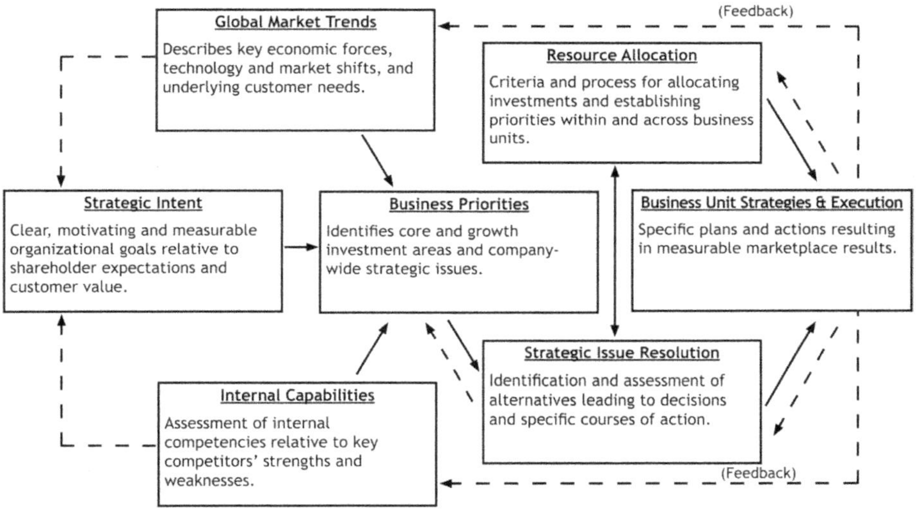

SOURCE: IBM CORPORATE STRATEGY

This early draft of a system view emphasized some key points:

1. The strategy process must be a continuous, closed-loop, and adaptive system.
2. Market feedback is critical and is what makes the process adaptive.
3. Execution is a key part of the strategy system, not a separate process.
4. And, as a cornerstone of strategy, resource allocation is the major end result.

Linking strategy and execution was vitally important, and it was a bigger cultural change for IBM than one might imagine. In the old days, for some unknown reason, the spring "strat plan" and the fall operational plan or budget were two completely separate events. In the spring during strategy season, it was OK to think big and boldly about aggressive growth initiatives and closing wedges of opportunity. But reality always set in during the fall, and attention turned to tactics, while most creative ideas went unfunded. Parallels abound in government legislation in which major public programs are readily agreed to but then not funded. By the way, recognized long ago was the critical need for strategy and execution and their tight integration. At least two and a half millennia ago, Sun Tzu said, "Strategy without tactics is the slowest route to victory; tactics without strategy is the noise before defeat."

This initial framework we created was not theoretical, but a pragmatic linking together of major efforts we were working on at the time. These included setting core and growth priorities for the company, realigning resource allocation, and resolving major issues, our "deep dive" process, which I'll describe later. The framework intentionally emphasized external market insights, since that was an immediate top priority and a major project—Global Market Trends—commissioned by the new CEO. In fact, it was widely perceived that insularity and failure to sense key market shifts was the root cause of IBM's "near-death" experience in the early '90s. This early model also called for an assessment of internal competencies versus competitors', although we never could figure out how to do that in a credible, unbiased way and keep it up to date. Resource allocation was another area that was problematic. Who owns the resources, corporate or the forty separate business units? And do you allocate company-wide resources including research and development investments to the current best performing units or to the most profitable or to the most attractive future growth prospects or to complete high-priority integrated solutions across units?

This first strategy ecosystem was a leap forward, but it also had its shortcomings. The picture relegated "execution," what 98 percent of our employees were doing every day, to just a single box and failed to deal with business design, innovation, or culture, three of the most critical determinants of enduring success.

A New Leadership Model

By the late '90s, the strategies we developed for the corporation were producing positive results and the IBM turnaround was credible and gaining momentum. However, it was clear we now needed to cascade strategic competence out to the business units. We needed to do a much better job in teaching strategy and helping the units—multibillion-dollar global businesses in their own right—to develop their business strategies.

We decided to design the Strategic Leadership Forum for the leadership team of each unit to help them apply effective strategy together as a team. We engaged two of the world's leading strategists, Professors Michael Tushman of the Harvard Business School and Charles O'Reilly of Stanford University, to help us design the program. We showed them our integrated model as a starting point, and they suggested that we first expand the "execution" section to include all dimensions of execution: critical tasks, people and skills, culture, and formal organization structure. This was their major focus area and the foundation of their research for over two decades. They also suggested that we devote more attention to the cold reality of market feedback, but do so in two dimensions, current "performance gaps" and future "opportunity gaps," how we are competing today and tomorrow.

With the execution dimension of the model clear, we went to work on the front end of the model, strategy development, including evaluation of strategic alternatives, which Tushman and O'Reilly had relegated to an input in their execution model. The result was a more balanced model that gave strategic innovation and strategic execution equal attention, along with more explicit

> *This model conveyed to the entire leadership team and employees that strategy is part of an ongoing, adaptive, synergistic, market-based system.*

market feedback. The two-headed arrows linking strategy, execution, and market results were to remind us of the continuous iterative nature of the model. Once and for all, we had to break the mind-set that strategy is a calendar-driven event that happens only once a year, resulting in a document that no one reads and projects that may not be funded. Instead, this model conveyed to the entire leadership team and employees that strategy is part of an ongoing, adaptive, synergistic, market-based system.

We needed to add one other element if this were to serve as a complete business leadership model for our line executives. During our transformation, we had developed a list of leadership competencies that were being demonstrated by our most effective role model leaders at the time. For IBM, the attributes included: innovation, thinking horizontally, informed judgment, strategic risk taking, dedication to every client's success, building client partnerships, collaborative influence across organizational boundaries, embracing challenge proactively, earning trust and demonstrating personal responsibility, enabling growth, having a passion for IBM's future, and developing IBM people and the community. These cultural attributes tailored specifically for our firm and articulated in "IBM speak," were another dimension that served as an umbrella set of leader behaviors over the ten process steps illustrated in the rest of the model.

Figure 8.
Strategic Leadership Model

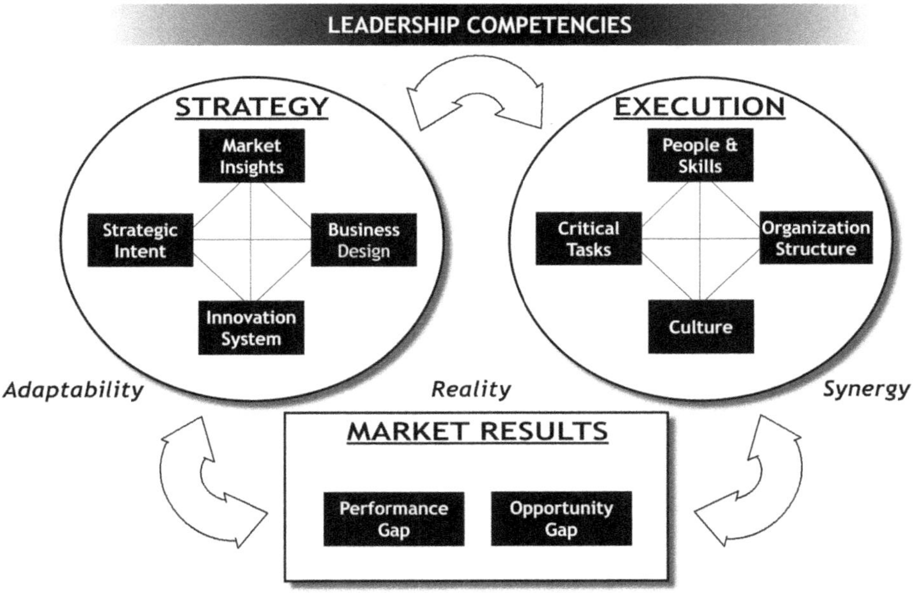

SOURCE: IBM STRATEGY

One ongoing debate we had was whether the innovation system deserved to hold such a prominent place on the strategy side of the model. In fact, we had started with a theory that we should be assessing internal core competencies as a balance to external market insights and a key input to the business model. When we attempted to do that, we discovered that assessing competencies across the company was an endless, nonspecific, and time-consuming exercise. Furthermore, we had already addressed people and skills in the execution portion of the model. On the other hand, by placing explicit focus on innovation, we were addressing one of the critical, but often overlooked, contributors to long-term success.

We based the leadership model on systems theory and feedback loops. That's a cornerstone of strategic competence, and links the seemingly unrelated pieces into a whole. While I've broken the components into discrete pieces to help readers understand each of them, it's the interrelationship and synergy among them that becomes the powerful aspect of the model.

In his study of learning disciplines, Peter Senge advocates the use of systems maps, but admits many people have a problem "seeing" systems, and it takes work to acquire the basic building blocks of systems theory and apply them to an organization. On the other hand, failure to understand system dynamics can lead to company failure. Senge argues that one of the key problems with many management techniques is we apply overly simple frameworks to complex systems. And we tend to focus on the parts rather than see the whole, and fail to see organization as a dynamic process. A better appreciation of systems will lead to more appropriate action.

In addition, Senge says, "We learn best from our experience, but we never directly experience the consequences of many of our most important decisions." We tend to think that cause and effect will be relatively near to one another. So, when faced with a problem, we often focus on the solutions that are close by, actions that produce immediate improvements. However, when viewed in systems terms, short-term improvements often involve very significant long-term costs. For example, cutting back on research and design or advertising can bring very quick cost savings, but can severely damage the long-term viability of an organization. We see the benefits in terms of immediate cost savings, and in turn further trim spending in this area. In the short run, there may be little impact on demand for our goods and services, but in the longer term, the decline in innovation and visibility may have severe impacts. An appreciation of systems will lead to recognition of the use of reinforcing feedback and the need to balance short- and long-term consequences.

Adaptability, Synergy, and Reality

As mentioned in the last chapter, adaptability, synergy, and reality are the three recurring themes of strategy. One of the important features of the Tushman-O'Reilly execution model is *synergy*, or what they termed "congruence," the alignment and reinforcement of the four dimensions of execution. Synergy applies to the linkage and reinforcement of strategy and execution as well. The lack of it is what Burgleman termed "dissonance," and possessing it is what Porter called "strategic fit." To what extent do a firm's current people, formal organization structure, and culture contribute to or hinder accomplishing critical tasks that must get done?

As we designed the strategic part of our model, we used the same concept of synergy and added the dimension of *adaptability*. To what extent are the market insights and innovation system in sync with the business design and strategic intent of the firm, and how responsive is our strategy to the ever-changing market forces and results? This strategic framework, if applied sequentially, rigidly, and on a periodic annual cycle, may serve to only reinforce industrial age planning disciplines; however, if it's applied continuously, responding and adjusting to market feedback, it can form the foundation for an adaptive enterprise.

The third element of the model deals with the *reality* of market results, the cold hard truth of *reality* of company performance, both current and future.

Summary

As we discussed in Chapter 1, the chaos of the new economy affects every one of these components. Your firm's strategic intent will be more powerful if it captures the essence of this new era, your company's role in it, and your empowered workforce.

Market insights are best captured as by-products of the direct interaction with your networked customers and partners. In a networked world, your innovation system can tap into every connected resource: employees, partners, and "prosumers," customers who contribute real value to a firm. Making your business design digital opens a potential tenfold growth in productivity, according to research conducted by Slywotsky and Morrison. We can first experiment with new processes and tasks in the marketplace and then adapt them based on market results. We can source, develop, and leverage skills via the Internet, tapping the millennial generation, who grew up digital. A firm's culture can adopt both traditional and entrepreneurial values to become truly ambidextrous. And the networked organizational structure can allow the creation of a more virtual enterprise and a more focused scope.

In the chapters that follow, we'll drill down into each of these ten elements of the leadership model, starting with the strategy section, followed by the execution section, and finally the market results.

SECTION II:

Strategy and Adaptability

༄

CHAPTER 4:

Strategic Intent: The Power of Inspiration

*Some men see things as they are and say "Why?" I dream of
things that never were and say "Why not?"*
– George Bernard Shaw

*Good business leaders create a vision, articulate the vision,
passionately own the vision, and relentlessly drive it to completion.*
– Jack Welch

We start the core discussion of strategy with the element of
vision or strategic intent, the overarching theme and purpose of
the firm. Vision is one of the most overused and least understood
aspects of strategy. Done well, it can be a powerful, motivating,
and integrating device; done poorly or superficially, a huge waste
of time or worse, a demotivator. And to be credible it must be reflected in a firm's actions and behavior. As Joel Barker once stated,
"Vision without action is a dream. Action without vision is simply
passing the time. Action with vision can change the world." Since
each of the components of strategy formulation—strategic intent,
market insights, innovation system and business design—all interrelate and get developed in an iterative continuous process, an
initial strategic intent may get drafted early, but then refined over
and over, and actually be the last to be finalized. And in this dynamic networked world, despite its role as a "distant beacon" or

destination, the intent must remain pliable and adaptive enough to remain relevant.

That Vision Thing

After Joel Barker's classic video *Discovering the Future* in the mideighties, every respectable U.S. company felt they needed to articulate their vision. Unfortunately, for many companies, the result of the initial visioning exercises became somewhat "Dilbertesque," as every vision developed by formula seemed to sound the same, a string of clichés, platitudes, and superlatives. "We intend to become the very best in the world, the unquestioned global market leader in serving our delighted customers through our extraordinary products and empowered people." Wow, how profound! What does that mean specifically? How does that make us uniquely different? Where's the emotional tug? Visions are supposed to be the energizing force for a company, building confidence for the future. But if the aspirations are unfounded, trite, or vague, skeptical employees will see through them as empty slogans and they will have an opposite demotivating effect, as Dilbert constantly reminds us.

Inspire a Shared Vision

It was also in the mideighties that Jim Kouzes and Barry Posner wrote their classic, *The Leadership Challenge.* They developed a short list of exceptional leadership behaviors based on extensive fact-based research of what followers thought of the best leaders they had worked for. The five key practices were: 1) inspiring a shared vision, 2) challenging the status quo, 3) enabling others to act, 4) encouraging the heart, and 5) being an effective role model.

In a 2008 interview, Jim Kouzes said, "*According to our data, the area in which leaders have the poorest performance is 'inspiring a shared vision.' Of the five practices, that's been the most difficult for leaders to master, despite all the emphasis on how important it is for leaders to have and convey a vision. Leaders come up short in the ability to make their vision compelling to their constituents. Leaders not only need a vision, but must be able to communicate it in such a way that other people want to join in and see that it's in their interests to further that vision. The way to enlist others is not through facts and figures. What we imagine or recall when we think about an exciting place or idea is the senses it evokes—the sights, smells, tastes, and feelings. That's what leaders need to communicate to inspire a shared vision.*"

> **The most successful companies articulate a vision that has two fundamental components:**
> **1) the core ideology of the firm, essentially its values, and 2) the envisioned future.**

Back in the last century when the "command and control" model of the industrial age reigned, having a vision was not a big deal. The firm was glued together by the force of power at the top and downward through the hierarchy, as well as the bureaucracy of rules. There may have been some value statements, but the real glue was the control system. In the more empowered, dispersed networked economy, shared vision and values become the glue. Even tough-minded "Neutron Jack" Welch said, in *Control Your Destiny or Someone Else Will,* that every firm needs to articulate a vision with simplicity, clarity, and vigor. Of course it's especially important for a firm as large and varied as GE. He said, "If you can't articulate your business vision, if you can't get people to buy in, forget it...companies need overarching themes to create change." After several tries, Welch created a complex two-dimensional matrix with key principles related to technical attributes (be number one or two in each market, pursue high growth businesses...), political attributes (integrated diversity, cross-functional teamwork...), and cultural attributes (speed, self-confidence, boundary-less, ownership...).

Jim Collins, who wrote two best-sellers, *Good to Great* and *Built to Last*, observed that the most successful companies articulate a vision that has two fundamental components: 1) the core ideology of the firm, essentially its values, and 2) the envisioned future. He said it's that cherished core value and purpose that provides an organization's glue, and that's the part that needs to remain constant and unwavering. Everything else that's not part of the cherished core should be challenged and changed to deal with current market realties and the firm's direction.

Strategic Intent

In the '90s, business visioning got relabeled and redirected to become something more practical, a way for a company to reconcile its purpose with its means. And the terminology sounded more businesslike than "visioning." Gary Hamel and C. K. Prahalad in their classic *Harvard Business Review* article defined "strategic intent" as an ambitious and compelling dream that energizes a firm. It provides the competitive thrust and the emotional energy for the journey to the future.

By their definition, a strategic intent has three distinct attributes:

1. <u>A sense of direction</u>: a point of view about a long-term market or competitive position that a firm hopes to build over the coming decade or so; it unifies and personalizes.
2. <u>A sense of discovery</u>: a competitively unique point of view that conveys how we are differentiated.

3. <u>A sense of destiny</u>: an emotional edge, something employees perceive as inherently worthwhile. They have to understand, believe, and live according to it.

The genesis of their thinking came from the dramatic ascent of the postwar Japanese corporations that aspired to global market leadership ten or twenty years hence, well beyond current planning periods. Hamel observed that the Japanese were able to energize their workforces to relentlessly pursue those faraway goals; workers actually became *obsessed* in pursuing their strategic intents.

At the center of the strategic intent concept are competitive objectives that are out of all proportion with a firm's current market power, resources, and capabilities. Many Japanese converted the obsession with winning these uphill competitive battles into rallying cries for their employees. Komatsu's ambition to "encircle Caterpillar," Canon's goal to "catch Xerox through technology differentiation," and Toyota's "beat GM" reflect the ability to zero in on the current market leader and surpass them over time. Although I wasn't around at the time, in 1924 IBM, a young midsized company with presence in just two countries, the United States and Canada, renamed itself International Business Machines, declaring a much loftier ambition than its modest capability justified. Developing strategy and strategic intent should be a stretch exercise, not a fit exercise, focused more on tomorrow's opportunities, not today's problems.

The other dimension captured by strategic intent is the purpose, the nobility of the quest, infused with the shared beliefs and values of the firm. Adrian Slywotsky observed that when an enterprise authentically stands for something of value, its employees' level of commitment becomes deeper and more enduring. Remember, an organization is a collection of people, each striving to find purpose. As Victor Frankl said: "What man actually needs is not a tensionless state, but rather the striving and struggling for some goal worthy of him. What he needs is not the discharge of tension at any cost, but the *call* of a potential meaning waiting to be fulfilled by him." The challenge with articulating a strategic intent is that it needs to inspirationally capture that "call" for the collective firm, a universal purpose, and at the same time be especially relevant to the company now and in the near-term future. Michael Tushman adds that "a widely-shared, strongly-held vision can provide a sense of psychological attachment and motivation that cannot be duplicated with formal incentives."

Corporate Social Responsibility: Motivation and Sustainability

Related to the need for higher purpose, the latest CEO study commissioned by IBM Global Services says enterprise leaders are becoming more socially minded, increasingly focused on their obligation "to do no harm." Whether it's environmental issues, social needs, child safety, or community or employee support programs, they are proactively dealing with corporate social responsibility (CSR) more now than ever before. One motivation is that current and prospective employees want to work for ethical and responsible corporations. So social responsibility can rally employees together in a cause that makes the world a better place. In addition, CSR makes good business sense as CEOs increasingly see it as an opportunity, rather than just an obligation, a key element of corporate sustainability. If genuine, this connects and reinforces a firm's values and basic beliefs.

Real Value from Visioning

Several major studies concluded that there is a direct correlation between a firm's management vision and their success. One was published in 1993 by Baun and Lucke from the College of Business and Management, University of Maryland, and the American Institutes for Research; another, "Organizational Beliefs and Management Vision," by Eric Van den Steen, MIT Sloan School of Management, was published in 2005. Both studies concluded that leaders who followed a practical methodology for developing, communicating, and implementing visions were more successful in every measure of a business than those who did not. Van den Steen's research also concluded that vision would be most important when uncertainty is high and actions are difficult to lock in, an apt description of today's chaotic world.

Some Exemplary Strategic Intent Statements

Nearly every firm has some articulation of its strategic intent or vision. Notice how varied the following examples are and how they reflect what's really important to each firm, capturing its unique personality. These are not cookie-cutter vision statements.

Cray Research, Inc.

We see the world challenged during this decade to address fundamental issues...global warming, defeat of cancer, economic competitiveness, national security.

All require effective use of the highest performance computing obtainable...with the highest possible "knowledge" content they can use easily day by day.

Performance leadership in its chosen market segment of the scientific computing market is the very reason for Cray's existence.

We will create the most powerful massively parallel system that can be built to deliver the power of our systems to researchers anywhere in the world, in a language they can understand and a form they can use.

Pepsico

...is in the business of selling soft drinks and snacks, as well as a whole lot of chicken, tacos and pizzas.

But we're really in the business of building brands...big and powerful...on a scale that most companies only dream of.

Big Brands that:
- *stand the test of time*
- *grow in good times and bad*
- *lead to a lifetime of loyalty*
- *travel well*
- *are more than a pretty face.*

Apple

Apple's original vision remains intact:

By putting powerful technology that was once available only to the few in the hands of as many people as possible, we can transform the way people think, learn and communicate.

University of Illinois at Springfield

UIS will be recognized as one of the top five small public liberal arts universities in the United States.

We will achieve this by creating a world-class liberal arts oriented undergraduate educational experience reflecting many of the characteristics and best practices of small private liberal arts colleges while building on our many strengths. Among those strengths are professional academic programs, graduate education, and public affairs activities.

Newport News Shipbuilding & Drydock Company

We will build good ships
At a profit when we can
At a loss if we must
But, always, good ships.

And finally for inspiration and imagination…

Star Trek's Vision and Mission

Space—the final frontier.
To seek out new life, to boldly go where no one has gone before.

How to Develop a Strategic Intent

One of the early mistakes made with vision and mission exercises was that many tried to develop it in a one-day strategy session or an off-site visioning workshop. The best ones are developed by the organization's leader with

A broad understanding of the marketplace landscape, a good grasp of the business strategy, and an imaginative feel for future business models are the foundation for creating a strategic intent.

lots of input, and they mature over time. A broad understanding of the marketplace landscape, a good grasp of the business strategy, and an imaginative feel for future business models constitute the foundation for creating a strategic intent that's unique, specific, and relevant. One approach for developing strategic intent is to envision how the future will look in five to ten years. If your business has a principal target customer, create a picture of that customer's daily life or business operations and then describe discontinuities and anticipated changes from the world of today. You can then describe future customers' needs and the success factors required for meeting those needs. To achieve great things, you need bold, ambitious visions, a significant stretch for your company. In effect, you use strategic intent to inspire radical innovation in contrast to the incremental improvements under way.

Engaging employees is key. At one point, DuPont asked its scientists to help the corporation "invent its way" out of the company financial malaise. Texas Instruments exhorted TI employees to "find new businesses in the white spaces" between existing business units. And Otis Elevator asked its people to pursue an industry "Holy Grail," to find a way to move people up and down a mile-high building. It doesn't matter that the vision cannot be laid out in detail. It's the direction, inspiration, and imagination that count.

IBM Visioning in the '90s

My first intensive work with visioning occurred during the summer of 1991 as the subject of strategic intent (SI) was becoming widely discussed, even as George H. W. Bush suffered publicly from his lack of that "vision thing." As IBM was sliding downhill, John Akers, the CEO, sensed we needed a new vision. He requested that I meet with him every week for six weeks in one-on-one work sessions to help him craft a new IBM strategic intent, a very personal one. IBM still had a very strong culture with a well-grounded belief system, so just restating the values in SI terms would be a waste of time. And the customer focus aspect was already covered in IBM's highly visible Market-Driven Quality program. His motivation and scope were broader and different than what I was anticipating. He saw the benefits as: 1) providing a framework for investment and divestment decisions; 2) being motivational, helping employees and workgroups to see how they fit in; 3) giving customers and partners confidence in our long-term relationship; and in a similar way, 4) giving shareholders confidence in IBM's long-term direction.

In the weeks of iterations that followed, we discussed his perspective on the driving forces impacting IBM at that time—the complexity and rapid pace of business and technology, the current worldwide economic climate, our disappointing business performance, the unrelenting strength of competition, and the value of the empowerment movement. In IBM, we tended to view strategy and execution as falling into one of three time periods. In the near term (next two years), we were focused on delivering on "plan commitments." In the midterm (three- to five-year period), we had specific strategies under way to improve and extend core businesses and create new ones with two different mind-sets, the "what" and the "how." On the "what" side, our major services and OEM thrusts were the two largest, and on the "how" side was the company-wide emphasis on market-driven quality. I thought the strategic intent should be focused in the third stage, our long-term future state, ten years out. But Akers was more impatient and wanted to foster a sense of urgency to change *right now*, even as he articulated the future state. And his focus was clearly on structure and our lack of competitiveness. We were too slow to respond or innovate.

What he envisioned was an IBM with many selected businesses and markets (enterprises, OEMs, consumers), each business highly responsive to the customers it served, each business highly accountable for results—growth, share, and returns—and each fully empowered to act as a focused competitor. The new IBM that he envisioned was adaptively linked to capitalize on IBM's broad capabilities, scope, and scale. It was a "federation of businesses" and markets greater than the sum of its parts, governed by a minimal set of rules and free market principles. In John's view, this was the prescribed antidote for the stranglehold of bureaucracy that had gripped the company and made it so slow and noncompetitive. The new IBM would be nimble, quick, and agile, selecting and innovating early, delighting customers, fulfilling proud employees, and enriching stockholders. And a new cultural attribute would be added. We would be *obsessed with winning* in the marketplace. Our basic beliefs encompassed quality, customers, and employees, but not competitiveness.

Students of IBM history will recognize in these strategic intent attributes the seeds of the new organization structure that Akers announced to the business world at the end of 1991 and began to implement during 1992. The mental picture was a fleet of agile speedboats or destroyers replacing a slow-moving battleship or aircraft carrier. Whether you agreed with the content of the vision or not, the point is, he saw the strategic intent process as an effective vehicle for the CEO to explicitly address the most critical issue facing the firm. In IBM's case, it was about structure, speed, and competitiveness. This was not a general, wishy-washy, or feel-good statement.

Visioning in IBM Revisited

Just a few years later, the "federation of businesses" vision was replaced with a renewed commitment to a fully integrated IBM; and a new leader with a new vision replaced John Akers. To capture a view of the future, the technique Lou Gerstner used was to create a task force called Team Future. He did this five or six years into his CEO position, when the company was back on solid financial footing. Team Future was a handpicked group of ten to twelve future senior VPs who received direction from and reported only to the CEO for a six-month project. I served as the team's strategy expert.

We interviewed dozens of internal and external futurists, product planners, entrepreneurs, and researchers. We eventually created a market landscape, a picture of what the future of our networked industry might look like when it was fully populated with e-marketmakers as we called them: e-communities, e-marketplaces, business process outsourcers, and e-commerce sites. Against that backdrop, we created four specific strategic initiatives that would take years to develop and require major shifts in direction and partnership, and hundreds of millions of dollars of investment. One additional benefit was that the future senior VPs who created the strategy would soon be responsible for turning it into reality.

Market Framework

The complexity for IBM was that although our forty different businesses were related, they were not tightly coupled. They all provided value to business customers and involved information technology, but everything else was different: the end customers, the market dynamics, the types of offerings, and the sources of competitiveness. We studied value migration and concluded that a simplified way to view our industry was to see it as three major segments: component technology, integrating systems or infrastructure, and value-added services. When we studied long-term industry profit trends, value was clearly shifting to the end points as component technology was fueled by miniaturization and by embedding it in other products and services, while at the other extreme, the application of technology and services was on a long-term high-growth vector. Gerstner visualized this as a vertical barbell shape with technology and services at the wide end points and everything else in the middle.

Over time, we did more analysis and refined the landscape picture into three specific value layers. The three-layer value model of the industry we created identified *component or technology value* at level one. The basic technologies we had developed for decades fed not only our own products but also major OEM companies such as Nintendo, Sony, Dell, Apple, and others. Scale economies drove low costs, and rapid innovation cycles drove success. For IBM, software components like database, hardware components like servers and storage, and microelectronics comprised this lowest level in which advanced technology provided the value.

At level two, we delivered *infrastructure value,* providing services and middleware to integrate the various pieces in the customers' shops, whether they were IBM components or others. Naturally, support of open architectures and standards are keys to success. The services opportunity included network service providers, Internet service providers, application service providers, managed service providers, content distribution networks, and business process outsourcers.

The top level was labeled *business value creation* and included the high-level business consulting services and industry and cross-industry applications to solve specific customer problems. At this highest level, business insight, collaboration, and process integration became the determinants of success. The layers helped our business units to relate and gave us a framework for our vision. This was the beginning of a shared view of the future and a long-term company-wide blueprint.

Figure 9.

Emerging Industry Landscape

Overall Value Proposition: Help Customers Become e-Businesses

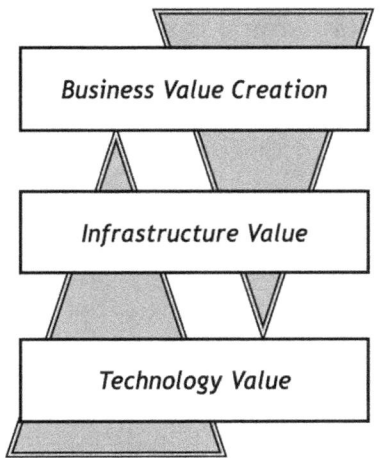

Business Value Creation

Infrastructure Value

Technology Value

Focus:

- Leverage e-strategy & industry consulting services and technology & implementation skills to help transform businesses

- Provide products and services integrated in an open architecture to enable e-Business

- Be a reliable supplier of leadership technology

SOURCE: IBM STRATEGY

As we examined this three-layer construct from a value migration standpoint, we enlisted the influential financial community inside IBM to add their perspective to the blueprint and intent. They applied long-term profit performance for both the industry and IBM against the market landscape. We were able to see how volatile some segments of the industry were, how some services counterbalanced others depending on the state of the economy in each country, and how we could sustain profits through periods of economic expansion and contraction and capitalize on geographic diversity to sustain growth. And we were able to see explicitly how IBM was "mixed" with the industry, where the industry was growing faster because of its greater intensity in one segment. As the CEO and CFO reviewed these financial profiles and projections with the IBM board and security analyst community, the strategic intent became specific and measurable.

81

Engaging the Entire Enterprise

Hamel and Prahalad suggested a logical sequence that begins first with setting the strategic intent, then identifying the major challenges to be overcome to accomplish the dream, then empowering the organization to pursue it, reversing traditional top-down communications to become more bottom-up. So the last aspect of strategic intent is about effective communications, the refinement of the intent, and cascading it downward or outward. In IBM, the company-wide strategic intent served as an umbrella under which business units, departments, and individuals were encouraged to create their supporting and reinforcing visions. It's this last step in the process that makes the strategic intent come to life and become relevant and vitally important to employees. It addresses the vision gap that Jim Kouzes identified.

Summary

Expression of strategic intent is to help individuals and organizations share the common intention to survive, endure, and extend themselves through time and space. Whether you call it visioning or strategic intent, it's an iterative process, which, done well, engages every individual in the firm. In this new era of empowerment, social networking, and the inherent importance of the individual, people need a philosophy of life that resonates with their day-to-day existence and personal life. Complementing the strategic intent is the need to fundamentally understand the market and the customer for whom we are creating value. That's the focus of the next chapter, market insight.

CHAPTER 5:

Market Insights: Scanning, Interpreting, Understanding

The fact is no company is going to succeed without a clear set of tough-minded strategies grounded in a clear understanding of what's happening in the marketplace.

– Lou Gerstner

Your most unhappy customers are your greatest source of learning.

– Bill Gates

Monitoring, analyzing, and responding to a highly dynamic marketplace make an enterprise adaptive. And how frequently, deeply, and insightfully a firm does that and then how quickly it responds determine ultimate success. Most companies say they're customer based or at least market based, but the reality is quite different. Too many are

> *We need to make better sense of our market, find those precious nuggets of knowledge, and translate the conflicting market signals into valuable insights.*

insular, suffering from an internal focus syndrome. In the industrial age, firms were nearly all product centric; it was a supplier's world, and market contact was typically left to sales or marketing. The flow of information was one way, from the firm out to the customer. "If we don't make it, they don't need it" was the arrogant mind-set of a typical product-driven enterprise. But in today's world, power has shifted to the buyer. We need to make better sense of our market, find those precious nuggets of knowledge, and translate the conflicting market signals into valuable insights. Adrian Slywotsky said, "One must have a clear and compelling point of view on one question: Exactly how is the customer changing? That means doing complex, demanding street eye detective work." We need to meet decisive moments with *informed* action; we need to pursue new opportunities with vision and foresight; and we need to preempt, outsmart, and outmaneuver the competition—all of which are dependent on one's capability in market insights.

New CEO Agendas for Market Insights

In the most recent CEO survey, respondents were upbeat about the growing global market for goods and services. In the rapidly developing emerging markets, the middle class is growing, becoming more prosperous, and demanding more sophisticated, higher-value products. At the same time, in developed countries, significant wealth accumulation among baby boomers and young affluent inheritors is boosting growth that otherwise would have been flat. In both emerging and developed markets, the consumer is much more informed and the enterprise is no longer calling the shots.

In one recent retail survey of a one thousand shoppers, 53 percent said they now use the Internet for comparing products, features, and pricing, and 25 percent use a mobile device to do so while in the store. Ten percent are actually sending text messages from the store, so the word-of-mouth concept has now become amplified, digital, and mobile over the billion-user Internet! Many of these young, informed, and wired consumers are willing to become collaboratively linked to a progressive enterprise.

The outperformers in the IBM CEO study are pursuing strategies that create new offerings that are relevant and valuable for the new markets. Recognizing that each market has its own culture, needs, and aspirations, companies are constantly experimenting and learning to find niches, white space, and complacent competitors where they can capitalize on their market insights and knowledge.

Leading firms are also pursuing strategies that discern the fine line between introducing innovations that are beyond, but not *too far* beyond, what a market can accept. The goal is to create offerings for early adopters and seize "first mover" advantage. Another progressive strategy is to connect employees at all levels directly with customers through real-time information so that deeper relationships can form and better market insights can be developed regardless of the function involved—warehousing, manufacturing, design, operations, or whatever. At the enterprise level, leading firms are connecting and collaborating with key early adopter customers to develop new products. The customer really becomes a partner, resulting in deeper loyalty and increased barriers to switching.

By capturing market insights through its many channels and then using advanced tools to actively mine that information, the enterprise can better anticipate shifts in customer demand and respond before the competition. For example, using *virtual worlds*, an online computer-simulated environment, companies can gauge customer reaction and receive crucial feedback well before a product is developed so that the creators know exactly what users want, a crucial competitive edge.

Evolution to the Adaptive Enterprise

In a world of accelerating chaos and rapidly growing customer power, businesses are evolving along a continuum from *product driven* to *market driven* to *customer responsive,* and ultimately to *adaptive enterprises.* As a starting point, think about the industrial age leaders, the traditional plan-based firms that succeeded through a one-dimensional focus on what they produced and sold. In the '80s and '90s, there was a broad awakening to the value of becoming more *market driven,* identifying and pursuing key market trends, using market maps to plot competitor positions, and to chart long-term market strategies. In this second phase, the focus began to shift from the product to the market, but the pace remained ponderous, governed by annual planning cycles and the limits of a pre-Internet unconnected world. Now, in the next phase, a combination of new technology, information, the Internet, multimedia digital content, and social computing is enabling higher levels of customer interactivity, one-to-one, and viral marketing. Satisfied customers are now becoming proactive advocates and contributors of value; or conversely, they can be vocal critics, and do so on the Web for all to see. The fourth phase is a transformational one as firms redesign the entire business, its structure, and processes to become truly *adaptive.* Ultimately, the goal is for every enterprise to rapidly *sense and respond* to each customer opportunity in near real time. For large companies, the challenge is to accomplish this without sacrificing the benefits of scale and scope. Let's follow this evolution of market insights at a level deeper.

Historical Background

The real wake-up call for U.S. businesses came in the early 1980s as they embarked on a widespread effort to become more market driven and customer focused. This was due in part to the waning of the industrial age and, in part, to respond to the successful Japanese firms that were achieving quantum leaps in quality improvements, customer satisfaction, and revenue growth. Research organizations such as PIMS (Profit Impact of Market Strategies) collected enough data to prove that improved customer marketing and service lead directly to improved profits. Said another way, gains in customer mindshare lead to gains in customer market share over time, which in turn lead to improved financial returns. But despite the analytical evidence, our industrial age mind-sets found it difficult to change and envision a truly market-based or customer-centric enterprise.

To be comprehensive, a market insight process should sense the changing needs and values of every influential stakeholder in the marketplace: customers, prospects, substituters, government regulators, partners, distributors, suppliers, industry associations, and even investors. And firms should strive to understand every important market shift, be it customer priorities, channel shifts, competitor positions, or profit trends. Valuable strategic signals can even be transmitted by investors and help us identify emerging growth patterns in our industry. But the highest priority should be on building customer understanding, perceiving competitor insights, and sensing major market shifts. For IBM, it took more than a decade to build an effective market insight capability.

An Emergency Intervention: The Market Analysis Task Force

IBM, a prototypical industrial age enterprise, felt little need for monitoring customer or market trends in the early '80s; business was going very well without it. It experienced record revenue and profit growth, was judged by *Fortune* magazine to be the world's most admired company for five years in a row, and dominated nearly every industry segment it was in. A cover story of *Time* magazine in mid-1983 was entitled "IBM: The Colossus that Works." As insiders, we pointed with pride to the core value system, the basic belief in "Best Customer Service" as evidence that we were truly customer oriented. Of course that addressed how well we serviced customers *after* they installed what we developed and sold them, not that they were involved in defining our offerings. As an enterprise, we were brimming with confidence, although critics termed it arrogance. Demonstrating the futility of basing business strategy on decade-long forecasts, the projections developed by my department during the Growth Task Force of '79 projected that IBM revenues, then around $30 billion, would grow to $100 billion by decade's end (1990). A more aggressive stretch case projected growth to $200 billion! Of course, "pride goeth before the fall."

In 1986 disaster struck, and many IBM core businesses went "casters up," to use a familiar computer industry term for business failure. The entire business, at least from a profit and market value standpoint, went into serious decline. To be fair, the revenue growth in the early '80s before the fall was inflated with the "lease-to-purchase" conversion of our customers and the introduction of the wildly successful PC, but the downturn of '86–'87 was real nonetheless, and the recession made matters worse.

To their credit, top management's knee-jerk reaction to the downturn was *not* to force people to work harder or just invent better products, but to go directly to the marketplace and listen to the customer base to discern what was fundamentally wrong. As a direct result of the Market Analysis Task Force of 1987, dozens of market-based actions ensued over the next five years. We had concluded through three hundred in-depth customer interviews that IBM needed to: accelerate the business remix by moving more resources into high-growth services and the small and medium business markets; step up our Application Solutions business and application development tools; address customer inhibitors like complexity and better articulate the business value of investing in IT; and revamp our corporate measurement systems to do more comparisons to industry growth. We also decided to emulate our midrange business unit in Rochester, Minnesota, the AS/400 team, who were obsessively customer centric and later won IBM's first Baldrige Award. In addition, we developed a universal customer satisfaction measurement system and added those criteria to the executive compensation formula; we invited customer CEOs into our internal strategy conferences and senior leadership meetings for firsthand feedback and to combat insularity; and we improved our Partnership Executive Program that teamed senior corporate executives with the assigned account executives in the field. We believed those initiatives, known collectively as the Industry Leadership Assignments, would drive the required turnaround. Most were designed to bring us into closer sync with a changing marketplace.

Early Attempts at Being More Market Driven

John Akers, CEO at the time, also commissioned a small group of us to create a company-wide Market-Driven Quality program, one that would engage both IBM marketeers and engineers in a disciplined proactive focus on both customers and quality. For the customer dimension, we created a simple premise: "If we can be the best at serving the needs and wants of those customers we choose to serve, everything else will follow." On the culture side, two major IBM traditions were terminated: the infamous "Contention System," which pitted corporate staffs against the line, to speed development and marketing cycle times; and the "Full Employment Practice," which implied lifelong employment, allowing us to downsize more quickly and take a swipe at entitlement.

There was a competitive insight program in place, but at the time, it was narrowly focused on the JCMs (the Japanese computer manufacturers such as Hitachi and Fujitsu), DEC (Digital

Equipment Corporation), and Microsoft, our one-time partner who had outmaneuvered us in PC operating systems. In many ways, the competitor insights were looking backward at previous competitors, not forward to the future. Our Ten-Year Technology Outlook, prepared by IBM Research, was fascinating from a science standpoint, but had no clear market connection or projections for the commercialization of technology. So rethinking was required in both of those areas.

To be more customer oriented, a new advertising campaign centered on "IBM: The Solutions Company." Our Leadership Development Center launched a broad developm ent program called Transformational Leadership. We also remixed IBM's portfolio of product businesses, exiting the typewriter and low-end printer businesses, and made two major strategic bets in services and OEM component technology. The services strategy we developed in 1991 was a classic and helped establish the foundation for IBM's eventual turnaround.

What was intensely frustrating at the time was that despite this broad-based, intensive, multiyear effort, the impact was not immediate. In fact, on the surface, things got worse. Downsizing was incredibly expensive, and the substantial write-downs, $8 billion in one year alone, delayed the financial turnaround and demoralized the workforce and investors. The real recovery didn't show results until years later when a new executive team was put in place with a new customer-oriented focus, new ideas, and new energy. They and we further attacked the culture and inertia and ultimately succeeded beyond expectations.

When the new executive team arrived in 1993, Lou Gerstner, the new CEO, made several important strategic decisions: recommit to the mainframe (IBM's cash cow), drive the emerging OEM and services businesses, invest in network-centric computing, and finish the work to become truly customer centric. As part of that last initiative to strengthen IBM's customer relationships and market insights, he took several important actions:

1. Increased customer focus by immediately reorganizing the marketing and sales part of the company along customer sector lines, the businesses our customers are in, away from the traditional product and piecemeal country organizations.
2. Increased competitive intensity by getting each business unit head to be accountable and lead an explicit competitor strategy targeted at a major rival.
3. Developed new market insights for alternative strategies through a renegade task force of mavericks called Arachnid, a spider web metaphor. This team, which I headed, presented alternative strategies for exiting the OS/2 operating system, reestablishing core systems, and promoting open systems.
4. Created a more traditional task force, which I co-led with John Landry, CTO of Lotus, to develop a proactive leadership Internet strategy, a huge ($16 billion) high-growth (44 percent) opportunity perceived to be "the next big thing."
5. Commissioned a major mega trends process, Global Market Trends, to sweep up and prioritize the most important market issues IBM needed to address. This became the centerpiece of our market insights process and my team's major focus for the next six years.
6. Hired a new marketing executive (CMO) from outside IBM and consolidated all of IBM's advertising worldwide for message clarity, consistency, and efficiency.

Gerstner made the point repeatedly that by hiring him to run IBM, the board had selected a former IBM customer. And going forward above all else, IBM would be *customer centric*! Of course, if IBM had been a true market-based enterprise, and truly committed to "Best Customer Service," it wouldn't have needed so many special task forces, emergency actions, and overlays on existing structure. If IBM's capital investments in R & D hadn't been so huge, we might have been more receptive to customer-driven priorities. Were the mind-sets and processes in place, the normal line organization could have identified and responded naturally to the key market shifts in their areas. But they weren't.

Global Market Trends: GMT

The centerpiece of our new market insights system was Global Market Trends. GMT became one of the most widely quoted and most recognized strategic documents in IBM and became a model for strategy professionals outside of IBM. Inside, it became a brand of its own and the fact-based reference point for strategic decisions. GMT focused outwardly on the marketplace and discerned what would come to matter most to customers over a one- to five-year horizon. The challenge is that business leaders are often confronted with a blizzard of contradictory consultant and academic-sponsored interpretations and opinions of what's happening in the marketplace. Those inputs are further confused by narrow anecdotal evidence delivered by a single customer or competitor event. Lou Gerstner believed we needed to synthesize all we knew about current market trends into a single integrated company view to identify the most critical themes, initiate debate, and focus our energies. So GMT provided senior management with a shared view of threats and opportunities, the most important customer trends, competitive issues, and the new technologies of the emerging network era.

Internal line and staff experts with a cross-section of external contributors collaboratively developed GMT. One of GMT's disciplines was to ensure that every insight was written in understandable prose and that the drivers of each trend were clearly identified and were supported by hard sourced data. Over time, that discipline spread to almost every strategy project and market study across the company.

On the face of it, the creation of GMT appears to be a study in chaos: hundreds of pages of trend data scattered on conference tables and tacked on walls, roundtable discussions escalating into heated debates, and presentations of conflicting trends by respected world authorities. The GMT contributors were a "who's who" of the technology, economic, and political landscape. During the first six years of publishing GMT, we had over two hundred contributors, eight major universities, and over twenty global research houses. I was invited to join the UN's Advisory Council on Technology and become an author of the UN's Human Development Report mainly because of the broad-based and fact-based research we had conducted on global business development. Despite the apparent chaos, GMT had an underlying discipline of a four-step process.

1. Gathering insights and creating "bumper stickers": We collected marketplace insights from industry thought leaders, customer visionaries, business partners, and IBM employees. One-on-one interviews and larger Delphi sessions generated rich debate and yielded a hypothesis on each trend. In the technology area, our Research Division conducted an "earthquake" process to identify the most significant emerging tech trends, with a ten-year view, to feed into GMT.

As the collection of trends grew, we captured the essence of each trend as a hypothesis in a short phrase we called a "bumper sticker," such as:

- "Investment in Information Technology (IT) Correlates to Productivity and Economic Growth"
- "Worldwide Venture Capital Strongest in Life Sciences and IT"
- "e-Markets Are Developing with Astonishing Speed"
- "Consumers Are Armed and Dangerous" (...armed with PCs and the Internet)

2. Synthesizing ideas and finding themes: GMT used two collaborative techniques, one face-to-face and one digital, to enable team members to debate and interpret trends en route to publication. In the first technique, the strategy "war room" at HQ became the physical staging area for posting each of about seventy-five bumper stickers and clustering them around dominant themes. In some cases, we created multiple scenarios if there was great uncertainty. With the help of the Global Business Network, we assembled a diverse and eclectic work team that included Research Fellows from other firms (like Disney), several high-tech CEOs and CTOs (like Apple), well-known technology journalists, venture capitalists, academics, entrepreneurs, and even a film producer. The goal was to see trends from as many vantage points and mental models as possible. The digital collaboration approach involved creating a Lotus Notes TeamRoom for access by our extended team around the world. They contributed supporting or disputing evidence to help enrich the deliberation.

Debate over specific trends centered on two criteria: (1) is this issue an *established trend* or simply a *critical uncertainty* to be monitored for future action, and (2) is it significant enough in its potential impact to IBM to be included in the final report?

3. Validating trends and themes: Once the triage of trends was finished, we validated the final list of global trends with an advisory council of customers, our internal strategy executive council, and finally with our corporate executive committee, which included IBM's CEO and top ten executives. Feedback from all three of these refined the trends and triggered action. The session with the CEO and executive committee was the toughest, and the intense debate could last eight to ten hours. All had read the report in advance, and each had strong opinions on the validity of the issue and the degree to which IBM needed to respond more strongly to, preempt, or lead a trend. The result was a short list of critical strategic tasks with deadlines, each assigned to a senior executive. Each was a major strategy, entering or exiting a market, or launching a new venture, not just adding product features.

4. Communicating and linking to action: Following these reviews, we published the hundred-page narrative and supporting graphics that became GMT. Although we created a few hundred bound copies, the broadest distribution occurred electronically, sending it to IBM's Senior Leadership Group and posting it to our internal intranet for all four hundred thousand employees to download and read. We encouraged them to provide online feedback. Publishing GMT served as a launching point for formulating unit strategies, driving key investments, reshaping the IBM business model, and broadly developing IBM's market insight competency.

Corporate strategists have long sought to have a larger impact on business direction, especially when businesses focus so intently on tactics. GMT provided IBM strategists with a means to achieve that impact, gaining agreement on market facts, forcing us to re-examine our priorities, and moving us toward a shared view of the future. Although it greatly increased awareness to the outside market, it was not a real-time, continuous sensing process.

Market Maps: A Fuller Picture of the Market

One simple tool that helps strategists understand market insights is the two-dimensional market map. This visual tool can provide a comprehensive and easy-to-understand overview of a total market, a snapshot that represents huge amounts of data. For either new or existing markets, we used the x-axis to plot the major segments of an industry in a logical sequence relating to how the offering was marketed, used, or developed. A market might include segments such as core technology, applications, services, content, tools, accessories, and related products. The width of each vertical bar indicated the amount of value—revenue or profit—associated with that segment at a point in time. On the vertical y-axis, we plotted the current industry players from high to low and our own market position. As we plotted each segment of a related domain, we could easily see where each competitor was concentrating, the intensity or strength of their presence, and the gaps in their offerings. As we contemplated our own business design and the planned scope of our business, this tool was invaluable. The example below shows a snapshot of the dynamic storage marketplace that ranges from large stand-alone devices to small, embedded devices and from storage management software to storage services. More mature market segments tend to have a concentration of competitors; emerging segments are often more fragmented.

Figure 10.
Market Map Example: Storage Marketplace

External Disk Drives	Embedded		Networked Storage		Storage Software				Storage Services		
	PC	CE	NAS	SAN	REPL	DEVICE	INFRA	SM	CONSULT	SI	OS
Other	OTHER	OTHER	OTHER	OTHER	OTHER	OTHER	OTHER	OTHER	OTHER	OTHER	OTHER
E	H	OTHER	OTHER	OTHER	OTHER	OTHER	OTHER	OTHER	OTHER	OTHER	C
D	G		I		H	M	M	N			
C	F	H	H		G	L	L	M	P	Q	Q
B	A	G F C A	D	K J H	F	G	L	M	O	C	
VENDOR A	B		A	D C	C	C	C	F	C	O	P

X-Axis: Opportunity Size ◄──────►
Y-Axis: Leading Vendors by Market Share

Advisory Councils

Another effective way to gain direct market insights is to form an advisory council of customers, partners, industry observers, and other insightful constituencies. We started one when I was running Insurance Industry Marketing for IBM early in my career. A small group of insurance CEOs, strong vocal customers, were willing to meet for two days every six months and listen to and interact with each other and us about the potential for technology to impact their businesses. They provided their feedback directly to us, helping to shape our offerings and programs. We later replicated the concept in the area of mobile computing with top industry consultants, analysts, and journalists. One key is to ensure that the advisers provide constructively critical feedback; what's wrong with our plans; what can we do better? We used the same approach with a nonprofit cancer foundation with major donors and former patients. The process was more or less the same each time. Invite six to ten experts to volunteer their time and serve as advisers for a fixed period of time, two years or so, on a rotating basis. Ask them to sign nondisclosures so council content can be very candid including unannounced programs or products. Pick a convenient and desirable location for the council, make the schedule accommodating for busy people, provide meaty content, ask for their input in shaping the offerings, and really listen and use it. Use dinnertime for a lighter work session. Provide an honorarium or appropriate memento and cover all their travel expenses. Ask for real-time feedback and a short written report afterward responding to specific questions, and circulate feedback comments to all.

Business Intelligence

While the focus of market insights is capturing data and information *external* to the firm, many companies have created a

Business Intelligence (BI) department within their marketing, strategy, or finance organizations to collect and control the vast amounts of data they've gathered about *internal* operations and performance. BI systems typically provide historical, current, and predictive views of business operations, using data that has been gathered and stored in a data warehouse. A variety of software tools have been developed to assist in the extraction, analysis, and presentation of this information. While the initial focus is internal, these tools and resources can be used for external analysis as well, for example, gathering information on comparable companies to produce competitive benchmarks.

Toward Continuous Market Sensing

As market pace accelerated to "Internet speed," the frequency of capturing market insights for many firms increased in parallel. In IBM's case, we launched a major market insight work effort in 1979, and not another one company-wide for eight years. We then moved to an annual Global Market Trends process, augmented by other market signals. Maybe in the industrial age, when the pace of developments was much slower, it was OK to check in on the market every few years or so, but not now. The next step was obvious: continuous and distributed customer monitoring. One unit in IBM served as a role model for us.

> *As you create a passionate customer-centric organization, ensure everyone in the firm knows what customers are experiencing.*

The AS/400 team in Rochester, Minnesota, continuously tapped partners and customers. In fact, they centered the whole concept of quality at Rochester on their direct open links with the customer. They crafted detailed offering features by analyzing the needs and expectations of existing and potential owners of the computer hardware and software manufactured by that division of IBM. A near-fanatical customer base was motivated to ensure IBM invested in their favorite architecture.

Today the Rochester quality process is a continuous loop that begins, ends, and begins again with the customer. More than forty data sources are analyzed to guide improvement efforts. Most provide information on customers' product and service requirements or ways to refine these expectations into detailed specifications for new IBM offerings. And customers are active collaborators in development. For example, customers and business partners from over 4,500 businesses worldwide have participated on customer advisory councils throughout the development of the AS/400 computer system. The Rochester quality culture has been transformed from reliance on technology-driven processes delivering *products* to market-driven processes directly involving suppliers, business partners, and customers to assemble *solutions*.

IBM Rochester and other leading customer-driven teams believe customer experience feedback is crucial to company success. But, to be most useful, the feedback must be real time while experience is still fresh in customers' minds. Stale information is useless. It also needs to be a continuous feed, a constant sensor on the "pulse of the market" to sense the subtle shifts in value, since the market is a moving target. And customer feedback should be gathered from everyone in the enterprise and the resulting insights shared throughout the organization.

Toyota: Meet Every Customer Need

In the automotive industry, one customer-focused firm is beginning to pull away from the pack. Toyota is now on track become the largest and most successful car company in the world. For Toyota, to carry out their policy of "customers first" on a global basis, they believe it's essential to respond to the needs of *every* customer and *every* market. That goes against conventional wisdom and the widely held belief that "selected markets" implies that you must explicitly decide which markets to serve and *not* to serve, to achieve maximum focus. Toyota apparently understands this focus point, but is doing it anyway, and doing it very well.

In implementing the strategy, Toyota decided to create different offerings for each market segment, not by price class, but by use and consumer type. So the Corolla line was designed for the utility-minded, Sienna for family-oriented, Lexus for the luxury-seeking, and Scion for the young sporty market, and they are now breaking into the truck market with the Tundra line of pickup trucks. With no experience in a truck market dominated by U.S. automakers, they decided to send their designers to logging camps, cattle ranches, farms, and construction sites to meet with truck drivers face-to-face. In the process, they observed how trucks were being used and discovered in each environment what was required for towing capacity. They hit upon the need for bigger handles for windows and knobs, since many workers wore bulky gloves. They also observed the emerging trend of using the pickup as a mobile office, hence the need for file storage and other office features. In all their markets, they've told their engineers they're building communities of users, not cars, and the best market insights come from directly observing the use in each unique community.

Customer Experience

As we extend the notion of market insights out to the farthest point of the enterprise, the next logical step is to fully engage the customers themselves. Over a decade ago, Joseph Pine and James Gilmore had the insight to foresee the coming of the "experience economy" and articulated the key role *experiences* play in building stronger, more personal relationships with employees and customers. The "experience business" is highly differentiated, charging customers for the *feel* they get by engaging it. Pine and Gilmore believe that today's business must deliver emotional, authentic experiences to ensure sustainable growth and future survival. Their prescription: first, create a consistent theme, one that resonates throughout the entire experience; layer that theme with positive cues, easy-to-follow signs; eliminate negative cues, those visual or aural messages that contradict the core theme; and finally, engage all five senses to heighten the experience and make it more memorable. An exceptionally positive experience can transform a passionate customer into a proactive advocate for your business.

Two firms that exemplify the experience economy concept are Chuck E. Cheese and Starbucks. The former is a cross between a frantic carnival and a fast-food restaurant designed exclusively for kids. It combines games, stage shows, animated characters, an amusement park atmosphere, bright colors, and lights, creating an environment where you can run, play, laugh, and scream. At the other end of the relaxation spectrum, Starbucks is designed to be a cozy home away from home. The comfortable couches and armchairs, soothing music, and lighting encourage customers to linger, meet with friends, or immerse themselves in a good book and cup of gourmet coffee. Each has created a memorable experience for its target audience.

To truly understand your customers' experiences today with both your offerings and your competitors', you need to go out into the real world, spend time with

> *You need to go out into the real world, spend time with them in their own environment. You need to live it to find the unarticulated needs and wants of customers.*

them in their own environment. You need to live it to find the unarticulated needs and wants of customers.

Philip Kotler, author of the classic *Marketing Management* and once called "the messiah of marketing," says, "Make your business a workshop where your customer can draw what he wants; *marketing is the delivery of experience.*" His example is the Four Seasons hotel chain that customizes hotel rooms for its guests. Whenever possible, the next time the guest visits the hotel, he or she gets the same room and the amenities he or she likes. "While the aim of business is to create satisfied customers, the truth is companies continue to lose unsatisfied customers." Kotler's message: plug the leaks by exceeding customer satisfaction and customer delight, moving to a higher level of customer astonishment.

Using the Web for Direct Customer Feedback

At the other end of the spectrum from direct observation of the market is the use of the Internet. The Web now provides dozens of market insight tools that weren't available just five years ago. Sensorpro, EZquestionaire, KeySurvey, and FeedbackFarm are just a few. One leader, SurveyMonkey, claims to provide "intelligent survey software for *primates* of all species." Its single purpose is: "to enable *anyone* to create professional online surveys quickly and easily, supporting every question type from multiple choice to rating scales to open-ended text; support any national language from Chinese to Arabic; and provide extensive survey analysis tools."

In my consulting work with the federal government, I used Zoomerang, one of the first online survey tools in the market. Introduced in 1999, Zoomerang has a variety of features depending on the price the user is willing to pay. The free "basic" version allows the user to create a survey with no more than thirty questions and view the results for a limited time. The pay versions permit larger numbers of questions, more complex analyses of results, and the use of a firm's own brand rather than Zoomerang's. They claim nearly a million users. For the military consumer, we were able to gather a very current, broad, and immensely valuable insight on what soldiers value and are willing to pay for communications and technology services around the world. The survey response rate was nearly 20 percent, far higher than the typical direct mail rates of 1–5 percent. If your customers are willing to "opt in" by providing an e-mail address, you can make them a voluntary standing army of market insight providers, something many are very willing to do.

Marketing 2.0

As we enter the age of Web 2.0, the world of social networking, customer–company dialogue changes radically and a new marketing paradigm emerges. "Word of mouth" spreads exponentially through the Internet and becomes a loudspeaker, much more powerful than TV commercials and print ads. The new tools of Weblogs or blogs, viral marketing, podcasts, videocasts, and wikis, all gathered under the buzzword banner of Marketing 2.0, provide a new way for customers to directly spread the news about a company or product. And in this hyper-interactive culture, it's also a new source of market insights. Simply Google your company name or brands and you can search the unfiltered conversations about your products, both good and bad. It's immediate and very candid market research. Personally, I use TripAdvisor because I always find the unfiltered and most current feedback on a hotel from travelers to be more valuable than what the hotel says about itself. Companies can't stop customers from speaking their minds, and they shouldn't stop employees from talking directly to customers and empowering them to act on what they hear. The only caution is that most customers don't want to hear "the party line" from the company itself, so be careful in creating your own blogs or trying to unduly influence customer opinion through them.

One of the best examples of the success of viral marketing is what Levi Strauss has accomplished. Levi's has successfully executed what few companies have managed to accomplish: create ultracool videos on YouTube that get viewed by millions of people and make their coveted "most watched" list. One features unbelievable young performers back flipping into jeans off rooftops and cars, another filling their Levis with helium to float above the crowd, a third features a chimp in Levis applying for an acting job. The secret to their success is that nowhere in the YouTube episodes is the Levi's brand pushed on the viewer. The subtle brand identification of their famous leather logo patch is all that's visible. Of course, you just need to convince your CEO that spending a few thousand dollars on an unbranded video makes sense. In Levi's case, they made the bet and have seen positive, measurable results in target markets around the world. According to my son, Vice President of Levi's Marketing, they've had six million aggregate views on the "Jean Jump," eighteen million in total, with nineteen thousand individual consumer responses—all for a meager production cost of $35,000 and no media buy!

A Boston start-up called Flimp takes this a step farther marrying video marketing with one-to-one marketing. Their technology enables a company to e-mail a video or other rich media marketing message to a single targeted customer and then track whether it's opened, viewed to conclusion, and acted on.

Competitor Insights

While the discussion and focus up to now has been on market shifts and customer value, another valuable market insight involves competition. In IBM we launched a separate initiative to capture and describe the competitive landscape, placing accountability on each product manager for monitoring competitor actions as a core part of his or her job. Like GMT, the periodic competitor update document was a comprehensive, fact-based view of every major competitor across thirteen industry segments ranging from semiconductors through professional services. For each of these segments, we analyzed market dynamics over a six-year period, key players, and the outlook, the challenges, and disrupters that will likely change the segment going forward. We created several standard graphic formats to show market share trends for the top five or six participants in each segment, their primary strategies, key investments, and standard profile data including revenues, profits, market capital, and share of total revenues. After doing this the first time and establishing a common format, we delegated it back to the line organizations for them to update as their markets changed. The process was a good start for competitor insights, but fell short of continuous market monitoring.

Continuous Monitoring of Competitor Activity

An early pioneer of real-time continuous market insight was Frito Lay. During one of our IBM Strategy Conferences, we invited several customers including Charlie Feld and Michael Jordan, CIO and CEO of Frito Lay, to discuss real-time information strategies. Working together, they had implemented an advanced mobile computer network for field sales that transformed the work of the company's ten thousand salespeople. Instead of filling out stacks of paper to record inventory levels and to account for special promotions, salespeople could enter data on handheld computers, saving hours of paperwork a week and freeing up much more selling time. An important by-product of this system was that the distribution people delivering new supplies to stores twice a week could record competitors' product mix, shelf space, and supplies on hand. They explained to our senior executives that they were now getting direct market signals on competitors twice a week; at the time, we were lucky to get secondhand feedback maybe once a quarter!

Frito Lay actually took the market insight design even further. Using artificial intelligence software, they analyzed sports results and weather patterns to better predict geographic demand and product mix. They then dynamically diverted supplies of their salty snacks to the areas of highest predicted demand, using the mobile onboard computers in their trucks. The project was an early case study on how information technology (IT) can partner with business units to create an advanced "sense and respond" system and achieve true competitive advantage.

The Adaptive Enterprise

Ultimately, to survive in a world of chaos, the enterprise needs to be redesigned to become truly adaptive to its customers and the changing marketplace. The "sense and respond" management model was the brainchild of Stephan Haeckel, articulated in his business classic, *Adaptive Enterprise*. The "sense and respond" concept turns a firm into a continuously adaptive system, a business on demand, rather than a business as planned. The model was developed at IBM in the late 1990s, and successfully applied in IBM Global Services in the early 2000s. It became the basis of the Department of Defense's Sense and Respond Logistics initiative in 2002, and a variety of leaders facing unprecedented change have since adopted it. Haeckel reasoned that if unpredictability is a given, leaders need to learn to manage their enterprises as adaptive systems. They need to sense earlier and respond more quickly to the abrupt changes in customer needs. As a metaphor he used the

OODA Loop, (observe, orient, decide, and act), of jet fighters to simulate high-performance business leadership behavior. According to Haeckel, a firm needs to develop five competencies to become a customer-centric, adaptive enterprise:

1. *Know earlier*, using advanced technology to anticipate and diagnose individual customer needs and recognize emerging customer preference patterns earlier than competitors do.
2. *Manage by wire*, using advanced information systems to provide a digital representation of the business that can be manipulated by decision makers to directly change business operations. The information system must support role-specific decision making to capture shifts in external conditions, invoke appropriate models, and translate decisions into operational changes.
3. *Design the business as a system.* Referring back to the systems concept discussed in Chapter 3, this adds the principles of systems *design* to the skills of systems *thinking.* Instead of bolting together existing processes to produce offerings, system designers work backward from what the customer needs to create capabilities the business needs and the interactions between them. In Haeckel's view, this means designing an organization around its customer value proposition. The system designs eliminate silos, alignment problems, and suboptimization issues. They create synergistic horizontal organizations, a concept we'll discuss in Chapter 9 on organizational structure.
4. *Change the business orientation* from "firm forward" to "customer back" by dispatching requests from the customer back into the firm, using customer metrics of value and success. In the process, the firm moves from prediction and optimization to knowing earlier and improvising in context.
5. *Develop bounded empowerment*, enabling employees to negotiate, collaborate, and innovate, using technology to track commitments and ensure people's actions are consistent with the

overall purpose, policy, and strategy of the firm. Recall the discussions of chapter 4 on strategic intent.

In many ways, the *adaptive enterprise* is the blueprint for the enterprise of the future in a world of permanent chaos.

Summary

Market insight is a broad, complex, and critically important input to developing a dynamic strategy. As companies increasingly democratize the leadership of their firms, empower all workers, and attempt to respond to market forces in real time, market insights are becoming dispersed and embedded in every employee's responsibility and action. At the same time, processes must be defined to see the big picture, the cross- business trends and long-term shifts in value that no one person can see. And given the hundreds or thousands of constant and conflicting market signals, some process needs to be defined and refined to bring order out of chaos, identify the patterns, and establish company focus on the most important priority issues. Listening to customers, responding urgently to their needs, and engaging them as collaborative prosumers are all valuable approaches to market feedback. But, of course, feedback is just inert data unless you, as a strategic leader, do something about it.

CHAPTER 6:

The Innovation System: Beyond Customer Imagination

Innovation is the spark that makes good companies great. It's not just invention, but a style of corporate behavior comfortable with new ideas and risk. Companies that know how to innovate don't necessarily throw money into R&D. Instead, they cultivate a new style of corporate behavior that's comfortable with new ideas, change, risk, and even failure.
– Fortune magazine

Logic will get you from A to B. Imagination will take you everywhere.
– Albert Einstein

The consensus among today's business leaders is that the way you thrive in this chaotic network economy is by innovating—innovating in technologies, in products, in new ways to serve the customer, and most important, in business models embracing creative new business strategies. *Innovation is not an option; it's a survival issue.* That's one of the conclusions of the latest study of global CEOs. Unfortunately, in many firms, the innovation process is informal, ad hoc, or nonexistent. And that's the purpose of this component of the model, to explicitly foster innovation, whether it's managed in a centralized organization, distributed to every business unit and department, embedded as part of every employee's responsibility, or a blend of all these. Very bluntly, failure to innovate leads to corporate death. In *The Innovator's*

Dilemma, Clayton Christensen uses the disk drive industry to make the point. Of the original 17 firms in the industry from 1976 to 1995, all but one failed; and of 129 new firms that entered the industry during those twenty years, 109 failed! The common cause was failure to innovate and move quickly to the newest technology platform of a very dynamic industry.

> *Innovation is not an option; it's a survival issue.*

The need for innovation now covers a wide spectrum of activities. A decade ago, it was mainly about technology, quality control, or more efficient ways to reduce costs; now it's about reinventing business processes and building entirely new offerings that meet unsatisfied customer needs, sometimes needs customers haven't even articulated or can't even imagine. As the Internet and globalization greatly expand the source of new ideas, innovation is about selecting the *right* ones and being the first to bring them to market.

Innovation and creativity are tightly linked opposite sides of the same coin. Creativity is more about the process, innovation the solution. What's important in the business world, in contrast to the art world, is that creativity must be applied to solve some specific customer problem and to develop a sustainable solution for it.

At the foundation of innovation is a fundamental concept that has parallels in both nations and enterprises: *creative destruction.* Austrian economist Joseph Schumpeter introduced the process in the last century and it remains today the essence of free market capitalism. Creative destruction is the process of incessantly destroying the old and creating the new...new markets, new methods of production, new leapfrog technologies. The attributes of openness, flexibility, entrepreneurialism, and technological advancements are its hallmarks. According to Schumpeter, the entrepreneur, or "wild spirit," disturbs the equilibrium of the status quo, creates innovation and is the driving force of long-term economic growth.

The nature and locus of innovation is also changing, especially in the high-tech field, where it's a required core competency. Innovation and research used to be centralized; now they are being dispersed and embedded throughout the enterprise, and even across enterprises as multifirm collaboration becomes prevalent. Boeing's breakthrough process in designing and developing the 777 in the early '90s, the first paperless-designed aircraft, was based on collaboration with Boeing's customers, fellow aircraft manufacturers, airline users, engineers, finance experts, technicians, and computer experts. That pioneering type of cross-enterprise collaboration decades ago is now almost commonplace.

Rethinking Centralized Innovation

Although some would call it a relic of the industrial age, *centralized* research continues to fuel industries that require a continuing flow of new products every year, such as pharmaceutical, automotive, aerospace, chemical, and high tech. Global firms that continue to invest in *basic* research include GE, Dupont, 3M, Genetech, Toyota, Apple, Dow Chemical, Google, and Lockheed Martin. But for years, CEOs have complained that traditional corporate researchers often play in their expensive "sandboxes," too focused on their own pet projects and pure invention, too disconnected from the market and the rest of the enterprise. Two major shifts are now occurring: the boundaries between research and development are fading, and partnerships are creating more market-based solutions with economic value.

Firms like AT&T, Xerox, and IBM created and funded a centralized research organization as the firm's main innovation engine from the outset. Historically Bell Labs was the biggest, twenty-five thousand researchers at its peak. In IBM's case, the function is still centralized even though the labs themselves are dispersed throughout the world in cities like Beijing, Delhi, Haifa, La Gaude, Palo Alto, and soon Shanghai, recognized centers of innovation. That approach with its current team of 3,200 scientists and researchers has been very successful as IBM has remained the worldwide patent leader for sixteen years in a row through 2008, and the team has accrued five Nobel Prizes.

Stepping back, the U.S. innovation engine appears relatively healthy, with a cumulative investment by the private and public sectors of $5 trillion since the year 2000 in R & D and higher education, the two key drivers. That puts the United States ahead of Japan, Germany, France, and the UK and on a par with South Korea with innovation spending as a percentage of GDP, according to the OECD. And, according to *Business Week*, the top twelve innovation companies in the world include strong U.S. representation: Apple, Google, Toyota, IBM, GE, Microsoft, Tata, Nintendo, P&G, Sony, Nokia, and Amazon. But the end results are disappointing in hot emerging fields like nanotech and biotech, and employment in cutting-edge fields is actually declining.

One key challenge for enterprises is how best to manage the creative process and creative people. The current head of IBM Research, John Kelly, says across all companies, innovators tend to be self-motivated, enthusiastic, and highly energized about the intrinsic value of their work. They really want to accomplish something and need the peer recognition when they do. Of course, they especially appreciate the freedom to act and perform on their own. But the needs of the business require that their inventiveness be channeled into strategic domains, solving specific customer-perceived problems or targeting specific future opportunity areas. In IBM's case, he now has Research focused on four top research priorities, rather than spreading investments on a hundred small opportunities. The four bets are huge, each project getting $100 million over the next two to three years, in hopes of generating at least $1 billion each in new revenue. The four projects are: inventing a successor to today's semiconductor, designing computers that process data much more efficiently, using math to solve complex business problems, and building massive clusters of computers that operate like a single machine, a concept called "cloud computing." All are big and bold.

Another innovation trend involves collaboration. Procter & Gamble is leveraging a partnership with Los Alamos and Sandi National Labs to create more eco-friendly consumer products. Goodyear's doing the same thing to help accelerate new product launches like their Triple-Tred. HP is working with their customer Dreamworks Animation to create a more sophisticated videoconferencing system called Halo. IBM is also becoming more collaborative, creating dozens of new joint ventures called "collaboratories," working with companies and countries. One venture announced in 2008 is focused on nanotechnology in a collaboratory with Saudi Arabia.

Emerging Business Opportunities: A Complete Innovation System

But increasingly in the network economy, we see power, influence, and innovation all shifting to the outer nodes of the network, closer to the market and where the freedom to interact and collaborate is the most advantaged. The problem is if you diffuse the responsibility out to tactical business units too soon or without proper

> *"Why do we keep missing emerging new industries and market opportunities?"*

executive guidance, support, and funding, the new innovations will fizzle and fail.

While IBM was pretty good at inventing new technologies in its research arm described above and in its product divisions, it was terrible at creating successful new businesses. That's starting to change. The new innovation system we developed in the late '90s began with a rant from then CEO Lou Gerstner, who sent a scathing letter to his senior execs demanding to know, "Why do we keep missing emerging new industries and market opportunities?" The task force I led to respond to his question was called Emerging Business Opportunities, or EBO for short. IBM had earlier unsuccessful runs at creating an internal venturing process, some without funding, some without process, and some without sustained top executive support. This time we attacked the problem comprehensively and aggressively. We met with venture capitalists and entrepreneurs, reviewed academic literature, and benchmarked against new business development efforts of other major IT companies like Microsoft, Intel, and Cisco. But the most convincing part was the in-depth assessment of twenty-eight internal IBM start-ups, both successes and failures, attempted over the past two decades, from the original PC to Web servers.

Rather than just theorize about venturing, we got very specific, assessing each internal start-up in enough detail to determine what caused the project to fail or succeed and to debate the naysayers. By project's end, we concluded there was a common set of root causes leading to failure and wrote a no-holds-barred report calling for abrupt change. The root causes were:

1. Our management system rewarded execution directed at short-term results and did not place enough value on strategic business building.

2. We were preoccupied with current served markets and existing offerings, as many established companies are.
3. Our business model emphasized sustained profit and EPS improvement, rather than actions to drive higher P/Es.
4. Our approach for gathering and using market insights was inadequate for embryonic markets.
5. We lacked established disciplines for selecting, experimenting, funding, and terminating new growth businesses.
6. Once selected, many ventures failed in execution due largely to the lack of entrepreneurial leadership, skills for building a small business, and sustained funding.
7. Senior management did not spend enough time on the new growth opportunities.

I've shown this list to other large company senior executives and have received strong head-nodding reactions: "That's our problem too!"

During the course of this project, we discovered a useful model developed by McKinsey that helped portray a company's investment profile. As described in the book *The Alchemy of Growth*, a simple framework divides a business into three horizons: 1) current core businesses, 2) future growth businesses, and 3) a portfolio of new ventures to feed longer-term growth. The concept reinforces the need for ambidexterity, maintaining short- and long-term growth. As the following chart illustrates, the appropriate leadership style, measurements, and cultures and goals vary widely according to the horizon business you're dealing with. For example, mature Horizon 1 businesses need to be led by operational leaders and measured on profit. High-growth new businesses, Horizon 2, need to be led by business builders or entrepreneurs and be measured on revenue growth and market share. The Horizon 3 portfolios of experiments need creative portfolio managers and entrepreneurs as leaders and project-based milestones.

Figure 11.
Three Horizons for Growth

Successful enterprises achieve a balanced portfolio of businesses across all three horizons of growth.

Profit

Horizon 3
Portfolios of Experiments

Horizon 2
New Growth Businesses

Horizon 1
Core Business

TIME (Years)

Leadership:	Operators	Business Builders	Portfolio Managers

Measures:			
	• Profit	• High revenue growth	• Project-based milestones
	• Return on invested capital	• Market share gains	• Option valuation
	• Costs	• New customer acquisitions	• Pace of conversion from idea to business launch
	• Productivity or efficiency	• Profit	• Number of initiatives

SOURCE: THE ALCHEMY OF GROWTH

The external research done of thirty sustained growth firms indicated that successful companies maintain a pipeline of investments balanced across all three horizons. Furthermore, McKinsey's conclusion is that market valuations of large companies are based more on the market's opinion of their Horizon 2 and 3 portfolios than on today's mature Horizon 1 businesses.

Back in the late '90s, we discovered that IBM's investment profile was strongly skewed to Horizon 1 businesses and we lacked sufficient Horizon 2 growth initiatives capable of replacing H1s in the next few years. Furthermore, our H3 portfolio was highly fragmented and random, not centered around any predetermined business domains and not on a measured course to become revenue-producing businesses anytime soon. Without the promise of new and large growth businesses, we had to rely on extending mature businesses well beyond their natural life, not a good thing in the fast-paced high-tech industry.

In essence, the EBO Task Force discovered that IBM, like many other large companies, suffered from the conflict of two cultures: a dominant one protecting and serving the existing customers and mature business, and a new start-up culture attempting to create brand-new businesses in new markets, but without sufficient organizational support.

EBO Recommendations

To overcome these obstacles and address the root causes identified above, the EBO Task Force recommended that IBM:

1. Adopt the "Three Horizons for Growth" model and use it as a way of assessing the health of IBM overall and each business unit. The profile of each business would help us determine where new pipelines are required. As part of this, we recommended that our senior leadership establish a company-wide priority on building H2 and H3 portfolios; allocate more time to encouraging, measuring, and inspecting these investments; and demonstrate a willingness to protect them during the inevitable periods of financial pressure.

2. Create a well-structured management system for emerging businesses. We needed a more streamlined business system that ensured we would rapidly and effectively identify, prioritize, select, fund, and, when necessary, terminate new businesses.

3. Develop an execution model for Horizon 2 businesses. As soon as an H2 is declared a "go," it should follow a model comparable to a fast-growing start-up competing for venture capital funding on an IPO track. As part of this execution model, we needed to attract and cultivate entrepreneurial leaders, provide personal wealth opportunities comparable to the outside, embrace speed as a critical criterion for success, add significant

marketing resources and support as external start-ups do, and measure the H2 on revenue growth and market share.

4. And finally, appoint an executive sponsor, a truly senior one, someone well known, well respected, and sufficiently powerful to oversee and help nurture these fledgling start-up businesses. Initially we identified eighteen EBO ventures to fund, later expanding it to twenty-five, so overseeing them all was a full-time job.

At the final approval meeting, Gerstner, who was notoriously gruff and intimidating, stared icily throughout the presentation without expression. He paused for a long time then finally said, somewhat sarcastically, "EBO? I thought that was some sort of African animal." He was also notoriously anti-acronym, and I regretted slipping into acronym mode, even if just for the title of the project. But his mood changed to one of determination. He next said, "OK, let's do it." He approved our overall recommendations and agreed we needed someone with "really big shoes" to manage this. A week later, he selected the most senior group executive, John Thompson, and promoted him to vice chairman of the board and executive sponsor, in charge of all emerging new businesses.

Role of the Executive Sponsor

The role we defined for the executive sponsor, what we called "Big Shoes," had three main elements:

1. Appoint an executive leader for each H3: This meant finding the most skilled individual in the company (or sometimes outside) to lead each new venture. For IBMers, that meant changing the culture to see the running of an emerging growth business as a valuable, positive, and exciting career step. Collectively, these ventures represented IBM's future. Entrepreneurial skills and the ability to manage an unstructured, cross-functional team were critical. The executive sponsor was to act as an adviser and coach to each H3 leader and create training sessions as required.

2. Champion the initiative among group executives and corporate: It was necessary to secure buy-in with the powerful group executives and senior corporate execs because they had the ability to provide talent, funding, and critical cross-IBM support. The executive sponsor was specifically tasked with providing visibility and status and resolving conflicts and funding issues. The executive sponsor was like a fullback running interference for the less powerful H3 leaders running behind him.

3. Actively manage: This was *not* just one of many assignments given to the new vice chairman. Actively managing the portfolio of new start-ups was his full-time job, requiring his full dedication. He was expected to create and then leverage the H3 management system. Over time, he had to oversee the process for refilling the H3 pipeline with new growth candidates and transitioning and scaling up mature H3s, ensuring a sustained flow of new businesses.

Role of the Executive Leader

Venture capitalists often say that no person is more critical to success than the start-up's leader. Each leader of a Horizon 3 growth initiative was selected because of his or her basic entrepreneurial skills and was given five specific objectives:

1. *Assemble the core team.* Create a small multi-disciplined, cross-IBM team with subject matter experts, a core leader team, and external hires and partners as required.
2. *Create a focused game plan.* Create a short, crisp business plan, a market map, and targeted focus areas; like a venture capital start-up, make a case for investment and secure the initial funding; and establish strategic milestones.

3. *Launch in-market experiments.* Build visibility via proactive market communications and initiate market trials.
4. *Continually <u>assess</u> progress, <u>learn</u> from the market, and <u>adapt</u> the business model* as the project progresses, and monitor and meet milestones.
5. *Scale the winners up fast.* Once a concept has tested successfully in the market, ramp it up quickly to lead the market.

Incubation and Transitioning EBOs

Running a line business from Corporate HQ is a recipe for disaster. We knew we needed to incubate the businesses for a while, guide them, and protect them from the internal antibodies that tend to attack new things. But, as soon as an H3 was done experimenting and was up and running successfully, we relinquished most control and centered the oversight in the line. We established three overall criteria for transition:

1. <u>Market maturity</u>: Is the value proposition clear, do we have paying customers, and are the two or three market beachheads secured?
2. <u>Business design well understood</u>: Is the IBM offering identified, is profitability clear, and are the main elements of the business model defined and reinforcing?
3. <u>Value net clarity</u>: Are the critical internal and external partners identified and signed up to support this new venture?

Notice we didn't say, "The business needs to be profitable." That's not expected until the next stage, Horizon 2, after the business has scaled up. To be clear, the H3s are first nominated and supported by the line that also provides some funding. If accepted as a corporate EBO, the venture becomes a hybrid partnership with shared responsibility between the host division and nurturing corporate staff. When ready, rather than abruptly transferring responsibility to the line, we develop a gradual transition plan. As the new business matures, the parent division assumes an increasing share of ownership and funding.

Measuring Success

Of course the ultimate measure of any project is its final outcome and contribution. Over 150 project candidates were nominated to be Horizon 3 ventures for EBO when we began the program in the year 2000. As a VC firm would do, we carefully selected twenty-five to bet on. Of those, three failed and the other twenty-two had some degree of success. Collectively, they contributed more than $6 billion in additional revenue to IBM in 2002, more than $10 billion in 2003, and $15 billion by 2004. Today fourteen of the EBOs have been transitioned out of the corporate system and have been delegated to the business groups and divisions so that operational issues can be better handled.

Important Lessons Learned

There are many lessons we learned from EBO; here are the major ones. To tackle any problem you must clearly define it, really understand its root causes, and then address them. Using facts about why earlier attempts failed, or in some cases succeeded, is a very humbling but

> *Commit to revolutionary goals, but take evolutionary steps. Use in-market experiments, assess, learn, and adapt.*

useful approach, much better than just applying some outsider's theory. Support from the very top is absolutely crucial, since many of these strategic ventures won't pay off for years. You need management system discipline; venturing is not to be viewed as high-risk gambling. But the management systems and processes need to be "venture-appropriate" rather than maintain the traditional focus on revenue and profits as mature H1s have. Provide funding like a VC. That means start small and invest more as you progress, not the opposite. Don't starve new growth initiatives. Commit to revolutionary goals, but take evolutionary steps. Use in-market experiments, assess, learn, and adapt. Select and develop a generation of entrepreneurial leaders; you'll need more of them as you pursue more growth opportunities. Build a pipeline process to keep new business growth flowing and keep reminding everyone of the continuing value that accrues from new growth businesses. In summary, the three-horizon model provides a simple framework or agenda for the CEO to explore long-term growth and pose some fundamental questions.

Figure 12.
Critical CEO Leadership Questions

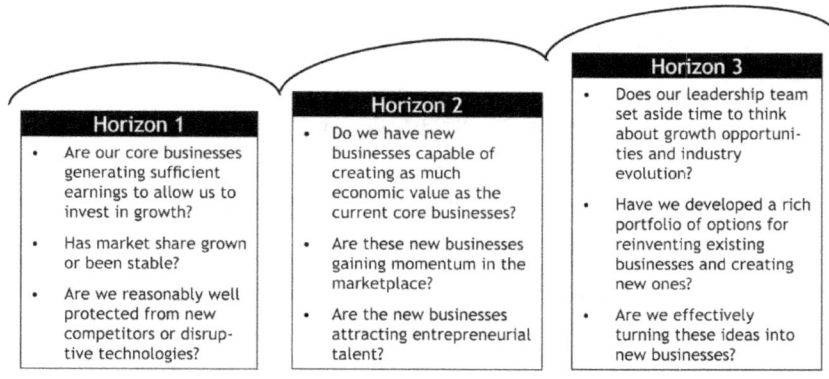

Horizon 1	Horizon 2	Horizon 3
• Are our core businesses generating sufficient earnings to allow us to invest in growth?	• Do we have new businesses capable of creating as much economic value as the current core businesses?	• Does our leadership team set aside time to think about growth opportunities and industry evolution?
• Has market share grown or been stable?	• Are these new businesses gaining momentum in the marketplace?	• Have we developed a rich portfolio of options for reinventing existing businesses and creating new ones?
• Are we reasonably well protected from new competitors or disruptive technologies?	• Are the new businesses attracting entrepreneurial talent?	• Are we effectively turning these ideas into new businesses?

Linking Market Insights and Innovation: Crossing the Chasm

In the last chapter, we discussed the role of market insights. One purpose for understanding the market is to decide whether to create or enter a new market. In pursuing emerging markets, we applied three criteria: 1) is the new opportunity area *technically* viable, that is, can you develop and manufacture the new innovation commercially, reliably and efficiently; 2) is it financially or *economically* viable at this early stage, are the returns better than other uses of capital; and 3) is the mainstream *market ready* for it, is there perceived customer need and value? It's this last criterion that relies heavily on external market insights.

Geoffrey Moore, in his classic book *Crossing the Chasm*, described the model that almost universally defines Silicon Valley's view of the high-tech start-up marketplace. Ironically, the adoption cycle was originated for the low-tech seed corn market of the 1950s, addressing the diffusion of new farm practices. Moore acknowledges that across the spectrum of continuous to discontinuous change lies a wide response on the part of consumers to new innovations. The technology adoption life cycle describes five distinct groups of consumers who have different psychographic and demographic profiles.

Figure 13.
The Technology Adoption Life Cycle

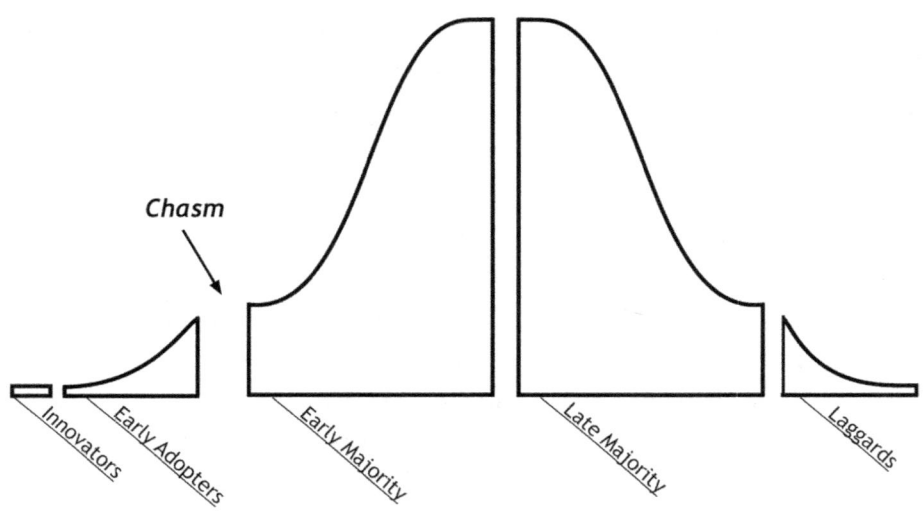

SOURCE: G. MOORE, CROSSING THE CHASM

Innovators tend to seek out new technology even before it's formally marketed, because technology is a central aspect of their lives and they are intrigued by the new features of a device, regardless of how well it performs. These are really technology enthusiasts, the sort of people who bought PCs when they had to be assembled from kits, or camcorders when they cost thousands of dollars. They want to be the first to get new stuff, regardless of the economics involved. As the bell curve illustrates, there are typically very few of them.

The *early adopters* or visionaries typically buy into new offerings very early in their development cycle, but they are not technologists. They have the ability to imagine the benefits of a new technology. They rely on their own intuition and vision rather than other people's references. Visionaries tend to be new entrants to the executive ranks, dreamers, and charismatic influencers. They pursue business goals not technology ones. They tend to be looking for a fundamental breakthrough in business design. This segment is key to getting a new product or technology adopted by the general market.

The *early majority* tends to be more pragmatic and wants to see how other reference customers do with the new inventions. This group comprises roughly one-third of the market and is key to profits and growth. These pragmatists are hard to win over, but are very loyal once they are.

The *late majority* are much more conservative and much less comfortable with cutting-edge innovations. In a sense, they are against discontinuous change and believe more in tradition than progress. They look for lots of support and assurances that this new product will be a de facto standard, to reduce their risk. They buy and use advanced products only because they must to keep up with the rest of the world. Like the early majority, this group constitutes about one-third of the total market.

And finally, the *laggards* want absolutely nothing to do with new products, for either technological or economic reasons.

The value that Moore contributed was in defining the gaps or chasms that exist between several of these life cycle stages. Especially important is the huge gap between early adopters and early majority. To illustrate the point, IBM, working with its partners CBS and Sears, invented a radically new concept in the late 1970s called "home networking" under the brand name Trintex, later relaunched under a new brand name Prodigy. The application and customer need was vague. IBM theorized that people could use it for asynchronous messaging, home shopping, and maybe, someday, home banking, but it was not at all clear in 1980. Furthermore, there were no other competitors in the field to legitimize the concept. AOL didn't appear until 1987. Innovators and a few early adopters were using the system, but no one else. There was no compelling reason to buy it. Most people could not even imagine sitting at home at a network-connected PC talking to friends online. Just use the phone! Technically and economically, the concept was feasible, but it was way ahead of the pragmatic majority markets.

As you gather market insights about emerging markets, it's critical that you perceive who's responding and telling you they'll consider buying the product. Are they technology enthusiast innovators or pragmatic early or late adopters? It makes a huge difference in terms of market readiness, market entry timing, and the appropriate strategic decision.

Innovation Depends on the Maturity of the Firm

Over time, fundamentally different innovation strategies are required based on the maturity of the firm and the stage of development of its primary offerings. Tushman and O'Reilly have observed that as firms or business lines move from emergence to growth to maturity, the rate or pace of innovation naturally slows down. While different product classes have different change cycles, the principle remains the same. Importantly at the outset, innovation may have more to do with dominant product or offering designs. In the growth stage, *process innovation* becomes the critical success factor. Then in the maturity stage, the opportunity exists for *radical innovation* to capitalize on the discontinuous change as new product or process substitutions become viable and offer a substitution.

Another way of viewing this progression is that, at its lowest form, innovation is about making incremental improvements to existing products. This can be valuable in its own right, as Toyota attests in making millions of innovations each year. At the next level, there are architectural or generational changes in a product line, which may require or benefit from major improvements in linkages and subsystems. At the highest level is radical innovation, the creation of an entirely new business, offering, or approach in response to a major market force. This requires entirely new subsystems and may require simultaneous change in the supporting execution elements of structure, skills, and culture.

Encouraging Individual Innovation

The Emerging Business Opportunities (EBO) project became a formal innovation system for IBM and for the thousand or so employees working on those specific ventures. But, at the same time, there's growing evidence that in the most innovative companies, it should be encouraged and embedded throughout the entire enterprise. Ultimately, in the new economy and in the intelligent enterprise we envision, power is dispersed to each individual employee. They need to increasingly feel like owners of the strategy and challengers of the status quo. Gary Hamel, the preeminent strategy consultant, makes the point this way: "How can we make rule-breaking innovation a systemic capability—how can we give everyone the chance to be an innovator? Look on the Web and you'll discover a world of hackers, mixers, mashers, bloggers, and podcasters. Yet at work, too many people are viewed as little more than semi-programmable robots."

Innovator Role Models

So how do you make innovation part of the culture of your firm and get everyone engaged? Whirlpool found a way, according to *IndustryWeek,* and their head of Strategy. They attribute $4 billion of their $19 billion in annual revenues to their innovation program, up from $2.7 and $1 billion in the two years before. That means they're measuring ingenuity and emphasizing it as a component of corporate culture. Their Innovation 101 program defines it specifically against three criteria: "Innovation allows us to have a unique and compelling solution that a *customer validates,* a real and *sustainable competitive advantage,* and we get *extraordinary value* from it."

Google says rigor or discipline is the key to their Innovation Factory. The company has eight brainstorming sessions each year with one hundred engineers. Six concepts are pitched and discussed for ten minutes each with the goal to build on the initial idea with at least one complementary idea per minute.

At Apple, it's all about the corporate culture. Apple COO Tim Cook says, "We hire people who want to make the best product in the world and provide an atmosphere to challenge each other to do that. And that's deeply embedded in the DNA of the company. This atmosphere is very, very unique. We don't have an issue attracting talent. We have so many things going on and innovation is so deeply embedded in the company."

One of the most sustained innovators, 3M, dubbed their innovation program "The Seven Habits of Highly Innovative Corporations," a play on Covey's popular best seller. Their Seven Pillars include:

1. A top-down commitment to innovation recognizing that organic growth and new products drive the company;
2. A corporate culture that says, "Hire good people and let them do their job in their own ways and tolerate mistakes";
3. Leverage the broad base of technology, allowing researchers to take an idea from one realm and apply it to another;
4. Share innovations through forums, collaborate and call for advice, and build on each other's ideas;

5. Set individual expectations and reward employees for outstanding work, selection by peers for their achievements;
6. Quantify innovation efforts to determine how much revenue comes from products introduced in the past four years; and
7. Link research to the customer so employees better understand what their needs are and design more-valuable products.

Toyota has really unleashed the collective wisdom of the corporation, implementing a million new ideas each year. That's creating new innovations at the breakneck speed of over 2,500 new ideas every day! How is this possible? Innovation at Toyota begins with three guiding principles:

1. The art of ingenuity: The key is to continually ask the question: "Is there a better way?" This is possible if the individual fully leverages his or her domain knowledge and expertise, continuously pursues every possible way to innovate and perfect, challenges opposition tactfully, does not accept the status quo, and uses organizational efficiencies to drive new ideas and methods.

2. The relentless pursuit of perfection: For a business to succeed at innovation, it has to rigorously search for an optimal solution—one that yields low-cost, low-risk, high-impact breakthrough. Innovation happens at Toyota through the systematic pursuit of perfection at every level, every department, in everything it does. Perfection equates to excellence, precision, flawlessness, and this chase for perfection creates better processes, products, and services. Lexus epitomizes perfection in the form of car design, function, performance, service, and total satisfaction.

3. The rhythm of fit: Great innovation has to fit—fit the innovator, the times, and the larger system. How can a great innovation shape and then change the attitudes and behaviors of people, the way they think, work, and live? For example, customers want a car that is economical to drive, is environmentally friendly, and does not sacrifice the inherent need for roominess, safety, and performance.

The three principles create both the policy and framework at Toyota for driving innovation and creating elegant solutions.

A Comprehensive Innovation Program

Putting these ideas and others together, here are ten suggestions that seem to recur among the innovation leaders, the companies that remain at the cutting edge of bottom-up innovation. Pick those that you think will work within the culture of your firm and combine them into a comprehensive innovation program.

1. Decide to make innovation a way of life: Commit from the very top to make innovation a very visible attribute of your corporate culture, and one in which everyone plays. As we'll discuss later in Chapter 11, that means demonstrating top management commitment, visibility of role models, symbolic actions, and both intrinsic and extrinsic rewards. For reinforcement, reserve time at operational reviews to discuss innovation.

2. Do the math: Create metrics to measure innovation. After defining it crisply for your enterprise, determine ways to value the contributions of innovation and run the numbers, whether dollar savings, revenue growth, or throughput advantages that are directly attributable to it. Examine fact-based benefits of past projects and publicize measurable value.

3. Lead with learning: As we did with quality and other cross-enterprise emphasis programs, develop innovators by conducting a broad-based education program on it, use outside experts if necessary, make it a central topic in leadership development programs, and encourage all employees to attend classes. And look for the attribute in the people you hire.

4. See customers as the fount: Customers, the users of your goods and services, are often the best at seeing the need for new innovations. Find ways to go out and spend more time through their vantage point. Learn about their emerging needs, even their unarticulated ones; learn to read their minds.

5. Encourage work teams: Urge them to come up with innovations and to share their ideas. Schedule group innovation strategy sessions and encourage them to find new ideas focused on today's current problems. And reward the creative for their efforts, whether it is compensation, public recognition, a free lunch, or a valued parking space.

6. Redesign the workspace: Make the office more conducive to innovation and creativity; knock down the walls so that people in different cubicles, departments, and business units can talk to each other and tap into their collective know-how. Create a common brainstorming space. Creativity abounds amid diversity, so encourage people with varying levels of experience and backgrounds to meet and share ideas.

7. Establish an innovation fund: Set aside a portion of annual expense dollars as an investment fund earmarked for bottom-up innovation efforts such as trial experiments. It's demotivating to hear, "That's a great idea, but we don't have the money to try it." Protect the funds from other "emergency" uses.

8. Provide incentive plans and rewards: If it's a strong measurement culture, people tend to do what they're measured on and paid on. Reflect innovation in performance plans, evaluations, and recognition, and especially in executive compensation plans.

9. Create an innovation portal: Give every employee access to a comprehensive suite of business innovation tools. In addition, give them access to a database of customer insights and competitor intelligence and an internal Web site that helps individuals gather peer feedback on their creative ideas. Enable employees to fully exercise their imaginations and become fully empowered business innovators.

10. Establish an innovation board: Create a team to review, assess, advise, and fast-track ideas. It's critical that the tone of this board be receptive and encouraging and that a high percentage of initial ideas be accepted or at least tried. The internal word-of-mouth factor is extremely powerful.

Summary

The conclusion of this year's CEO study was unmistakably clear. If a company plans to survive and be an "Enterprise of the Future," it needs a mainstream innovation strategy: one that stimulates innovation beyond customer imagination; one that benefits from deep collaboration across enterprise lines, and mutually benefits both partners; one that creates groundbreaking offerings to open new segments and new markets; one that extends the enterprise globally; and one that taps into the collective genius of the enterprise.

Ultimately, the question is: "Are you building sustainability into your company through systemic innovation, not just bells and whistles on existing products, but an ongoing flow of customer value, and an innovation attitude woven into the fabric of your company culture?" As *Fortune* magazine's editors once observed, "Innovation is the spark that makes good companies great!"

CHAPTER 7:

Business Design and Explicit Strategic Choices

*By business design, we mean the fingerprint of the unique way
a company does business.*
– Adrian Slywotzky

*The challenge for organizations is to recognize that all of the business de-
sign variables need to be open to question all the time. Because if they're
not, someone else is going to come along and take some dimension of that
that you never regarded as important.*
– Gary Hamel

The business design is the central point of integration of the
strategy process, the area all the other components feed. During
this stage in the leadership model, strategic alternatives are carefully considered and decisions are explicitly made. In essence, the
business model describes exactly how a firm plans to create value
for customers and then how it will capture and sustain a portion
of that value. The business design embodies the uniqueness of the
company and all the critical success factors in an integrated, synergistic way.

During the 1970s and 1980s, leading companies in every industry began to falter and fall into a "no-profit zone." Two forces seemed to be working at once and against each other. Customers gained extraordinary power through better information
and began to search globally for the best deals and best prices.

Consequently, customer loyalty declined and churn increased. At the same time, too many companies mindlessly pursued market share or pure growth at all costs. Share leaders like A&P, DEC, Ford, GM, IBM, Kodak, Sears, United Airlines, and U.S. Steel, all household names, followed an age-old maxim that if you pursue high growth and market share, profitability will automatically follow. But that old business maxim and model seemed to be forever broken.

We have come to learn that there are many strategic problems with a single-minded growth strategy. Michael Porter called it the "growth trap," which has a perverse effect on strategy. In the mindless quest to serve all customers, uniqueness becomes blurred, compromises are made, strategies become confused, and competitive advantage is undermined. High growth is much harder to manage, especially during economic downturns, and high growth with the wrong business design actually destroys value faster than low growth, as less profitable activities are performed. Growth, achieved by stretching a company into new market domains, to new customers beyond its core competencies, or beyond selected segments, presents huge challenges and business risk. Not surprisingly, companies tend to be valued more by their P/E ratios and profitability than profitless growth

The Business Model Defined

If customers are increasing their relative power, why not reverse the "product push" model of the industrial age and replace it with a "customer pull" model?

Enter Adrian Slywotsky and David Morrison in 1997 with a crisp definition of the heretofore vague concept of "business design," articulated in their classic book *The Profit Zone*. In retrospect, it all seems so logical. If customers are increasing their relative power, why not reverse the "product push" model of the industrial age and replace it with a "customer pull" model? Start with the customers' priorities and then work inward with their preferred channels, offerings, and features. This definition of business design complements the concept of market insight and the need for every function in the firm to interact and understand customer needs, preferences, and values. With this inward flow in mind, Slywotsky and Morrison defined five key elements to a business design:

1. Customer selection: Which customers do we choose to serve? To which customers can we add real value, which customers will allow us to profit?
2. Unique value proposition: What makes our value proposition unique? Why do they buy from us?
3. Value capture: How do we make a profit?
4. Strategic control: How do we sustain that profitability over time?
5. Scope: What activities do we perform? And consequently, which functions do we want to subcontract or outsource to others?

As businesses increasingly adopted and applied business model thinking at the beginning of this century, Slywotsky and Morrison added two more dimensions in subsequent books:

6. Organization system: What organizational architecture and culture should we create that supports the first five elements of the design?
7. Information and network technology: What digital assets do we need to support the overall business design? How do we manage and distribute intelligence in the system?

Figure 14.
Business Design Framework

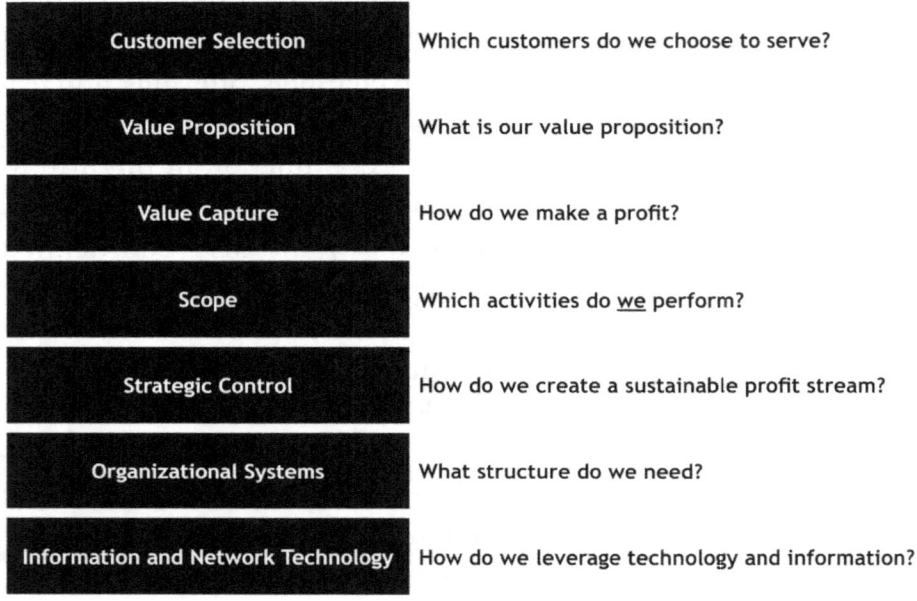

Customer Selection	Which customers do we choose to serve?
Value Proposition	What is our value proposition?
Value Capture	How do we make a profit?
Scope	Which activities do <u>we</u> perform?
Strategic Control	How do we create a sustainable profit stream?
Organizational Systems	What structure do we need?
Information and Network Technology	How do we leverage technology and information?

SOURCE: A.J. SLYWOTSKY, D.J. MORRISON

Here's a fuller description of each of those seven elements.

Customer Selection

At the foundation of a customer-focused organization is market segmentation and selection. Established firms may have thousands or even millions of customers. Separating the customer base into segments based on buying behavior, current and future needs, and priorities is a logical first step. In-depth market analysis can also reveal which segments are a firm's most profitable and attractive customers. Research by Don Rogers and Martha Peppers concluded that the contribution of the best customers (the top 20 percent) actually exceeds the total profit of a company and, in effect, they subsidize customers who cost more than they're worth. Their research shows that a new customer costs money to acquire and satisfy; a long-term customer is more self-sufficient and profitable. And a landmark study by PriceWaterhouseCoopers of 427 high-growth firms indicates that extraordinary customer service is the top contributor to both revenues and profits. If you've defined a market map showing all the participant groups in an industry, you can also be more precise in customer selection, understand who else in the industry has unmet needs, and expand the customer set to new unserved buyers.

One of the most powerful tools for understanding the unarticulated needs of customers is to do an economic analysis of the customers' total costs of ownership, or total system economics. This technique can be applied to either industrial customers or individual consumers. The fact is most customers don't really know their total system costs, although they have a rough sense of them. It's one area in which a supplier can use information to his or her advantage and counter the growing power of customers. Disney provided a classic example when they analyzed the total cost of a family vacation and decided to enter the lodging, food, and cruise line businesses to gain a greater share of total vacation dollars while reducing the consumer's hassles.

Unique Value Proposition

To determine your firm's strategic uniqueness, consider the following questions. Which priorities are your competitors satisfying, and which can you satisfy better? Which can you provide at a lower cost, or which will your customer pay a premium to you to satisfy? The goal here is simply to add more value than your competitors do. Remember, competitive strategy is about being different, explicitly deciding to provide differentiated value for customers. Jack Trout and Al Reis defined the one or two major differentiators as the "beachheads" that must be defended at all costs.

Value Capture

There are literally dozens of different profit models. This step requires a level of specificity to find the most appropriate one, given your industry structure, your firm's strengths, and its strategic goals. Slywotsky identified several of the typical models including: a) *customer solutions focus*, in which you learn the customer's business, create a total solution, and develop a strong relationship; b) *product pyramid profit*, in which you provide a wide range of products from low-priced entry ones to high-end more profitable ones with a variety of styles, features, and colors; c) *switchboard profit*, in which your firm connects multiple buyers with multiple sellers; d) *time profit*, in which fast innovators get to market one or two cycles ahead of the competition; e) *install base profit*, in which initial products have low margins, but follow-on products are very profitable; and f) *low-cost business design profit*, in which you achieve lower costs through new routes to market or manufacturing.

Strategic Control

One of the most critical aspects of business models is the approach used to sustain profitability over time. Many firms enter a market or provide a radically new offering in a market and achieve immediate attention and profitability. But over time, that initial market power erodes as competitors respond and imitate, and powerful customers demand more. The landscape is littered with "one-product wonders" that had a small window of fame but were unable to sustain success through successive product cycles. We always felt that Slywotsky's term "strategic control" sounded too deterministic; in a free market, no supplier really *controls* a market or customer base. But, whatever the label, the concept is sound. Enduring firms need to use one or more of the many strategic mechanisms to sustain profitability over the long haul. As the following table shows, many well-known firms have succeeded in doing so. The best business models have at least two of these mechanisms, and the higher the index number, the better.

Strategic Control Point Index

Power	Index	Strategic Control Point	Example
High	10	Own the Standard	Microsoft, Oracle
	9	Manage the Value Chain	Intel, Coke
	8	String of Superdominant Positions	Coke International
	7	Own the Customer Relationship	GE, IBM, EDS
Medium	6	Brand, Copyright	Countless
	5	2-Year Product Development Lead	Intel
Low	4	1-Year Product Development Lead	Few
	3	Commodity, 10-20% Cost Advantage	Nucor, SW Air
None	2	Commodity with Cost Parity	Countless
	1	Commodity with Cost Disadvantage	Countless

Scope

This element describes which activities we plan to do ourselves using our own assets, our own financial and human resources. It connects naturally with our recognized core competencies. Do we want to create the broadest possible line of activities and be fully integrated, or zero in on narrow specialties and leverage a large network of partners building to our standards? Global outsourcing now allows for effective leveraging of low-cost partners from around the world.

Organization System

Is our organizational design more hierarchical or networked to support collaboration? Is it more product- or customer-based? What are the strongest cultural attributes: collaborative, innovative, accountable, nurturing, conservative, engineering-based, adaptive, assimilative, reactive, preemptive? And, of the above, which are the most appropriate for our strategy and reinforce the other elements of our business design?

Information and Network Technology

This element, which Slywotsky called "Bit Engines," introduces the concept of a *digital business design*. The fundamental components are the digital systems for capturing, storing, processing, distributing, and leveraging information within and outside the company. To what extent does your design use the Internet to reach existing or new customers? Can customers use those linkages to customize offerings, receive service and support, and communicate with each other? In strategic control, are we building a repository of each customer's buying patterns, proactively recommending offerings, and building a stronger bond with them? And, organizationally, are we using online collaboration with customers and partners to enhance our offerings?

As we adapt our business design to the digital network economy and cross the virtual "e-line" to develop a *digital* business model, each of the seven elements changes in some fundamental ways.

Figure 15.
It's About Business Design
"Crossing the e-Line"

	TRADITIONAL ENTERPRISE		NET GENERATION ENTERPRISE
Customer Selection	· Local to stores		· Global buyers
Value Proposition	· Broad selection · Browse, cafe ambience		· Ultimate selection · One-click purchase convenience
Business Scope	· Selection/purchasing · Distribution · Chain of large stores		· Outsource fulfillment · Associate program
Value Capture	· Sales revenue · Profit from low-cost design	e-Line	· Sales revenue · Asset efficiency · Customer info capture
Strategic Control	· 10-20% cost savings over small stores · Frequent buyer programs		· Preference database · Exclusive links to key websites
Organizational Systems	· National advertising · Store management · Training		· IT intensive · Negative working capital · Employee stock options
Information & Network Technology	· Back office systems · Customer databases · Targeted direct mail		· Recommender engines · Network links · Online, hybrid marketing

Translating Business Design into Financial Plans

Once these reinforcing elements, the qualitative substance of the strategy, are agreed to, the next task is to develop the supporting quantitative model. The financial model, constantly adjusted as we learn from the market, is an important element of the measurement system and the baseline for assessing performance. There are three fundamental variables that need to be determined: What levels of investment are we prepared to make—enough to create and lead the market, or something more expeditionary and conservative? How and when are we going to implement this new strategy—in gradual market-test phases or in a full global rollout, or something in between? And, as detailed in the scope, how much of the value creation do we plan to do ourselves versus relying on partners and others?

The financial expression of the business model really gets people's attention because real funds need to be expended or at least earmarked. One recurring question is, how do you lock in a financial plan for a new expeditionary venture when you don't know which growth vector the new business will develop on? To answer this, we typically created a series of cases or models; the base case is what we most likely expected to happen, then a growth case and stretch case at two higher levels of performance, and a risk case at a lower level. The most important inputs were the expenses, the human resources and capital expenses required. We then set upper limits on how much investment we could make on each of the four tracks before going back for more approvals. The intent was to behave more like a venture capital firm and release funding as major milestones were met versus promising a large investment at the outset and then cutting back because of softer performance or competition for funds from other areas.

Applying Business Design: Making Explicit Strategic Choices

Understanding business models is the foundation for evaluating and deciding among strategic choices or alternatives. The starting point for developing a new business design is to first identify the most significant business issue(s) facing the enterprise. Market insights are especially critical in determining if we are truly addressing customer needs, losing competitively, or missing a major market shift. What is the most important performance or opportunity gap? This is an area we'll discuss in chapter 12.

The next step is to explore the smartest business design choices for responding to those issues. The attributes of the new design should include high relevance to customers; a consistent set of decisions about scope; a terrific profit model; a powerful, defensible source of differentiation; and an organizational system that supports the business design and best leverages company strengths. One of the fundamentals of strategic decisions is that you must be explicit about the strategic goal. Firms have four distinct alternatives or levels of investment to consider:

1. *Invest to lead the market*, helping to shape it and become the top share leader
2. *Invest to play in the market*, become one of the top three players
3. *Invest to reserve the right to play*, making a judicious conservative play, monitoring the market from the inside
4. Explicitly *decide not to play*, or exit a market if already there

Corporations have limits to their capital resources and need to carefully allocate or consider their bets. Which of the four levels (invest to lead, play, reserve the right, or exit) is appropriate depends on the variables of the market: the readiness of the customers, the current financial attractiveness, the firm's total resources and level of risk, and technical viability. Failure to be explicit on the intended goal of the investment will leave employees frustrated and confused. In IBM, we created a definition of "market leadership" so that the term was used with clarity and consistency. By our definition, the leader of a market or segment must have revenues twice that of the next player, be growing at a rate to sustain that lead, and have perceived quality and relative customer satisfaction measurements to support the perception of sustained market leadership.

An Integrating Example

Pulling several of these ideas together, here's an example of a strategy map that will help you to visualize four areas for major

THINK BEFORE YOU LEAP

IBM strategies in the late '90s. As a starting point, we created a strategic landscape to identify and help analyze alternative strategic initiatives. While there are many market variables, a simple 2 x 2 product-market matrix can define the boundaries of the market space. In IBM's case, we defined markets along the spectrum between institutions and individuals on the x-axis. On the y-axis, we defined the product spectrum from well-defined technology components as small as microchips to high-level activities and processes such as consulting services or new activities.

The accompanying figure illustrates four separate strategic initiatives. First, in the triangle at the bottom left was IBM's core business at the time, a range of products and services sold primarily to institutions. There was inherent synergy, leading with services to pull products, or selling products and then adding services. Here the strategic decision was obvious: strengthen the core and the synergy, "invest to lead," and exit unprofitable and disconnected businesses related to consumers. Pervasive computing would become the major initiative to reach consumers through game consoles or technology embedded in other products such as autos and cell phones, our OEM strategy.

Second, in the middle, was the initiative to create an infrastructure platform to link businesses with individuals and support higher-level applications and emerging e-business concepts. The key to the infrastructure was to assemble it using *open architecture* components such as Linux from IBM and other industry players, another "invest to lead" strategy.

The third initiative was more exploratory, addressing the unstructured emerging businesses with purely digital business designs, such as e-markets, e-exchanges, and e-communities related to Web 2.0. Here, the strategic decision was more venturesome, an "invest to play" or "reserve the right to play," until market viability was proven.

The fourth initiative complemented the other three, but was on an entirely different dimension, almost orthogonal to the others. Supporting all other strategies, we needed to shape a new corporate culture to encourage speed, innovation, and adaptability, topics we'll discuss later in the chapter on culture.

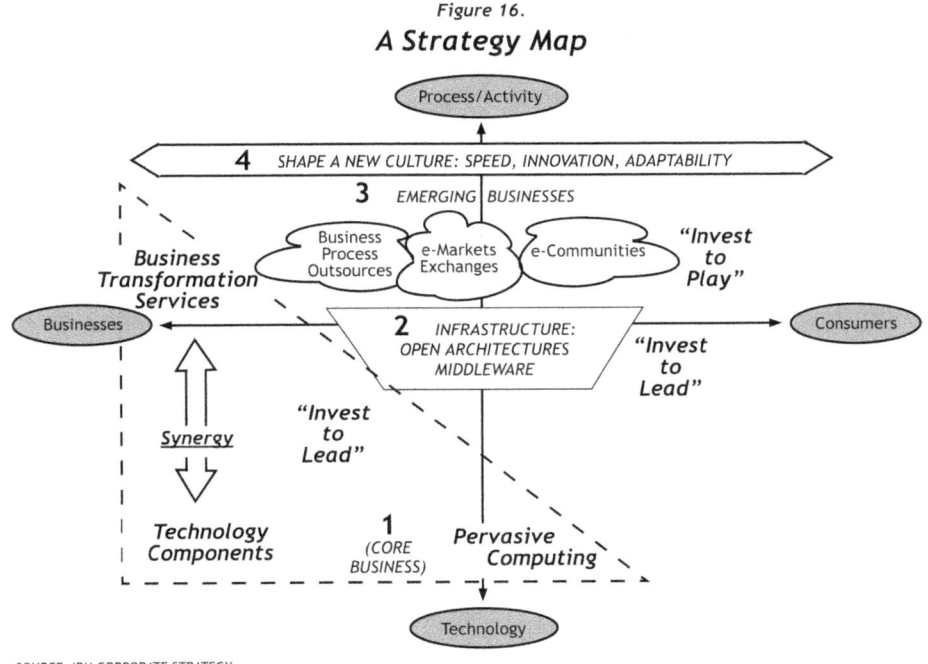

Figure 16.
A Strategy Map

SOURCE: IBM CORPORATE STRATEGY

A Case Study in Market Leadership: IBM's Commitment to Lead in Services

In the spring of 1991, IBM conducted one of the most memorable and decisive strategic planning conferences in its hundred-year history. The decision to "invest to lead" the IT services industry actually changed IBM's center of gravity and its performance for decades to come. Some IBM security analysts have said recently that services has become "the soul of IBM," its new core competence.

145

As of year-end 1990, IBM was generating only $2.9 billion in services revenue, a mere 3 percent of a hot market growing rapidly at 17 percent per year. By comparison, the total IT market was growing at less than 10 percent. And although IBM's services revenues had been fast growing for the previous five years, it was off of a very small base that was practically irrelevant. IBM's traditional focus was on hardware technology followed by software, leaving the customer or others to integrate all the solution components. An entire industry of IT services firms had grown up in the void including giants like Electronic Data Systems (EDS), Cap Gemini, NTT Services, Perot Systems, Computer Sciences, and Andersen Consulting, later renamed Accenture. Perhaps worse, IBM had been relegated to the role of an IT equipment vendor, while other firms were working with the top client executives to establish the strategic value of IT.

John Thompson, formerly the president of IBM Canada and the new head of the Corporate Marketing staff, joined me in 1990 to co-lead a services study team. We analyzed in depth ten major segments of the global services industry (e.g., industry consulting, IT strategy/planning, systems integration, outsourcing/operational services, systems management, network design...) and determined the financial attractiveness of each and the linkages between them. That involved calculating long-term trends in net earnings before taxes, return on assets, and return on equity for an industry that was largely privately owned or had complex integrated financial statements. This analysis was critical because we challenged the widely held assumption inside IBM that services was not sufficiently profitable, at least compared to the existing IBM technology businesses.

We also interviewed dozens of customers across six major countries and spoke to several CEOs of leading services firms to better understand critical management issues. The customers essentially told us they needed services help in reengineering their businesses, reducing structure, increasing value to their customers, improving quality and innovation, shortening cycle times, and empowering flatter organizations. Customers also told us they'd like to deal with one major supplier versus handing off pieces of a project to different specialty services firms and then playing the role of integrator.

In doing our analysis, we realized that one challenge IBM leaders had was that the services business was fundamentally different than our core product business and that we were evaluating it through the lens of a traditional product development company. Any services that we offered before 1991 were done to augment our core product sales. The following chart summarizes the fundamental differences.

Figure 17.
Services — A Different Business

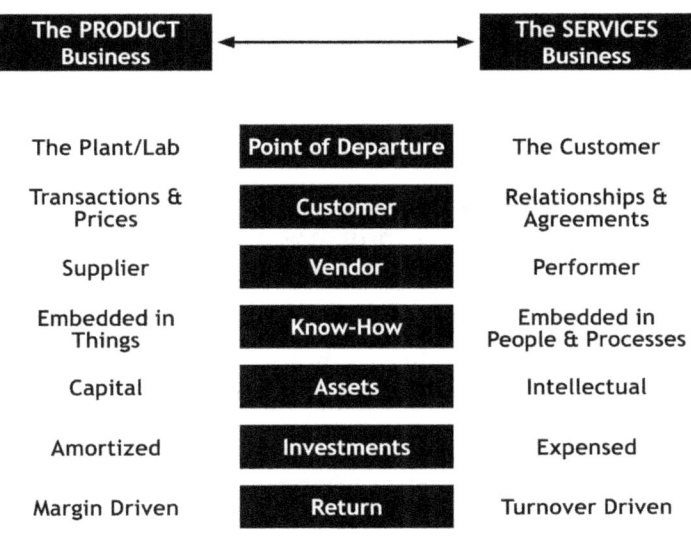

The PRODUCT Business	←——————→	The SERVICES Business
The Plant/Lab	**Point of Departure**	The Customer
Transactions & Prices	**Customer**	Relationships & Agreements
Supplier	**Vendor**	Performer
Embedded in Things	**Know-How**	Embedded in People & Processes
Capital	**Assets**	Intellectual
Amortized	**Investments**	Expensed
Margin Driven	**Return**	Turnover Driven

SOURCE: IBM STRATEGY

To summarize, IBM had a critical need for growth; our customers had major business needs that required services; and our detailed financial analysis concluded that many of the services segments were good businesses in their own right. At the end of the three-day strategy conference, we committed to a new strategic business design. It was to invest aggressively in services, enough to ensure a 30 percent per year growth over the next five years from $2.9 billion to $14.3 billion by 1996. That translated into $9.5B to $22.3B in total services revenue including maintenance. The strategy also capitalized on IBM's strengths and ensured that each services business was a good business in its own right.

The new business design could be summarized as follows:

1. Customer selection: Focus on our largest global customers, selling to the C-level at the CEO level and just below—i.e., COO, key functional executives, and CIO, at a strategic level. In fact, the services strategy provided the opportunity for IBM to reengage with more senior-level executives, as we had traditionally done, and help our clients to use IT more strategically. It was certainly higher-level selling than competing with other technology providers for, say, a disk drive bid.

2. Unique value proposition: Differentiation by having industry expertise in every major industry and country, close ties to advanced technology through IBM Research and Development, strengthened customer relationships, ability to take on the largest and most complex global projects, and ability to offer consulting, systems integration, and operational services all from a single vendor.

3. Value capture: High, stable financial returns from major long-term contracts. An added benefit was that operational services are strong during periods of economic weakness, while

consulting services are strong during economic expansion periods, creating a counterbalancing effect.

4. Scope: Provide a full complement of services in three major categories (consulting, systems integration, and operational services). Lead with services and pull technology, versus the current approach of leading with technology and offering add-on services.

5. Strategic control: "Own the customer relationship" and a string of super-dominant positions across the services spectrum; leverage the IBM brand, scale, and reputation for quality and customer service.

6. Organizational system: Create a separate, fully integrated Global Services profit center with the authority to deal with other competitive technology companies as necessary.

7. Information and network technology: Developed just before the network era, the major leverage of technology was in capturing and reusing engagement experiences and methods learned throughout the world.

To illustrate the reinforcing elements of the strategy, we created a framework reminiscent of the 7-S model, with a set of core imperatives: invest aggressively, capitalize on IBM strengths, ensure the highest customer and IBM impact, and establish each as a good business. These were surrounded by eight critical elements of the strategy: services to be offered, organization structure, practices/tools/methodologies, skills/competencies/professions, offerings that were designed to include services, business partners, implementation, and the resources strategy. It was this last topic that received the most attention because of the inherent risk of creating such a large people-intensive business. Our study team proposed adding 28,500 people to the current team of 11,500, bringing the total to 40,000, within three years!

Figure 18.
Integrated Services Strategy

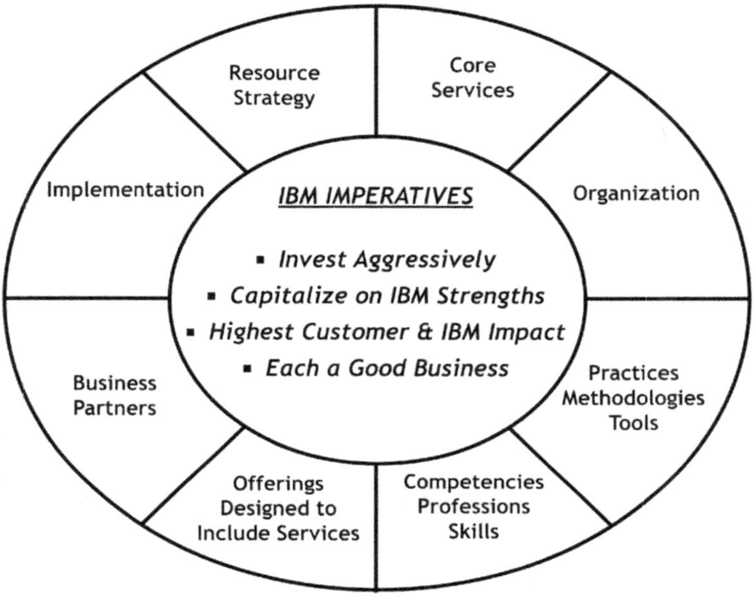

Resource Strategy

Core Services

Implementation

Organization

IBM IMPERATIVES

- *Invest Aggressively*
- *Capitalize on IBM Strengths*
- *Highest Customer & IBM Impact*
- *Each a Good Business*

Business Partners

Practices Methodologies Tools

Offerings Designed to Include Services

Competencies Professions Skills

SOURCE: IBM STRATEGY

After two days of debate, the senior executive team agreed to go forward, but we all recognized that the skill shortage issue in terms of hiring qualified consultants and services leaders was overwhelming. For consulting, we decided to hire Bob Howe, one of the top executives from Booz Allen Hamilton and then for market credibility completed forty major engagements before announcing the unit was officially open for business. To staff the services business, we moved resources from our Federal Systems group into commercial services, transferred over many of Marketing's systems engineers, hired well-known industry experts from the outside in each of fifteen industry segments, and acquired several boutique services firms. The eventual acquisition of PriceWaterhouseCoopers Consulting Services added 30,000 employees to help build a critical mass of skills. IBM Global Services is today a 190,000-person team that produces revenues of over \$60 billion, more than the revenues of EDS, Accenture, and CSC combined. It now contributes more than half of IBM's total revenues. As important, the long-term services contracts tend to smooth earnings and revenue flows for IBM during volatile economic periods. The commitment to "market leadership" was achieved.

Figure 19.
IBM Services Growth — "Invest to Lead"

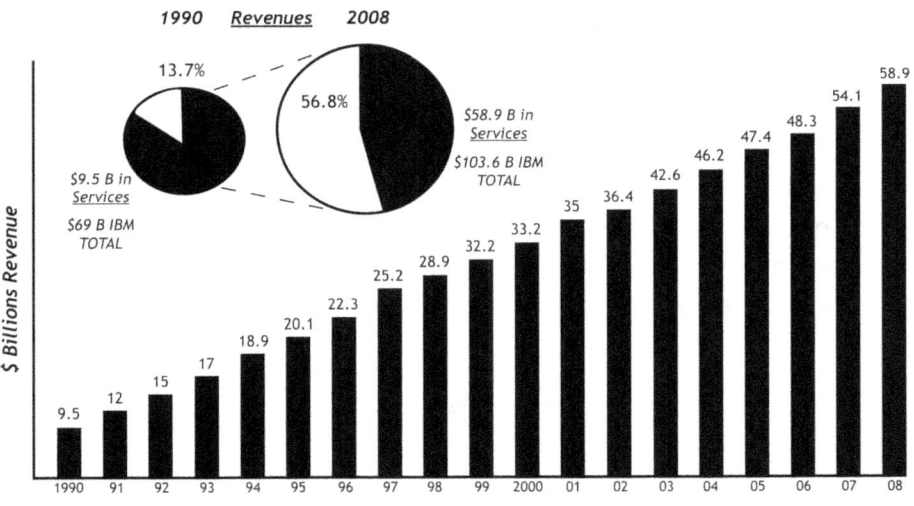

*Services include Maintenance Services

SOURCE: IBM ANNUAL REPORTS

Six Ways to Play

The services strategy decision was one of the boldest and most successful in IBM's history and was accomplished with the full support of our chairman, CEO, and board of directors, and access to all the company resources required. But our business units had more limited resources to apply to strategy, although most were billion-dollar businesses themselves. To help guide them in working their way through their own business designs, we created a simple template to describe some of the many successful ways to compete in the IT industry. Our principle goal was to help the unit leaders to think through alternative strategies that could be more effective than just imitating the market leaders or simply providing hardware, software, or services. While these serve as an example in just one industry, they may prompt you to think about the ways to play in your industry. These became known internally as the Six Ways to Play. Figure 20 portrays the overall industry transformation that was shifting competitive power from tight vertical integration to disaggregated horizontal layers. Michael Treacy and Fred Wiersma introduced the trichotomy of operational excellence, customer intimacy, and product leadership as the three overall sources of competitive advantage in *The Discipline of Market Leaders*. They argued that a firm's value proposition can be centered on any one of the three, while maintaining threshold levels in the other two. Each "way to play" emphasizes one or more of those three fundamental strategies.

Figure 20.
Six Ways to Play

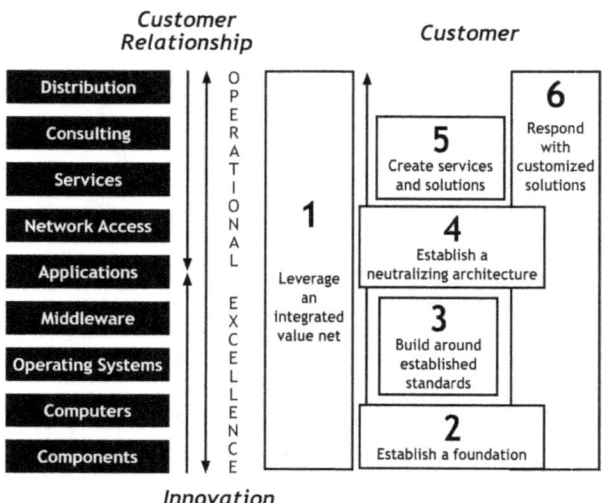

SOURCE: IBM STRATEGY

1. <u>Leverage an integrated value net</u>: The traditional way products were designed, developed, and delivered was around proprietary architectures that one company owned and controlled. Offerings were built from the ground up starting with components and ending with software and services. This strategy of vertical integration was the legacy of the last era when IBM and "the BUNCH" (Boroughs, Univac, NCR, Control Data, Honeywell) each had its own competing architectures and attempted to lock customers in. In the '70s and '80s, value migrated to horizontal strategies and vertically integrated businesses declined. This was due largely to customers demanding that vendors move from proprietary architectures to more open system components, so they could mix and match solution components. All three fundamental strategies play a role in an integrated stack.

2. <u>Establish a foundation</u>: By setting the de facto standard, and then attracting the rest of the industry to invest around that standard, firms like Microsoft, Intel, and Cisco became "shapers" of a value net and enjoyed a huge percentage of industry profits. This is the beginning of capitalizing on a horizontal disaggregated industry. Here product innovation is the key to success.

3. <u>Build around established standards</u>: Firms like Dell, HP, and Compaq became very successful as "adapters," building on the established architectural standards of others. This remains a very valuable point strategy. Operational efficiency is required for success.

4. <u>Establish a neutralizing architecture</u>: As control points move higher in the "stack," many of the leading software firms, such as Oracle and Lotus, are pursuing a "shaper" strategy by defining middleware standards across multiple component technologies at a higher level. The advent of open systems architectures furthers this neutralizing layer approach. As in

foundation standards, product innovation is the key to competitive success.

5. <u>Create services and solutions</u>: There are two categories of services-based strategies. One seeks to leverage proven methods and complete standard software applications across many customers and industries. Customer relationship is the critical strategy.

6. <u>Respond with customized solutions</u>: The other emerging approach is to let customers *pull* or select required solution components from one or more firms through the network and then integrate the pieces together in their shop, either by themselves or with outside services help. This is the core of the on-demand strategy. Customer relationship is the key here too.

Each of these strategies can be effective, but they are highly dependent on the competitive profile or intensity of the industry you're competing in and your own relative strength and position. In your industry, what are the major strategies that are being pursued? Which firms seem to be running away with the highest shares of profit, and what are their strategies? Which firms and strategies appear to be in decline? Which of the strategies should you be using to counter the current market leaders?

Digital Business Design: An Industry-wide Strategy

Leading firms that are striving to maintain leadership and entire industry sectors are adopting digital business designs. The automotive sector, for example, is actively investing to address three major opportunities for value creation through technology. They include: 1) Reducing the cycle time for designing a car, with the stated objective of condensing the current four-year design cycle to fifteen months. Half of that improvement is expected to come from advancements in the collaborative design process. The real-time collaborative service being created for automotive information exchange includes drawing databases and flexible workflow systems to manage design and engineering changes across departments and enterprises. 2) Transforming the manufacturing model to build-to-order, which entails a radical transformation of the manufacturing model and logistics system. The goal is to reach five-day order-to-delivery, which requires a full-scale business-to-business commerce infrastructure. A real-time supply chain and procurement system represents a paradigm shift for the entire industry. 3) Enhancing customer loyalty by improving customer service through existing distribution networks and creating direct electronic service links with the firm.

Achieving customer loyalty programs requires rich business-to-business (B2B) and business-to-consumer (B2C) portals as channels for sales and support services. The best differentiator may be telematics technologies, to support in-vehicle services including remote diagnosis and maintenance, personal productivity, entertainment, and wireless access to the Internet. The point is that as entire industries pursue progressive digital business designs, failure to strike a bold creative strategy for a single firm can leave that company far behind.

Better Strategic Decision Making: The "Deep Dive" Process

Ultimately, strategic leadership is the result of thorough, well-reasoned decision making that considers all logical perspectives, trade-offs, and long-term impacts on profit. For most strategic decisions, there can be dozens of variables, major unknowns, and the conflict of strong advocates arguing from opposing positions. Complex decision making needs a market-based process that optimizes the most profitable and successful strategy from among dozens of choices. It also needs to reconcile the multiple informed views held by different

> *Complex decision making needs a market-based process that optimizes the most profitable and successful strategy from among dozens of choices.*

constituencies in the firm. The most effective approach that we found for in-depth analysis is a four-step collaborative process that we discovered at GM and adapted for IBM. It was also widely used in Procter & Gamble, Kodak, Alcoa, DuPont, and many other large firms. Known variously as the Dialogue Decision Process, Decision Risk Analysis, or Strategic Decision Process, in IBM we just called it "Deep Dives." Michael Kusnic and Dan Owen headed a boutique consulting firm specialized in collaborative decision making. They helped introduce the technique into IBM and led several of our early projects.

The dialogue takes place between a small work team of four to six people analyzing the data for the decision and an executive decision team of two to four people who will ultimately decide. The process is based on collaboration, not consensus or compromise. Unlike the old task force approach, in which the task group returns at the end to the senior executives with *one* answer to the problem, the interaction of the dialogue promotes learning in stages along the way and helps shape a much better decision. Here are the four steps of the Deep Dive.

Figure 21.
Deep Dive Process

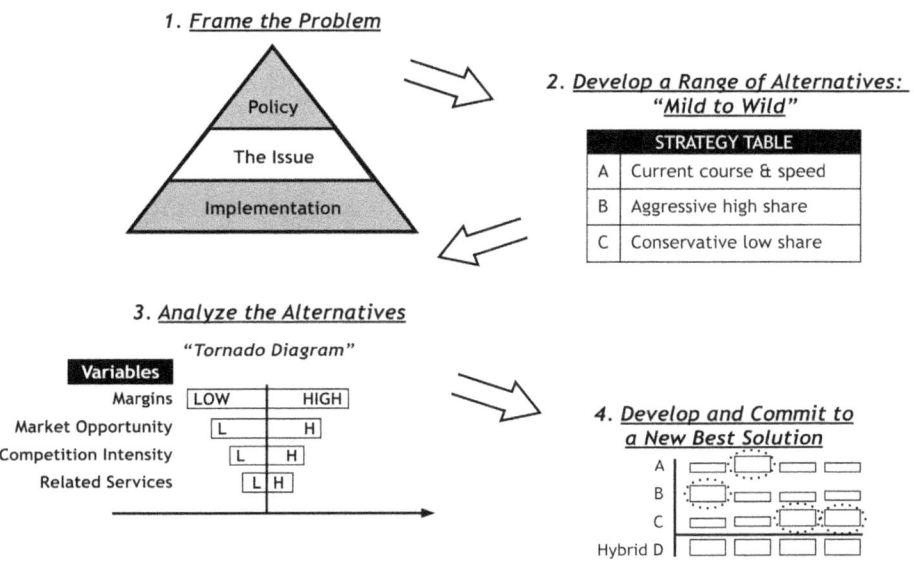

SOURCE: M. KUSNIC, D. OWEN

1. Frame the problem: Having a commonly shared definition of the issue and the decision to be made is the critical first step. We know any problem poorly defined will never be solved. In this first step, the team develops a comprehensive problem description that encompasses all points of view. One of the techniques is to create a decision hierarchy. At the top, list the policy or given boundaries on the problem, the things the firm has already committed to do. At the bottom are the downstream tactical aspects that can be postponed to a later time. In the middle is the heart of the issue, the strategic decision that needs to be made, and the reason the team was formed. As part of this framing, a list of knowns and unknowns are also developed. I always find it amazing that whenever the work team reviews the decision hierarchy with the executive decision team, there is always some misunderstanding on the scope of the issue or the assumptions on its constraints.

I remember many times when a senior executive surprised us by saying, "You don't need to assume we will stay in this market or operate it the way we do today."

2. Develop strategic alternatives: In this step, the team articulates at a high level each of the potential solutions to the problem, the underlying rationale, and the resources required to implement it. Each of the participants should ensure that there is at least one alternative he or she can support. The alternatives should ideally represent the whole range of alternatives that are available, from "mild" to "wild." One way of thinking of the alternatives is to envision them as test wells as used in oil exploration. Where the wells are drilled does not mean that's where the oil is, but it begins a triangulation effort. The alternatives represent all the creative and plausible ways to achieve the ultimate objective and, in the process, surface all the important conflicts inherent in opposing views. Three or four test wells will typically cover an issue. But it's important to realize that the final solution is rarely one of these alternatives, but a hybrid solution that encompasses the best thinking of each. Therefore, getting the alternatives defined with careful precision is not critical. Remember, they are just test wells.

3. Analyze the alternatives: The third step in the decision process is to do side-by-side analyses of the risks and returns of each alternative. The objective is still not to pick the best alternative at this stage, but to uncover the value that is embedded in each, expressed in profit terms. It's here that we engage experts in each of the variables. We ask them to identify factors that matter the most and sequence them from high to low based on their impact on the decision. For the many unknowns, we established a range in which the answer will lie 80 percent of the time. If one of the major factors at the top of the list is an unknown, the team may decide to collect more information to reduce the level of uncertainty. Interestingly, at the outset, there may be a hundred unknowns, but analysis shows that only three or four uncertainties really matter to most decisions. The tornado diagram illustrates the impact of the top factors.

4. Develop and commit to a new best solution: This final step is the most powerful. Based on the shared insights derived from the analysis of the prior step, the team develops a new best solution, a hybrid strategy that optimizes profit and combines the best elements of each test well alternative. It also minimizes the risks. As part of this step, the underlying rationale is also documented. But the step is not complete unless there is commitment to the decision, an allocation of resources, and accountability assigned to one leader to implement. The psychological value of this step and the entire process is that a team that entered with entrenched opposing positions, a potential "win-lose," can now point with pride and support to a new unifying "win-win" solution.

There are several benefits to the strategic decision process. First, because of the profit-based analysis, the results of the new hybrid solutions can be tracked and compared to any of the initial alternatives proposed or against "current course and speed." Second, with the support and buy-in of all parties to a decision, it is less likely that anyone will sabotage the shared new strategy. Third, as the process is used more and more widely, organizational learning increases as elements of the Deep Dive process can be used in smaller decisions, such as framing a problem more succinctly and exploring various alternatives before leaping to what appears to be an obvious decision.

Benefits of the Deep Dive Decision Process

We completed dozens of Deep Dive projects and then paused to assess the value of the technique. Our overall conclusion was that Deep Dives significantly increased the quality of decision making and we could calculate millions of dollars in improved profit as a result. The specific benefits of better decisions accrued from five areas:

1. *Focus on enterprise-wide issues*: Issues attacked were the most important, most complex cross-company ones, not confined by organizational boundaries.
2. *Breadth of alternatives considered*: A much better range of innovative solutions was generated and considered; a higher quality decision emerged.
3. *Extent of reality testing*: Process tools helped validate or rebut core assumptions, which were often unfounded.
4. *Timeliness*: Commissioning a Deep Dive at any time helped create a rapid response to emerging issues, harnessing the energy of the moment, even though the Deep Dive itself could take several weeks to do thoroughly.
5. *Better buy-in*: Unquestionably, we gained better collective support across the company and achieved better implementation success.

Summary

Great business design is like a gourmet chef preparing a magnificent and unique meal with a mix of fresh ingredients. It's the culmination of all we collectively know about our customers, added together with our knowledge of our offerings and the sources of industry profit, combined with inspired choices from among the many alternatives before us, and seasoned with the collective imagination of all our people. Over time, traditional business designs lose their luster, their competitive edge, and their uniqueness as each industry player tries to imitate those of the leaders, the ones that work best. So the challenge is to constantly adapt and reinvent new business models that are responsive to or preemptive of the marketplace changes around us, innovating beyond customer imagination. The most dangerous strategy of all is to stay with an old business model too long when value has migrated elsewhere. In the midst of creating new business design, we must explicitly choose among viable strategic alternatives. In an adaptive enterprise that requires collaborative decision making. Once decided, the next step is execution.

SECTION III:

Execution and Synergy

∽

CHAPTER 8:

Critical Tasks: The Art of Doing

Effective leadership is putting first things first. Effective management is discipline, carrying it out.
– **Stephen R. Covey**

Attempt easy tasks as if they were difficult, and difficult as if they were easy; in the one case that confidence may not fall asleep, in the other that it may not be dismayed.
– **Baltasar Gracian**

We begin the discussion of execution with the all-important area of tasks because the essence of execution is accomplishing the key tasks necessary to achieve the strategic goals, the vision, and new business model. Critical tasks, one of the two "hard" elements of execution (structure being the other), often get immediate top management attention. The action plan is what leaders think of first when the topic of execution is raised. But that's just the beginning. Once tasks are agreed to, we then need to evaluate how well the company-wide culture, organization structure, and skilled people work together to either help or hinder us in accomplishing those

> *Synergy, focused intensity, and urgency are all keys to successful execution.*

strategic tasks. Synergy, focused intensity, and urgency are all keys to successful execution.

It's important to remember that our focus here is on the critical tasks driven by our bold, unique strategy and business model. As Michael Porter reminds us, "The essence of strategy is choosing to perform activities *differently* than rivals do." Think about the strategic tasks Jet Blue set about to execute when they wanted to create a different airline experience, or Amazon in creating a different book-buying experience, or Wikipedia in creating and maintaining a free online encyclopedia. The focus is not on the mundane, imitative, or non-differentiating tasks required for operational efficiency. In general, there are five attributes associated with strategic tasks:

- They are directly tied to and driven by the new strategy we are executing.
- They embrace a high degree of innovation and differentiation, reflective of the unique strategy.
- There are relatively few of them, and most are of very high priority.
- They are synergistic with other elements of execution and the strategy.
- There is clarity in terms of accountability (who owns it), scope (specifically what it covers), goals (a clear definition of successful completion), time frame (due dates and checkpoints), and measurement (how and when we'll monitor progress).

Industry Leadership Assignments

At the conclusion of the 1987 Market Analysis Task Force mentioned earlier, we needed to execute about a dozen major strategic actions over the next three to four years if we were to regain industry leadership. Each of the high-priority tasks was a complex initiative requiring multi-year investments, the addition of skill sets around the world, marketing and communications actions, new development, and in some cases, alliances or outright acquisitions. To maintain attention and accountability, we put a simple mechanism in place called the Industry Leadership Assignments, or ILA process.

The CEO, John Akers at the time, assigned each ILA to a senior vice president who had the influence and clout to devote resources and to secure cross-unit commitments. Each owner had to report progress quarterly against the strategic goal and target dates, and self-score progress as an A, B, C, or D. The format required a summary of positive and negative market results, the highlighting of specific issues, and actions required, which we tracked from review to review. A higher degree of accountability, consistency, and strategic perseverance was achieved, although some of the bolder ILAs proved too difficult to accomplish in just three or four years. Some proved too vague, too broad, or simply unachievable. In retrospect, I think there were too many ILAs—most employees couldn't remember them all—and since they were each assigned to different units, little cross-unit teamwork ensued. A shorter list of three or four goals with the entire company integrated behind them might have been more effective.

Core/Growth/Issues

Several years later in the late '90s under a new CEO, we reinvented the corporate wide priority list. The simple one-pager entitled "Core/Growth/Issues" had three columns. The first column was the single most important action or goal that each *core business* had to achieve, such as "reinvigorate mainframe growth," "improve

Websphere share," or "increase consulting services engagements." The second column included *strategic growth* initiatives, whether product or geographic, such as "increase investment in India, China, and other emerging economies," "invest in mobile e-Business," or "launch life sciences." The third column listed major company-wide *issues* such as how to support Linux and Open Software, or exit a major product area like printers, typewriters, or desktop PCs. Rather than keep this list close to the vest, we socialized it widely inside and out so that employees, customers, partners, and investors had a clear sense of our investment and disinvestment priorities. As with the ILAs that preceded them, each item on the "Core/Growth/Issues" list had an assigned owner, a high level of accountability, and predetermined goals and milestones. But the list was more malleable, and the issue and growth portions changed frequently.

Critical Tasks in Strategic Projects

Maintaining a short list of top company priorities is pretty straightforward. It gets more complicated when the number of tasks and interrelationships expands to the hundreds or thousands as happens with major strategic projects. A fundamental tool for breaking a complex project into pieces is the Work Breakdown Structure (WBS), which we can trace back to NASA and the aerospace industry in the early '60s. To this day, it's used by the DoD for defense system development of missiles, aircraft, ships, and spacecraft. And since the late '80s, it has been expanded to wide general use for commercial project management.

The WBS tree structure permits the collection of subordinate tasks into their successively higher-level "parent" tasks. For each element of the WBS, a description of the task to be performed is generated. A well-designed WBS is organized around primary outcomes, instead of the actions needed to produce the products or services, making it easy to assign each project activity to one and only one terminal element of the WBS. It can also feed Pert and Gantt charts for overall project flow and scoping and can be used to subdivide a long-term project into phases, such as design, development, test, launch, and operations.

Collaborative Project Definition

Most experts recommend using the entire team to develop the initial project plan, using Post-it notes and a blank wall or two to create the first draft of the Work Breakdown Structure. This technique is easy and an active team-building exercise. Assemble the team into a large workroom and start by writing the names of the major deliverables on Post-it notes or index cards, one deliverable per sheet. If some of the deliverables are too large, create new cards that describe the deliverable at a lower level and arrange them under the higher-level deliverable.

Next, for each deliverable, describe the activities that must take place to complete it, each on a separate note. Arrange the activities under the specific outcome they refer to and sequentially in the order that they need to be completed.

Next look at each activity and estimate the work associated with it. If the effort associated with an activity is longer than eighty hours, break it into a set of smaller activities and add more Post-its. Continue with this process until the work required to complete all of the deliverables is defined, as best you know at this stage.

A key advantage of this large wall-mounted approach is that your entire team can envision the scope of the whole project, walk in and immerse themselves in it, and see their specific roles. And obviously the Post-it notes give you the ability to easily move things around.

Applying WSBs in the Extreme Humidity of Boca Raton

In the early '90s I was asked to assemble a new team and head a venture that we located in Boca Raton, Florida. We were given space in portable classroom-like buildings moved onto the main lab site. The work team numbered 125 people, and the project involved developing and launching a cutting-edge mobile communications service code-named "InTouch." With a new business domain, unproven technologies, new customers, new development team, new development processes, new partners, and a radically new business model, the project was fraught with uncertainty and risk.

Early in July in the midst of a hot tropical summer, we assembled the team leaders, about twenty of the managers, our architects from the Research Division, and a few consultants in the large war room. We worked for two days building the entire WSB structure on three walls encompassing over 950 separate work items. We used different colors of Post-it notes to indicate levels of the tree, the nature of the work, tasks, and activities, and used colored yarn to string related WSBs together. Friday night at 6:00 p.m. we finally completed the entire plan and, both exhausted and exhilarated, headed home for the weekend. Unbeknownst to us, to save on utility expenses, IBM turned off the A/C units that supported the mobile offices on weekends.

On Monday morning, amidst the humidity of the war room, we discovered a pile of 950 Post-it notes on the floor along the edges of the room. We began the process all over again. Fortunately, Building Maintenance had the good sense not to sweep them up and discard them. The key lesson: in humid climates, always use pushpins to reinforce Post-it notes!

WBS Shortfalls

Almost all project schedules are now built using a Work Breakdown Structure. One common problem I've observed with the WBS approach is that if too many detailed tasks are identified and tracked, micromanagement can result. A current project we're working on with the federal government has 1,350 WSBs and too many are being tracked on a weekly basis. In a firm encouraging creativity and empowerment, micromanagement of detailed tasks sends the wrong message and encourages dependency on the project manager (PM) rather than the team members doing the work. PMs are more effective when they hold people accountable for reaching measured milestones or interim goals rather than monitoring a long list of tasks.

Generally, most assignments in a project plan should have durations that are between one and eight weeks long. This coupled with weekly status reporting of hours worked, percentage complete, and an estimate of the hours of work remaining to complete the assignment allows the PM to maintain good control while placing the responsibility for achievement on team members.

Go back and look at the five attributes of strategic tasks in terms of their being strategic-driven, unique, few and focused, synergistic, and clear. In a complex project, do the few, major, and most strategic tasks bubble to the top for focus?

So Why Do Strategic Tasks Fail?

Here's the big question: if critical tasks are so important to the success or survival of the corporation or strategic project and have been assigned by the top executive, then why don't people just execute them? Are they insubordinate, incompetent, confused, or just plain lazy? There are many contributing factors. Strategy execution takes place over a much longer time frame than does formulating the strategy. In addition, the small group of people creating the strategy is typically located far from the front lines and far from the on-the-ground experience of those executing it. And the number of people implementing the strategy is much greater than those creating it. In the IBM services example, it took ten of us roughly four months to formulate the initial strategy, but implementation took nearly two decades and involved nearly two hundred thousand people.

> *Why don't people just execute strategic tasks? Are they insubordinate, incompetent, confused, or just plain lazy?*

One school of thought concludes that *execution discipline* is the key and that a combination of better focus, measurements, specificity, and peer accountability will solve the major barriers to effective execution. Stephen Covey says the bottom line is that most employees are not committed to a firm's most important priorities and may not even be aware of them. In his book *Four Disciplines of Execution*, he says that employees in today's downsized world have too many things on their plates, too many tasks, and too many roles. They just can't deliver excellent results when they're multitasking, trying to do everything at once. They or their management must narrow their focus to what matters most to the organization overall. *Focus on the wildly important goals!*

Second, Covey's research says too many firms don't have clearly defined measures about priorities, don't effectively track results, and don't really hold people accountable. Recognize that most people play differently when they're keeping score. And firms need to do better in rewarding performers and managing underperformers.

Third, top management often fails to translate lofty goals into specific actions. The actual tasks to achieve the strategy will ultimately fall on the shoulders of your employees. They must be able to make the connection between the organization's strategies and their daily jobs and work processes to truly deliver those results.

Finally, Covey says we need to hold each other accountable all the time. Many decisions fail because organizations do not maintain the *collective* discipline of performance and execution toward the goal. Organizations produce exceptional results when each team member makes it a habit to keep his or her commitment and helps others to deliver on their performance. Knowing that colleagues are counting on you raises your level of commitment.

I would add two other ideas to Covey's list. The first is to amplify his point on accountability with follow-through. The simple discipline of recording committed actions after each meeting can be powerful if you follow up by questioning, "Did you do what you agreed to do? If not, why not?" Of course, appropriate consequences reinforce accountability. The second is to add the consistency and synergy of reinforcing elements, ensuring that the tasks are being implemented by the right skills, in a supportive culture, and with the best possible structure.

Strategic Fit or Synergy

Michael Porter really emphasized that point of congruence or synergy when he first introduced the concept of *strategic fit*. He saw it as a central component to competitive advantage. His main point was that company success is not dependent on just one core competence, but on the entire collection of activities a firm performs. Everything matters. He described it as occurring on three levels. At the lowest level is the simple consistency between each activity and function of the overall strategy. Consistency ensures that the various activities don't cancel each other out or present conflicting brand attributes to customers and employees. Whether the strategy is centered on low cost, customer convenience, premium quality, broad choice, or extraordinary customer service, all activities should complement all the others. At the second level, activities are more than consistent; they are reinforcing and purposely feed or lead to other activities. And the third level is optimization, driving volume to the most valuable functions. In this highest level, redundancy is eliminated. Companies make strategic choices like deciding that customers can perform self-service or contribute content and innovations. Information exchange is critical at this highest level.

Competitive advantage accrues from the totality of all the activities working together. The more fine-tuned, synergistic, and tightly interconnected they become, the more difficult it is for rival firms to imitate the strategy. Consider, for example, the reinforcing elements of Wal-Mart's "Always Low Prices" strategy: extraordinary operating efficiency, huge buying power, supplier contracts, and advanced supply chain management processes. Or in the digital world, consider Amazon's reinforcing technology strategy: deep customer knowledge of its thirty million online customers, recommender engines, digital publishing, and now the e-book.

Lack of Synergy among All Elements of Execution

Tushman and O'Reilly built on this idea of strategic fit but did not use the activity maps that Porter suggested or the three levels of fit. Instead, their congruence model was more straightforward in its emphasis on the reinforcing power of the four building blocks of execution. Put simply, the complementary fit or synergy among tasks, skills, structure, and culture is key to unlocking effective execution. Diagnosing and resolving only one or two inhibitors, not all four, may lead to continued performance shortfalls and further problems.

To begin to understand synergy, we need to examine the nature of the specific tasks at hand. For example, what is the level of uncertainty associated with the tasks? Are we rolling out the next generation of a core product line we know well, or are we plowing into new markets, new offerings, or new business designs? If it's the latter, there is a high level of uncertainty and most of the tasks can't be preplanned or outcomes predetermined. The culture, skills, structure, and leadership styles need to be more adaptive and reflect the entrepreneurial spirit.

Another important element is how the work is performed. Is it within the bounds of a single business unit or in collaboration with other organizations inside or outside the firm? The simplest form of workflow is obviously performing all the key work inside a unit, with the exception of relying on corporate for shared services, such as human resources, real estate, or investment capital. It gets complicated when there is interdependence with other units. If the steps in a process flow sequentially from one unit to another, tight coordination is required across the units, and consequently the structures and skills must reflect coordination, negotiation, and interpersonal competencies. If, however, the interdependence is nonsequential or reciprocal, in which every function dynamically impacts every other function, then the structure and skills required are much more complex. A high level of collaboration, trust, and coordination are required for the whole system to adapt in sync. A highly adaptive enterprise is akin to a high-performing doubles tennis team that dynamically and instinctively adapts to each other's positions, to the shots, and to the competitors. Typically, business design innovation involves extra-enterprise linkages and collaboration among customers, suppliers, and partners. These reciprocal interdependencies rely on an adaptive value net of companies for market success. That may explain why implementing an innovative new business design is so hard to do. And, for the *ambidextrous* organization, it means doing this while simultaneously performing the more routine work of sustaining the mature business.

There are three main connections we explored in each of our workshops with our business unit leadership teams. The diagnosis or root cause analysis was aimed at finding and resolving inconsistencies in the following areas.

Tasks—Skills/People: There are two important synergistic concepts here. To what amount do the skills, abilities, and motives of the workforce fit with the tasks now required? And how are the individual needs of the employees being met by the tasks? As a "strategy execution" leader, he or she must personally engage with the employees to really understand the depth of their abilities and personal motivations. There are only two options: invest to retrain the people or replace them.

Task—Structure: Does the current structure adequately meet the demands of the task? As I'll discuss later in the chapter on structure, the scope includes the formal structure, the linking mechanisms, and the management system, with its formal rewards, measurements, and controls. And, of course, there's an informal structure operating as well.

Task—Culture: Does the culture facilitate task performance? As we'll discuss later, culture comprises a company's values and its norms, the behaviors, and the attitudes. One simple way to view corporate culture is to see it as one of four dominant forms: a *competence culture* that reinforces individual accomplishment, a *control culture* that follows well-articulated plans and a high degree of accountability, a *collaboration culture* that uses the power of teamwork to accomplish company goals, or a *cultivation culture* that fosters the creative expression of individuals. Which of these styles best fits the tasks at hand, and how do we go about changing the culture?

Synergy and Control Systems

While the subject of *culture* may appear to be too abstract to some managers, the subject of *control* is not. One way to view the congruence model of execution is to consider it as two intersecting control systems. The horizontal dimension of execution comprising critical tasks and organization structure is the formal control mechanism of the corporation or business. Most managers are comfortable dealing with this aspect whether it's managing budgets, sales operations, reengineering efforts, restructuring, or performance-based compensation. The vertical dimension, comprising skills and culture, is the social control system, the softer aspects of control. Here many managers may feel out of their element, as if they need to be psychology majors. Of course they don't. In case after case, however, the soft control mechanisms have been shown to be the most important determinants of company success or failure.

Summary

So, executing strategic tasks requires a high level of clarity, discipline, focus, accountability, measurement, and follow-through on each of the assigned work efforts. They must be executed with intensity and urgency. But beyond that, the tasks must be executed with synergy, fully supported by the right organizational culture, skills, and structure. We'll address each of these in the three chapters that follow.

CHAPTER 9:

Organization Structure: Fluid, Flat, and Networked

We trained hard...but it seemed that every time we were beginning to form up into teams we would be reorganized. I was to learn later in life that we tend to meet any new situation by reorganizing; and a wonderful method it can be for creating the illusion of progress while producing confusion, inefficiency, and demoralization.
– Attributed to Petronius AD 27–66

You will appear to be a visionary planner if you decentralize everything that is centralized and centralize everything that is decentralized.
– Dogbert

A firm's structure can have a significant impact on strategy execution. Unfortunately, it's usually negative. Organizations exist to execute strategies. They are supposed to make it easy for employees to work together, to innovate, and to achieve. Lou Gerstner once said, "An organization is nothing more than the collective capacity of its people to create value." It is supposed to be the means for creating a community of collective effort that yields more than the sum of each individual's efforts. And yet few organizations are able to do that or maintain their strategic advantage for long in a dynamic market.

As bold new strategies are developed in response to market forces, the deeply ingrained organizational heritage of the firm is often suddenly out of sync. The organizational inertia that keeps companies from adapting may be due to the imprint of the founder, the deeply ingrained routines of workers, or long-held traditions. And, as we've discussed, new structure requires alignment with new cultural behaviors and new skills to successfully accomplish key tasks. That means everything is changing at once. Consultants used to advise that structure should follow strategy, not precede it. My view is that structure evolves alongside strategy and synergistically supports its execution.

This element of execution may encompass the structure itself, as well as roles, procedures, measures, and systems that managers use to direct, control, and motivate. As Sumatra Ghoshal advises, "The key organizational task is not to design the most elegant structure, but to capture individual capabilities and motivate the entire organization to respond cooperatively to a complicated and dynamic environment." And structure can apply to the entire company, a business unit, a department, or a work team. Back in the industrial age, we tended to think there was a limited number of structural choices—organize the company primarily by product, by geography, by function, or by market. In most large companies, multiple dimensions of the structure get expressed through a matrix combining two or three of these elements, a concept introduced in the late '70s. Not surprisingly, these complex arrangements are often the source of conflict, role duplication, overlap, or all three. Today, creative new structural forms are emerging.

Informal Organization

To make matters more complicated, every firm has an informal organizational structure as well: the way work *really* gets done, where power *really* resides, how decisions

It's not uncommon to have inconsistency or a mismatch of structure with desired goals as new strategies unfold.

are *really* influenced, and how communications *really* occur. Of course, *informal* power is not conferred on an individual the way rank is, but rather earned through experience and expertise or seized through strong interpersonal skills and the ability to influence others. We've all known people who attempt to engineer their personal power through job assignments and experiences to gain access to more information or the right people and hence gain more influence in the informal organization. Obviously, it's important that the informal structure also be synergistic with the strategy.

From an enterprise standpoint, it's not uncommon to have inconsistency or a mismatch of structure with desired goals as new strategies unfold. For example, a company striving to serve global customers with global solutions and high consistency of service will find it nearly impossible to do so if the primary power in the matrix resides in strong disparate country organizations, localized career paths, and national rewards. That was one of IBM's strategic dilemmas in the midnineties, a company with deep traditions of very independent country businesses. Or another mismatch may occur when a highly disciplined hierarchy with rigid job specs and work rules attempts to execute a strategy that requires speed, flexibility, and market responsiveness; or when a company engineered around very narrow job specialties attempts to promote collaboration across functions and boundaries, both inside and out.

Organizational Trends

Organization structures are changing on several dimensions at once including:

1. The continuing dis-integration, downsizing, and flattening of the vertical hierarchal organization into smaller autonomous units yielding benefits of cost, productivity, and quality.

2. The expansion of the enterprise horizontally to the extended enterprise, tying in partners, suppliers, subcontractors, distributors, even customers to better address globalization, effectiveness, and market response.

3. The convergence of industries, the dissolution of current industry structure, and the formation of new alliances within and across industries for market supremacy and survival.

4. The creation, sharing, and distribution of knowledge that is dictating organization structure in enterprises that view themselves as a collection of competencies.

5. The dynamic reconfiguring capability that is embedded in the design of firms striving to be more nimble, recognizing the permanence of market change and the need for firms to adapt.

6. The emergence of the network organization, value net, or virtual organization, either by itself or in combination with remnants of the hierarchy, which may be required for legal purposes.

While various companies are moving in many different directions, most firms have concluded that vertical bureaucratic hierarchies are smothering. And as the hierarchies crumble and are replaced with flatter, more fluid, and networked structures, the old language of hierarchies (superior versus subordinate, top-down, bottom of the org., etc.) is suddenly out of place. Innovation is the key to competitiveness in this new century, so enterprises need to emulate smaller, faster start-up companies. In optimizing a company for innovation, you need to encourage every employee to develop the entrepreneurial spirit and give every employee the freedom to be

> *In optimizing a company for innovation, you need to encourage every employee to develop the entrepreneurial spirit.*

creative, to experiment, and even to fail. Creativity leads directly to productivity, a value even industrial age management understands.

In many ways, we are seeing the unfolding of the learning organization that Peter Senge described in *The Fifth Discipline*, "...organizations where people continually expand their capacity to create the results they truly desire, where new and expansive patterns of thinking are nurtured, where collective aspiration is set free, and where people are continually learning to see the whole together."

In his book *The Future of Work*, Thomas Malone of MIT calls the dispersion of control the "get small movement" and points to the development of advanced collaboration tools as the catalyst. They enable firms to build offerings across the value net of different partner enterprises. The "Federation of Businesses" plan that IBM designed in the early '90s was a harbinger of "get small," as was the forced divestiture of AT&T at the same time. But preserving global consistency and scale while simultaneously becoming smaller, faster, and lighter appear to be at direct odds with each other.

The Transnational Solution

One solution to that dilemma came from the groundbreaking advances in global strategy and organization developed by the late Sumatra Ghoshal and Chris Bartlett in the early '90s. In *Managing across Borders*, they laid out a new organizational form for the twenty-first century, calling it "The transnational," a dispersed and interdependent model in which remote units provide differentiated contributions back to the integrated corporation. Their research is considered the harbinger of the networked or virtual firm. In their view, it used to be that firms traditionally fell into one of three organizational types.

1. *Multinationals (MNC)*: Firms like Phillips, Unilever, and ITT operated a portfolio of strong local firms designed to be responsive to national differences. The mind-set of the MNC was that each country in a decentralized federation was an independent business.

2. *Globals*: In contrast, strong Japanese companies like Matsushita, Kao (soaps and detergents), and NEC built strong centralized g*lobal* firms to leverage their scale and scope. In this model, the mind-set was that overseas operations were merely a pipeline to a unified global market. Here, most strategic assets, resources, and decisions were centralized.

3. *Internationals*: In this third group of firms, the parent retained considerable central control and expertise, but exploited that capability through worldwide diffusion and local adaptability. GE, Procter & Gamble, and Ericsson are classic examples of firms that traditionally followed this approach. The mentality here was that overseas operations were appendages to a central domestic corporation. Even as some decisions were decentralized, they were controlled from headquarters.

Each of the organizational structures worked reasonably well if it fit the nature of the industry, product, and competition. But, the marketplace changed dramatically near the end of the last century. In *The World Is Flat*, Tom Friedman pointed out that after the fall of the Berlin Wall, countries that had followed the Soviet economic model, including India, China, Russia, and the nations of Eastern Europe, Latin America, and Central Asia, began to open up their economies to the world. When these new players converged with the rest of the globalized marketplace, they added new brainpower to the whole playing field and enhanced horizontal collaboration across the globe. He believes this convergence is the most important force shaping politics and economics in the early twenty-first century. To survive, large firms need global competitiveness, multinational flexibility, and worldwide learning simultaneously. The transnational model seeks efficiency, not for its own sake, but as a means to achieve global competitiveness. Local response is important, but mainly as a tool for achieving flexibility in international operations. And innovation is part of a larger process of organizational learning.

What exactly is a transnational? First of all, the sources of core competencies and assets are neither centralized nor decentralized, but dispersed, specialized, and interdependent throughout the firm. The role of the remote national units is to provide differentiated contributions to the integrated worldwide operations. And knowledge is not retained in the local units, but developed jointly and shared worldwide. When Dr. Ghoshal worked with IBM, we had successfully dispersed manufacturing and development missions around the world and had established eight research centers in different countries where specific skills existed (India, China, Israel, Switzerland, France...). But on the marketing and sales side, we were very U.S.-centric. With his guidance, over time, we established marketing missions for Germany, for example, to be a center of competence for large systems marketing and Italy to do the same for midrange customers through agents. These were worldwide marketing missions assigned to local countries.

In many ways, the transnational was a forerunner of the network organization structure, an emerging form in which the end points far from the center are empowered and dynamically reconfigured as market needs demand. The remote nodes are empowered and feed value back to the center for all to share and use.

Breaking Up IBM: Thirteen Baby Blues

Back in Chapter 4 on strategic intent, I described the work done with John Akers in designing the Federation of Businesses, the massive restructuring of IBM in the early '90s. As reported in *Fortune* magazine's cover story of mid-1992, "Chairman Akers is forcing perhaps the most complex company in the world onto a course of vast, painful change. His goal: to uproot a structure and culture formed when IBM had no serious competitors." The federation we had designed was to be governed by a minimal set of rules and free market principles, the antidote for a lethargic, bulging bureaucracy. The new IBM would give much more autonomy to the businesses and make IBM more nimble, quick, and agile. One chart that *Fortune* magazine created was for the benefit of shareholders. It compared IBM and AT&T over a ten-year period. IBM's market value had grown from nearly $34 billion in 1982 to $56 billion, up 66 percent, while during the same period AT&T's market capitalization, including the baby bells it spawned, had grown from $48 billion to an aggregate of $180 billion, a growth of 279 percent!

The newly announced structure was difficult to explain even to IBMers familiar with the acronyms. For some, it was energizing and exciting, a complete shakeup. It wasn't just a reorganization; it was a radical restructuring and, in retrospect, overly ambitious. The new IBM would be decentralized into nine huge global manufacturing and development businesses called Lines of Business (LOBs) ranging in size from $2 to $22 billion in revenue. Then four marketing services companies would market the offerings in a single monolithic sales force to each part of the world.

One conflict came from the LOBs that wanted specialized sales forces of their own, since they were now encouraged to sell to other industry firms as part of a new OEM strategy. The new structure was also intended to drive a high level of internal competition, a Darwinian notion that would better determine where to invest resources. The notion of the Personal Computer LOB competing for a customer's computing business against the mainframe and midrange LOBs was a scary notion. To further complicate things, the federation was based on an internal market-based, transfer-pricing scheme, a complex and untested financial mechanism. Additional aspects of the restructuring included a heavy emphasis on growing the services business, measuring and increasing customer satisfaction, cutting staffs without layoffs, reducing costs, and growing external partnerships. And one part of it entailed changing the culture by adding outside high-level executives to each LOB, extremely countercultural for organically grown IBM.

Consultants of every sort publicly weighed in on the IBM restructuring plan. Tom Peters of McKinsey & Co. agreed with the concept but said it should be broken into five pieces not thirteen; he also agreed the industry was too immature to be dominated by a big, slow $70 billion behemoth, IBM at the time. Several analysts and consultants said we should have separate sales forces for all but a few select customer accounts. But Esther Dyson, a well-respected industry voice, was more prescient, saying, "The key value IBM offers is integrating all the pieces together, never lose that." The ever-critical Bob Djurdevic of Annex Research said services is the key to IBM's future and IBM should focus there and organize that group along customer/industry lines, as EDS had done. And Noel Tichy, a University of Michigan professor guiding the GE transformation, felt the restructuring was right, but much more needed to be done on the *cultural revolution,* reducing the complacency and comfort levels, and reinvigorating the employee base.

Of course, to get the full benefit of financial restructuring, we envisioned some way to enable shareholders to invest purely in one IBM business or another. But the SEC required three years of audited financial reporting before allowing any spin-off. Before that could happen, the IBM board lost its patience and replaced much of the top management team, and with it, the federation concept. Within a year, a new team was in place and IBM was recommitted to its fully integrated structure. There was some consolation for us strategists: the bold new services, OEM, and customer satisfaction elements survived.

Small Business Too

Small businesses are not immune to the organizational problems of industrial age hierarchies either. They may not have the deep layers of management as large bureaucratic organizations do, but they often have dominant bosses—founders or owners—with strong personalities who like being in charge. Small businesses may also have the added complication of nepotism as family members and friends comprise an ad hoc succession system and informal power network. Often small firms are hindered in growing past a size threshold, limited by the tight hands-on control of the owner and lack of empowerment. The employees generally accept the hierarchy and informal power system, know how it works, and may think it's inevitable. Some small businesses try to ameliorate hierarchy's bad effects, but few question the basic idea. In every small business, whether you're a boss or a subordinate, and however hectic the pace of business life, it's worthwhile to stop and consider whether organizational hierarchy is as inevitable or as valuable as you've always believed. It is worthwhile thinking about alternatives, especially those that put more power in employees' hands, and trying them out. You might find better ways of working—more effective, less stressful, less dependent on key individuals, and more supportive of new strategies and a growing business.

The Internal Corporate Venture

As we discussed in Chapter 6, "The Innovation System," one chronic problem for large companies is creating new internal ventures to address emerging market needs. Once established and funded, the critical success factors include creativity, speed to development and market, in-market experiments and adaptability, and extraordinary teamwork. Based on our research and experience, the structure most appropriate for internal ventures can be characterized as follows:

- Stand-alone/independent from the core business
- Physically removed from corporate HQ
- Multi-disciplined team versus siloed, specialized functions
- Flat, thin, or network structure versus hierarchical
- Staffed with competent subject matter experts
- Leverages shared services from parent to retain focus
- Leverages non-core components from partners via an extended value net
- Led by an entrepreneurial leader/executive
- Measurement system based on milestones, not yet a profit center
- Supports fast, innovative, agile, distinctive culture
- Relatively small in size, strong group of core leaders
- Minimized administrative burdens
- Strong executive sponsorship and funding

Of course, one of the downstream benefits of internal ventures is that many of their successful ideas and processes can be transferred back into the core business, so the arm's-length relationship from the core business shouldn't be *too* arm's length.

InTouch: Intelligent Communications Services

InTouch, the first venture that I managed for IBM, failed on about half of those attributes listed above, ultimately becoming one of our best learning experiences. Our start-up team was too large and unwieldy at 125; we were too functionalized, too slow, too tightly controlled by CHQ; and its GM had no entrepreneurial experience. Our team was enamored of the technology, which included breakthrough software development processes, an extraordinary architecture, a unique user interface, and the first ever "personal agents," the forerunner of digital avatars. The concept was clearly "ultra-cool," and with such cutting-edge innovations, the enthusiasm and excitement level was high. But we had one major problem. Our structure preserved the traditional IBM functions of product development, marketing, business development, and finance as separate departments with strong leaders, and they each soon retreated to their traditional contentious roles.

InTouch made a huge splash at COMDEX when it was announced in the early '90s, but a combination of execution missteps meant it never saw the light of day as an operational service. Some pieces were salvaged for other projects, but many were just discarded. The learning experience was the most valuable aspect of InTouch.

A decade later when the Emerging Business Opportunities (EBO) project launched over a dozen new ventures, the lessons learned from InTouch were still painfully in "active memory." In areas as diverse as Life Sciences, Linux, Pervasive Computing, Autonomic Computing, and Storage Networking, we addressed InTouch's shortfalls and as many of the checklist items as possible.

The Saturn Venture

In working with GM's senior management and strategy team in the late '80s as partnership executive, I had an opportunity to see the genesis of their Saturn venture up close. Saturn was an extraordinary and initially successful effort within GM to create a company from scratch. Without any preconceived notions, they combined the most advanced techniques and ideas in all areas, with the goal of building a small car of superior quality and value as efficiently as possible. The separate GM venture employed the most advanced technology with the newest approaches to management, embodying a model of corporate enlightenment. Across the board they focused on environmentally responsible plant design, completely computerized operations, robots used to reduce direct labor costs, flexible manufacturing techniques, just-in-time inventory systems, dealer training to avoid traditional high-pressure sales tactics, community and employee involvement in decision making, and innovations in product design and production methods.

Roger Smith, GM's CEO at the time, chose to distinguish the venture with a separate structure, making it a wholly owned subsidiary called Saturn Corporation. He committed $5 billion to the venture, with an initial capitalization of $150 million, and the first nameplate added to the GM ranks since Chevrolet in 1918. Critical to its success, the United Auto Workers (UAW) approved a unique labor contract for Saturn. It allowed unprecedented flexibility in job content, eliminated work rules, and set pay rates at 80 percent of the base rate at other GM plants, making up the difference with performance incentives. All Saturn workers were salaried and participated in a "risk-reward" system in which they actually lost 20 percent of their pay if the company did not reach its sales goals but earned good bonuses if goals were exceeded. Each team was empowered to manage its own budget, inventory, and hiring.

Saturn realized its goal by producing a car ranked only behind Lexus and Infiniti in the 1992 J. D. Power & Associates customer satisfaction survey. And, as recently as 2008, the Saturn Aura was named North American Car of the Year. Saturn has been regarded as a successful product line and in many ways the embodiment of GM's vision of modern corporate ideals. The separate structure and new culture were key contributors. Designed with the young consumer in mind, Saturn was to play a key role in GM's green strategy as their first full hybrid arrived, the 2009 Vue Green Line Two Mode Hybrid. However, now all bets are off. Despite the initial successes, GM top executives since Smith have been less committed to the Saturn concept. In fact, GM has said it will stop making Saturn vehicles in 2010-2011. Saturn has been starved for product, consumers have flocked to SUV's and GM is fighting for survival. Among the options being considered is the possibility of spinning off Saturn as a retail channel for electric cars, leveraging its strong dealer network, the Saturn Distribution Corporation. This network could be converted to a chain of boutique stores selling various small cars made by others for the youth market. In a world of chaos, Saturn's fate is clearly unpredictable.

Department of Defense

No bureaucracy is larger than GM's except the U.S. federal government. One of my major consulting projects after my IBM career was to support a large unit of the U.S. Department of Defense. Our consulting firm recommended a long-term strategy to significantly enhance the communications systems on military bases throughout the world. To develop and manage the project, we proposed the creation of a small, stand-alone business unit with forty to fifty people in a relatively flat structure. The new unit was radically different than the parent corporation on many dimensions: culture, structure, and skills. Given its huge potential global market, the business was designed to be highly leveraged, relying on the core business for shared services and a network of business partners for all operational functions from network operations to customer support, Internet presence, and billing. As with most ventures, the critical success factors were speed, flexibility, innovation, and, in this case, strong customer centricity.

In designing a matrixed structure, we decided to make the product managers the quarterbacks. They'd define what the customer wanted and needed based on extensive market research using focus groups, online surveys, and on-the-ground base visits and interviews. Marketing and specifically the product managers were the customer advocates inside the unit and ensured everyone was designing offerings to deliver customer value.

While the core business grew organically from within, we went outside for fresh talent. The business unit hired several specialized experts from outside, from both the private and public sectors, including some recently retired military officers. These hires were invaluable because they were an in-house sample of the customers we were targeting to reach. One valuable piece of work was the creation of a life cycle template of the soldier's military life from boot camp through retirement that identified the specific service member's needs at each stage, a real insider's view. The point is that even in the public sector, creating a separate structure and culture for new ventures can be valuable and effective.

Current CEO Views

The most recent CEO study reveals that companies across the entire spectrum of size and geography are making radical changes to redesign their business models for global integration. As the world becomes more connected and more accessible, there are tremendous opportunities to expand reach and coordination, but with local sensitivity. The global market calls for business designs that facilitate faster collaboration and rapid reconfiguration when new opportunities appear. The actions CEOs say they are

> *The global market calls for business designs that facilitate faster collaboration and rapid reconfiguration when new opportunities appear.*

taking include changing the mix of capital, knowledge, and assets; partnering more extensively; actively entering new markets; globalizing brands; optimizing operations globally; growing through mergers and acquisitions; and driving multiple cultures. As they globalize, they are moving away from an operational focus and toward a redesigned client interface, which demands a new culture and new skills. One conclusion of this is that you just can't use the domestic team to drive global or international business. Of the CEOs surveyed, 85 percent plan to use local partners as they go from national to global, because it's an excellent source of valuable talent.

Developing a View of the New Structure

As you develop a new structure, explore various alternatives using some of the decision tools described in the Deep Dives process in Chapter 7. Consider the following factors:

1. How does the broad-based shift to a more global economy affect your industry and company?
2. What influences, opportunities, and challenges does the new digital network economy present to your industry and company? Who's gaining market share: new online companies, traditional established firms, or hybrids combining both?
3. How is your industry structure changing? Are the leaders consolidating their power, or is it becoming more fragmented?

Is convergence with adjacent industries occurring? Where is value migrating to in the industry?

4. What does our new strategy and business model suggest is the optimal structural design? What design will enable us to most effectively complete the critical tasks identified? What unique advantage and strength does the model expect us to exploit? What activities of the scope will be outsourced, and how will we create those partnerships? Does the strategy emphasize customer relationships, product innovation, or operational efficiency as our core strength?

5. What's the role of the center and how much control do we need? How much control are we willing to delegate to the units domestically and overseas? How much control are we willing to share?

6. What structural design will best facilitate the culture and skill changes needed to execute the strategy?

Summary

An enterprise's structure, in combination with the firm's culture, can either enable or hinder the ability of employees to work together, innovate, efficiently serve customers, operate at market speeds, and achieve extraordinary performance. Rather than accept the structure as it exists, as a strategic leader, you have the opportunity to shape a new structure, one that complements your strategy and is more open, more flexible, and more competitive. Whether you lead a large company or a small department, your responsibility remains to remove the structural and hierarchical barriers and as Sumatra Ghoshal once said, "*motivate the entire organization to respond cooperatively to a complicated and dynamic environment.*"

CHAPTER 10:

People and Skills: The Most Valuable Asset

Labor is the superior of capital, and deserves much the higher consideration.
— **Abraham Lincoln**

If a man has a talent and cannot use it, he has failed. If he has a talent and uses only half of it, he has partly failed. If he has a talent and learns somehow to use the whole of it, he has gloriously succeeded, and won a satisfaction and a triumph few men ever know.
— **Thomas Wolfe**

Virtually every enlightened corporate vision statement acknowledges that *people* and the skills they possess comprise the most critical and valuable company asset. And as we compete in a more knowledge-intensive economy and one beset by a global skills shortage, the value is accentuated even further. It's a well-known fact that no strategy can be executed without enough of the *right* people—motivated, willing, competent individuals with the skills appropriate to accomplish the specific critical tasks. Unfortunately, if your staffing needs require that you go to the external market to hire, you will find the U.S. data on talent and the pool of skills to be pretty sobering. By 2010, there will be a shortfall of ten million workers in the critical age range of twenty-five to forty-four years old, according to the Bureau of Labor Statistics, and 43 percent of companies now say "skill shortages" is their top business concern. Fully 40 percent of the U.S. workforce will be of retirement age by year 2010, according to the Conference Board. And one of every five large U.S. companies will lose 40 percent of their top-level talent as their executives reach retirement age. Of course, in our world of chaos, forecasting retirement statistics is virtually impossible with retirement savings accounts losing nearly $2 trillion in 2008. As baby boomers defer retirement and return to work, the percent of the nation's labor pool who are 55 or older will grow from 14% to 19% between 2009 and 2012, according to the AARP. But even during periods of rising unemployment and ample supply, the most critical skills in the fields of science, engineering, energy and technology remain scarce, an issue that is exacerbated by protectionism and reduced immigration. The U.S. manufacturing sector sees looming and widespread skill shortages in part because the younger generation perceives that manufacturing just isn't cool.

Scarcity of human talent is not just a U.S. problem. In the IBM CEO study, global leaders identified three major forces having the

> *Insufficient talent is now the top barrier to global integration.*

greatest impact on their organizations: market forces and people skills are tied as the top two issues, followed by technological factors. The survey respondents said they are searching for industry, technical, and especially management skills to support geographic expansion and replace the aging baby boomers who will exit the workplace. They said insufficient talent is now the top barrier to global integration. One CEO said we are making acquisitions *not* for the assets themselves, but to get the people, as Hewlett Packard did with Compaq and IBM did in acquiring PriceWaterhouseCoopers several years ago.

Skills Assessment

As you align the people component with strategic execution, the first step is to determine if you have the right *number* of resources appropriate for the task at hand, and whether you have them deployed or accessible in the right places, trained and ready when required, with the right mix of experience and skills, and have them organized into the right sized work groups. For example, when we started IBM Consulting Services, we determined that the optimal size of a consulting practice unit was seven consultants and a practice leader or manager. If we were to offer a particular discipline in a specific country, we'd need at least three or four practice units to be able to work in parallel. So in total, that would mean a minimum of twenty-four professionals per country per services offering. Considering IBM's operations in 166 countries, it was easy to see how we'd need thousands of trained consultants deployed worldwide to ensure discipline, quality, and consistency of our global offerings. In Google's case, they determined that the optimal team size for software engineering was three to four people. Anything larger creates unnecessary complexity and coordination, reduces individual accountability, and slows things down. They also keep every project slightly underresourced and attempt to solve problems *roughly*, rather than spend a lot of time smoothing out the final product. Customers can help do the refinements.

Looking beyond the *quantity* of resources to the *content and quality*, as you assess the current and required skill base of your team, recognize that there are several dimensions to the element of skills:

1. Competencies: What are they good at? Do they have the base knowledge, technical proficiency, and ability to perform the tasks at hand? Steven Covey's research concludes that there are five dimensions that comprise a person's competence: 1) talents, our natural gifts or strengths; 2) attitudes, our paradigms or ways of seeing things about work, life, and ourselves; 3) skills, our proficiencies, specific tasks we do well; 4) knowledge, learnings, insights, understandings, and awareness; 5) style, our unique approach, and personality. Competencies include job-specific skills and more general capabilities such as interpersonal skills, written and verbal communications, teamwork, flexibility, listening, open-mindedness, and so on—whatever is especially needed for the strategy you're executing. You need to develop some objective way to gather data about the workforce and workers' comparative skills. And if you're leveraging partners for key skills, you need to gauge their capabilities as well. This also includes assessing all the leaders' skills on the team as well as your own.

> *You need to develop some objective way to gather data about the workforce and their comparative skills.*

2. Motivations: Do you have reward systems appropriate for this team of people? That means understanding the difference between what motivates young brash untested workers and older, more experienced ones. For your strategy, are team incentives more appropriate than individual ones, or do you need a blend of both? The objective is to design a reward system that is aligned to meet individual needs and achieve the critical tasks. As you design a skills strategy to complement your business model, you need to be careful to attract the type of people who would naturally be motivated to work on it. For example, is the business model being created for an unstructured, entrepreneurial venture or a highly disciplined engineering project?

3. Team dynamics: What is the mix and level of team cohesiveness? How long has this team worked together, if ever? Are there great differences in age, background, and experience?

The greater the diversity of the team, the greater the opportunity for conflict. When I assembled our InTouch venture team, I was able to transfer in an entire intact team of eight bright young developers to create our virtual personal agents, or avatars. They had their own work style, typically working from 1:00 p.m. to 4:00 a.m.; ordered pizza in every night; and sometimes slept on the floor of the conference room or in a local motel. They were all single, mobile, highly motivated, and radically different than the traditional IBM development team in every way. They were fiercely loyal, but more so to their team leader and one aspect of InTouch than to the overall project. They were a high-performance sub-unit, but didn't assimilate well into the larger team. Strengthening teamwork through a specific development program is typically one of the most valuable contributors to long-term productivity and success.

4. Cultural diversity: How much geographic or national diversity is there on the team? How do the different cultures work together, resolve conflicts, work under pressure, and relate to the larger organization? Our Corporate Strategy team always felt like the United Nations. IBM was operating on every continent and needed a good balance of Asian and European strategists along with our North Americans to adequately develop and assess global strategies. At one point in time, we had three professionals from India, two from Japan, and one each from Italy, the UK, Germany, and China. Lunch conversations were practically unintelligible, but we always had a global view of opportunities and challenges. We also learned about cultural distinctions, such as respect. When you ask a Japanese employee if he understands his assignment, he'll often say, "hai," or yes, in response, which may mean "I don't really understand, but I'll figure out a way to understand it somehow," or, "I respect you as my boss and would never say 'iie' (no)." For Germans, respect is demonstrated by the tradition of gently knocking on the table to acknowledge a good presentation or speech. For Italians, especially in the north, business is more formal, so respect involves punctuality, being well dressed for a meeting, and having materials printed in both Italian and English.

Perhaps one of the most critical factors affecting success is the selection of the right team leaders. Strong team leaders form the core of the business unit. Recall that Kouzes and Posner said effective leaders visibly model the way, encourage the heart, and enable others to act. These subordinate team leaders don't need to be clones of the general unit leader and should certainly use their own styles, but they need to enthusiastically participate in the visioning process and support the overall change process and strategy with consistency. If some individuals or leaders can't do that, or do not respond to coaching, it's better to change them immediately, before too much damage is done.

Core Competencies: A Strategic Advantage

So skills encompass employee attitudes, styles, motivations, team dynamics, and cultural diversity as well as the competency itself. Back in 1990, C. K. Prahalad and Gary Hamel added one more dimension by connecting skills with strategic advantage in a classic *Harvard Business Review* article called "Core Competency of the Corporation." They wrote that a core competency is "an area of specialized expertise that is the result of harmonizing complex streams of technology and work activity." As an example, they used Honda's expertise in internal combustion engines. Honda was able to leverage this pervasive competency to develop a variety of quality products, from lawn mowers and snow blowers to trucks and automobiles, under a well-known corporate vision statement: "Five Hondas in every two-car garage." As we began an in-depth assessment of IBM's core competencies at the time, we also used the example of the Vermont Tubb Snowshoe Company, which exploited their ability to bend wood to transform into an entirely different business as a leading bentwood furniture company.

By Prahalad and Hamel's definition, a core competency is something that a firm can do well and meets the following three conditions:

1. It provides customer benefits. It's perceived to be valuable, a capability that allows a firm to exploit opportunities or neutralize threats.
2. It's not easy for competitors to imitate. The capability is rare to the extent that few, if any, competitors possess it, and it's very costly and difficult for others to reproduce.
3. It can be leveraged widely to many products and new markets, as our snowshoe example illustrates.

Core competencies are capabilities that serve as the source of competitive advantage. They can take various forms, including subject matter expertise, a distinguishing process, or tight relationships with customers and suppliers. They may also include product development or culture, such as employee dedication. Competencies develop over time by accumulating and learning how to deploy different resources and capabilities. Capabilities can include management (ability to envision the future of the industry, effective organizational structure), marketing (effective promotion of brand-name products, effective customer service, innovative merchandising), human resources (motivating, empowering, and retaining employees), manufacturing, distribution, IT systems, and research and development.

The value of the core competency perspective is that it elevates the discussion of skills to a higher strategic level. It's not good enough to have as many certified or skilled professionals as a rival. Yours should be measurably better if they are the source of your competitive advantage and directly deployed to fulfill your strategy.

The Fit between Skills and Strategy

To assess the new Strategic Leadership Forum we had designed with our team of business school professors at Harvard, we decided to take the Corporate Strategy department through one of the first new classes. As part of that forum, we did a candid assessment of our current skill base versus our new strategy and mission. My team at the time was a collection of about thirty competent and motivated executives and professionals, most with very full and impressive IBM résumés. They were bright, quick studies, and generally excellent communicators. We were fortunate to have a good mix of European and Asian-Pacific professionals on the team, some on rotation and some full time. The team had high morale and high performance, so why disrupt it? Here's why.

Our new department mission had six major thrusts:

1. Serve as strategy adviser to the new CEO and the inner circle of a half dozen senior corporate executives, helping to architect the company's long-term direction and turnaround. That meant formulating a continuing flow of fresh, bold, and global approaches to strategy and business. Specific tasks were to co-lead new efforts like Team Future, EBO, and other high-visibility strategic projects.

2. Lead in-depth Deep Dives on critical issues, requiring strong business acumen, team leadership, conflict resolution skills, industry knowledge, and sharp analytical skills. As with our major move into services, each of the Deep Dive projects required intensive analysis, creativity, and strong interpersonal and influence skills.

3. Proactively guide the forty business units in the development of their strategies through the Strategic Leadership Forum. In addition, evaluate unit strategies, perform in-depth analyses

and performance reviews, and recommend corrective strategic actions.

4. Assist the vice chairman in managing the portfolio of Horizon 3 (H3) internal ventures, manage the H3 pipeline, help select and develop entrepreneurial leaders, propose a continuous flow of new ventures, guide the transition of H3s to H2 growth businesses, and interface with the venture capital community in Silicon Valley.

5. Develop and publish the comprehensive Global Market Trends document on an annual basis, with a focus on actionable items for IBM overall as well as groups and units.

6. Develop strategy communications messages and presentations for the IBM board, Senior Leadership Group meetings, and major employee, partner, and customer executive forums.

Current Skill Base

Our team of thirty professionals included eight to ten experienced strategy executives at the director level or a step above but not full corporate VPs. Their individual ability to influence a division president or group executive, one to three levels higher, was a major challenge. In addition, many strategy executives had recently rotated out of line positions and were no more experienced in strategy development than the clients they were asked to guide. Another challenge was that we were managing a portfolio of start-up ventures, eighteen initially that grew to twenty-five, and exploring a hundred others. But few of the strategy team had worked in the VC field or in entrepreneurial companies. And we were geographically disadvantaged being located on the East Coast with the center of VC activity being in California. In addition, we strove to drive IBM into new technology leadership areas like open software/Linux, but our strategy team of mostly IBM veterans had little experience outside of IBM proprietary software architectures.

Developing a thorough Global Market Trends was an area that fit neatly within our strike zone as we had several experienced market analysts. But new trends involving social networking, for example, heavily used by the younger Generations X and Y, were not an area of experience. We did reasonably well in the area of strategy communications because we had good content material and selected good communicators.

Immediate Skill Adjustment

Our overall conclusion was that we needed to significantly upgrade our skills in three areas:

1. Attract three or four line executives at higher levels who could more effectively influence senior line executives. That meant recruiting a group of VP-level executives with strong strategy acumen. It would be good for influencing new strategies and good for their personal development before they took on future high-level general management positions.
2. Improve age diversity by hiring some young "newly minted" MBAs who were working in top-tier consulting firms. Develop them into future strategic leaders. We decided to hire six to begin with and eighteen over the next three years.
3. Hire senior people or executives from other leading high-tech firms who could bring fresh insights on technology-related businesses, especially those with some VC or entrepreneurial experience. We hired two of them that first year to oversee our VC efforts and establish a West Coast strategy outpost.

All said and done, we changed the profile of our small department within a year to better align skills with our new mission. Most of the changes and new individuals were effective; a few were not. But in the new IBM, experimentation, learning, and adjustment were now accepted and encouraged.

Saturn's Skill Strategy

In working with GM, I learned that when they conceptualized their new venture Saturn, they realized they needed a radically new way to approach skills, to create a highly motivated, empowered, and dedicated workforce. They decided to approach organizational design in a way that made the union, the UAW, an institutional "partner," participating in consensus-based decision making from the shop floor to the top levels of senior management. This structure was overseen by a series of "decision rings" at the department, plant, and business unit levels, as well as at the manufacturing and strategic policy levels of the organization. Through the partnership's arrangements, the UAW became an important part of strategic decisions regarding supplier and retailer selection, choice of technology, and product development. An initial collective bargaining agreement outlined the basic principles governing the relationship and the team-based organization.

The partnership process was complemented by employment practices designed to ensure that employees had the knowledge, skills, and motivation to contribute to the performance of the enterprise. Saturn required all employees to take a minimum of ninety-two hours of training each year, and 20 percent of compensation at Saturn was contingent on the completion of this minimal amount. In addition, more than 80 percent of the workforce was guaranteed employment security for life. Work at Saturn was based on self-directed work teams of ten to fifteen members, who were cross-trained and rotated responsibility across the tasks in their unit. Teams had collective responsibility for hiring new members and electing their own team leaders. The next level of organization, called modules, covered about five to seven teams and conducted weekly governance meetings in which teams were represented by their leaders. Teams also had responsibility for quality assurance, job assignments, record keeping, safety and health, material and inventory control, training, supplies, and housekeeping. In essence, the radical new business strategy reflected in Saturn was complemented by an equally radical skills strategy, even in a more restricted unionized environment.

Global Skills Shortage and Solutions

The discussion of skills wouldn't be complete without addressing the serious skill shortages that exist across countries, industries, and firms of all sizes. A mid-2008 survey by KPMG, a global professional services firm, concluded that the lack of skills is the number one issue facing the global energy sector for the next decade, topping their CEOs' concerns about material costs, political instability, climate change, government regulations, and geological challenges. A study at the end of 2007 of small and medium-sized enterprises in South Africa found that 75 percent had severe skill shortages and only 37 percent were satisfied with the adequacy of their current skill base. In Australia, 78 percent of companies identified global competition for skilled IT resources as the greatest strategic impact, and 70 percent said retaining talent was their biggest people challenge. The Israel government announced they are attempting to stop the "brain drain" by establishing a $45 million fund to promote research and technology, since 50 percent of Israel's scientists have left for other countries. And, according to PriceWaterhouseCoopers, which interviewed over three hundred CEOs of privately held and fast-growing U.S. manufacturing and services companies in late 2006, 49 percent said the shortage of qualified workers will be the major barrier to their business growth.

In the IT sector, the estimates of the skill gap approach 1 million people in the United States, 1.7 million in Europe, and nearly 4 million in Asia, which will slow revenue growth and the transformation of companies worldwide. In hot specialty areas like networking, the shortage has grown from 18 percent to 33 percent over a five-year period. A contributing factor to the personnel disruption is shortened tenure within one firm, now only 3.6 years on average, and even less in Silicon Valley.

In the past, the continued flow of immigrants coming to America was a major driver of our economy and especially helpful for new business creation. Because of our political stability, personal freedoms, excellent university system, rich venture capital process, and progressive immigration policy, we were able to attract some of the best and brightest minds from around the world over the past century. That opportunity to attract highly skilled labor and entrepreneurs has changed dramatically with the soaring economic growth of China and India, ubiquitous global communications allowing services to be performed anywhere, and the end of the cold war and accompanying rise of democracy and capitalism, which means more and more skilled workers can stay "home" and be reasonably productive.

There are two obvious and immediate solutions to the chronic skills shortage issue. One is to outsource specific tasks to contract employees or entire business processes to outside firms. In the IT sector, the countries reporting serious skill shortages include the United States, United Kingdom, Australia, Germany, Japan, Korea, India, and even China. As this global trend intensifies, several countries see a strategic opportunity. The Philippines is creating a software development capability and is being called the next India. Brazil is specifically growing a tech-savvy workforce and is targeting the IT services market. Hungary, the Czech Republic, and Poland are emerging as major IT and telecom investment areas, setting up application development centers. And South Korea is becoming a major outsource center for software programming with aspirations to move up the value chain.

Other creative and collaborative solutions are emerging. Using advanced software development tools, IBM decided at the turn of the century to pursue a "follow the sun" twenty-four-hour development process by having teams in Russia, Canada, and India work on major projects, handing off the work product to the team in the next hemisphere as each shift ended.

The other solution is to step up education and retention programs for the current workforce. Educate current employees in the required skills through either in-house programs or college programs, with the added benefit of increased employee loyalty. Like it or not, some larger enterprises may need to enter the education business if they're not already there, either by themselves or in partnership with local colleges.

Skill Sourcing from the Next Generation: The Millennials

As you build a skills and people strategy with a plan to recruit fresh young talent, it's important to understand the mind-sets of

> *"Recruitment 2.0" is a way of describing new thinking, new channels, and new approaches to talent attraction.*

the youngest group entering the workforce, Generation Y, or the Millennials, typically born in the 1980s. As a starting point, you'll probably find these potential hires on one of the many Internet job sites like Yahoo!HotJobs, JobCentral.com, Career-Builder, or Monster.com, or one of the industry-specific Web sites. With an ever-growing competition for talent, the Internet offers a fresh approach to candidate attraction. "Recruitment 2.0" is a way of describing new thinking, new channels, and new approaches to talent attraction. For example, firms now use Internet search engine marketing to attract candidates; engage candidates through blogs, feeds, and dynamic content; allow candidates to respond to recruitment campaigns via Short Message Service (SMS)/mobile Internet; use direct response television as a cost-effective route to large passive communities; and use the unique power of the Internet to interact with diverse communities to expand candidate lists.

Naturally, in hiring and managing Millennials, you must also understand their mind-sets and motivations. A 2008 survey of over 1,000 people by a UK recruitment consultancy, FreshMinds Talent, concluded that Generation Ys are generally more ambitious, are brand conscious, and tend to change jobs more often than others. A 2007 segment on *60 Minutes* entitled "The Age of the Millennials" concluded that this new generation is exceptionally tech-savvy, especially tuned to their own value in the job market, have limited loyalty to any particular employer, and insist on working in a stimulating job environment. They are described as overachieving and overscheduled. As an aside, these are many of the same characteristics previously attributed to the older Generation X, so these behaviors may be consequences of modern culture rather than qualities of a particular generation.

In today's collaborative world, the Millennial Generation may have an advantage over their older colleagues in both their technology savvy and their natural inclination to keep in constant touch with others. Gen Y started online social networks, so you might want to think about how you can leverage them in the workplace to encourage team collaboration and knowledge sharing. Generation Y is much less likely to respond to the traditional command-and-control type of management still prevalent in much of today's workforce. They've grown up questioning their parents, and now they're questioning their employers. Some have jokingly referred to them as "Generation Why?" They don't know how to shut up, which is great, but that can be aggravating to an older task manager who says, "Just do it, and do it now." Despite the weakening economy, the Millennials have a different take on corporate loyalty and tend to job-hop, so you may need to find creative ways to appeal to their career goals, ambition, and resume building.

Kouzes and Posner, authors of *The Leadership Challenge,* have also done some research that suggests that Millennials have clear needs and are bold enough to articulate them. In summary, they want to know that they are valued, want to be challenged, and want to be treated with respect. They prefer to work with positive people and want to learn new skills and acquire new knowledge. They expect flexibility in their work schedules and want to work in a friendly environment. They learn best through teamwork, technology, structure, and experiential learning. And, they want to be paid well. Of course, these wants are really no different than what the rest of us want from jobs. The only difference is that Millennials don't hesitate to ask for them. And, of course, age is not the only factor that affects employee or leadership styles. Unique combinations of culture, age, ethnicity, gender, and life experiences all play a role.

Summary

It was Peter Drucker who first suggested a half-century ago that employees should be regarded as valuable assets as we enter a knowledge-intensive world. He viewed the corporation as a human community built on trust and respect for the worker, not just a profit machine. And, it was Peter Senge who articulated the values of and approaches to a learning organization, and his belief in continuously developing those assets individually and as teams. Unfortunately, too many firms still see employees as costs, overhead, or liabilities and even account for them in financial statements as a salary expense, headcount cost, or benefits expense. By contrast, top-performing organizations that consistently outperform their rivals see their employees as a significant source of competitive advantage, as a wealth-creating asset, their core competence. If you truly believe that, then those assets of skill and talent should be acquired and developed with as much care and diligence as is applied to expensive capital equipment. The return on investment in people will pay off as richly as those investments, or more so. And aligning the long-term skill strategy with the business strategy and the other elements of tasks, culture, and structure will better ensure that expected payoff.

CHAPTER 11:

Culture: A Powerful Hidden Ingredient

*Shun the incremental and go for the leap. Most bureaucracies
still think in incremental terms, rather than in terms of fundamental
change. Changing the culture, opening it up to quantum change,
means constantly asking how fast or how well am I going versus
the outside world.*

– Jack Welch

*Organizational inertia in the face of discontinuous change is
caused by management's inability to deal with the cultural
changes these market forces require!*

– Michael Tushman

Company Culture and Its Impact

Culture—the shared values, norms, attitudes, and behavioral patterns that groups pass on from one generation to the next—is one of the most powerful and yet elusive forces impacting company performance. It can either provide a firm with significant competitive advantage and success or severely hamper progressive change and transformation. And while skills, tasks, and structure can be easily altered over time, culture is more stubborn, one of the most difficult characteristics to change inside a firm.

Furthermore, culture's impact is pervasive, affecting every other box in the strategic leadership framework. On the strategy side of the model, a strong market-based culture encourages every employee to contribute to market insights; a creative culture invites everyone to play a role in innovation and, in an empowered culture, the strategic intent is reflective of the valuable role of all employees, motivational, and deeply supported by all. The business design should reflect appropriate ways to leverage culture to your competitive advantage. In the execution section, culture defines the desired attributes of the talent you attract and develop, the key tasks that need to be done, and the organization of the future that reflects cultural strengths. So, in one way or another, culture is a pervasive ingredient that determines the effectiveness of every other element.

Culture is a social control system and is already operating inside your company or business unit. Because of the intangible nature of "culture," we need to clarify exactly what it is in a business context. Culture is comprised of two elements: values and norms. Values reflect the core, shared beliefs, while norms reflect work behaviors, the shared agreements of what's important in our company. While values are usually more consistent across a firm, norms can vary by geographic location and by function. For example, in IBM, employees in the Rochester, Minnesota, site reflected U.S. Midwestern values, and there was a discernibly higher level of teamwork, politeness, and a "family first" mind-set. Functionally, it was also widely known in our firm that manufacturing and development people tended to be more confrontational and direct than the marketing people. Norms can be further divided into attitudes, orientation toward customers or employees, relationships with others, and conflict resolution.

Norms can also dictate appropriate and acceptable behavior and define the limits of what is *not* acceptable. I've always been fascinated with the variance among firms in their acceptance of humor.

Compared to other firms I've worked with and the federal government, IBM always seemed to have a high humor quotient, especially in marketing. It was demonstrated by outrageously funny kick-off meetings, skits, songs, costumes, pranks, and self-deprecating humor. When I worked in Bridgeport, we created a marching band in Marx Brothers costumes complete with kazoos, drums, a trombone, and a ladder. In the New York Media office, we created a film of employees using feedbags to boost productivity at lunch, even coercing the regional manager to wear one for the video. At our more staid corporate headquarters, one Christmas party featured our "follicly-challenged" managers and executives with a "NOEL" message painted on their bald pallets. We bought a Dilbert costume that someone wore to department meetings to skewer any overly bureaucratic pronouncements. Of course, off-campus promotion parties were even more unconstrained. We thought we were pretty outrageous until IBM acquired Lotus, a much smaller, younger, and more informal company, with a level of humor a notch above ours. One of their senior executives regularly showed up at major customer executive meetings dressed as Spider-Man, an obtuse reference to the web, climbing across the ceiling. But in both companies, the norms dictated that humor never crossed the line. The values on diversity and respect for the individual were so deeply ingrained, it was clear, though unwritten, what type of humor was inappropriate.

Cultural statements become operationalized when executives articulate and publish the values of their firm and then reinforce them in a variety of ways. Many of the cultural norms are unwritten and just seem to sustain

> *Firms with strong deeply held, and positive cultures tend to achieve higher results because employees sustain focus on what to do and how to do it.*

themselves, passed on from one generation of leaders and employees to another, constantly reinforced by role models. Companies with strong cultures and strong norms have less variation in attitudes and behaviors; there's consistency across the business. And firms with strong, deeply held, and positive cultures tend to achieve higher results because employees sustain focus on *what* to do and *how* to do it. But firms with ineffective, weak, negative, or conflicting cultures tend to focus on problems, not opportunities. They tend to lack trust, blame others, and do not tolerate failure of any sort. Turnover is often high, and over time, the people who stay lose confidence in their leaders and the company itself. Ultimately, market performance suffers.

Strong Culture and Success Can Lead to Failure Too

In the late '80s, when IBM launched a flurry of initiatives to transform itself into a leaner, faster, and more competitive company, the actions focused on quality, customer satisfaction, cost-cutting efficiency, downsizing, and entry into the services and OEM businesses. Little criticism or action was centered on the IBM culture, which was still viewed to be a strength and instilled by the founder's enduring Basic Beliefs of "Best Customer Service," "Respect for the Individual," and "Pursuit of Excellence." Who could possibly argue with any of those? There was some question as to whether these were just espoused values or really practiced all the time—that is, were we really "walking the talk"? But the fact remains that during our plummeting decline, most insiders and outsiders still viewed the strong culture of IBM as its one enduring plus. Employees worked hard, valued discipline, and were fiercely loyal to the firm, a refection of the culture that was almost paramilitary in nature. The three Basic Beliefs were also a source of pride, providing a more noble purpose to the firm beyond just generating profits. In many ways, IBM was caught in what Donald

218

Sull called "the active inertia trap" in his book *Revival of the Fittest*. He concludes that past success is one of the best predictors of future failure because current and often obsolete commitments limit organizational flexibility and response to new challenges.

It was at this time that two Harvard Business School professors, John Kotter and James Heskett, provided the first comprehensive analysis of how the "culture" of a corporation powerfully influences its economic performance, for better or worse. Challenging the widely held belief that a "strong" corporate culture leads to excellent business performance, their research showed that while many shared values and institutionalized practices can promote good performance, those same cultures can also lead to arrogance, inward focus, and bureaucracy—features that undermine an organization's ability to adapt to change.

This wasn't just academic theory or anecdotal evidence. Kotter and Heskett had studied more than two hundred enterprises in twenty-two industries over an eleven-year span and measured performance against benchmarks like income growth, returns on invested capital, and appreciation in stock prices. They admitted there's as much art as science in evaluating culture, and their research also conceded that cultures adequate for one economic context might prove disastrous in another. One key conclusion they came to was that firms need an adaptive culture that automatically aligns an organization's interests with those of its employees, investors, customers, and other stakeholders. One action they prescribed for insularity was to force more external focus, more market insight. They discovered that the best cultures were those that continuously adapted to changing markets and new competitive environments.

Their research was so relevant to IBM's current predicament that it prompted us to invite John Kotter into the inner sanctum of our Strategic Planning Conference in 1989 to candidly discuss his perceptions of IBM with our top twenty executives. He began by acknowledging that Machiavelli was right; change is difficult, frustrating, risky, and vexing. He said that forging a new culture in a far-flung enterprise as large as IBM is nearly impossible and would take years to accomplish. Of the dozens of firms Kotter had studied, he found only ten that had succeeded in changing enterprise-wide culture, including GE, Xerox, and British Air. And because of deeply ingrained resistance, it's typically a ten-year effort, well beyond the tenure of most senior executives, and all those in the room. And most often it requires an outside change agent, a real revolutionary. None of that was good news.

He then put a model up on the screen that illustrated the origins of an unhealthy culture, one that starts with a firm creating a strong culture, achieving sustained success, celebrating that success based in part on that strong culture, and then hiring and developing more people to reinforce that same culture. Inadvertently, the long-term unintended consequence is a hardening of the enterprise, making it impervious to change, inbred, unsupportive of diversity, and completely resistant to new external forces.

Figure 22.
The Origins of Unhealthy Corporate Cultures

Combination of visionary entrepreneurship and/or luck creates and implements a very successful business strategy.

A dominant position (and thus lack of strong competition) is established in some product or service market(s).

The firm experiences much success in growth and profits.

| The firm hires and promotes managers, not leaders, to cope with the growing bureaucracy, to keep things from getting out of control. Top managers allow these people, not leaders, to become executives and sometimes actively prevent leaders from becoming senior executives. | The pressures on managers come from inside the firm, not outside. Building a bureaucracy that can cope with growth is the biggest challenge. Top management does little to remind people of the importance of external constituencies. | Managers begin to believe that they are the best and that their idiosyncratic traditions are highly superior. They become more and more arrogant. Top management does not stop this trend; often they exacerbate it. |

A strong and arrogant culture develops. Managers do not highly value customers and stockholders. They behave insularly, sometimes politically. Managers do not highly value leadership and employees at all levels who can provide it. They stifle initiative and innovation. They behave in centralized/bureaucratic ways.

SOURCE: J.P. KOTTER, J.L. HESKETT, CORPORATE CULTURE AND PERFORMANCE

IBM's resource strategy resembled major Japanese firms and at the time was admired throughout business. In fact, business historians said modern Japanese firms modeled much of their business culture after IBM's. We carefully selected top college graduates, trained them in the IBM ways (as late as the 1970s teaching them IBM songs like "Ever Onward"), and provided them essentially with lifelong employment. It was easy to see why midcareer external hires and employees from new acquisitions found it incredibly difficult to assimilate.

IBM's senior executive team became immersed in Kotter's model at the conference, provided evidence of its validity, and debated the impacts. During that memorable conference, a palpable pall came over the assembled executives who, perhaps for the first time, began to understand the long-term effects of perpetuating an inbred culture and how IBM's traditional confidence and pride had somehow morphed into a pervasive arrogance. The unresolved issue was what to do about it, especially if it would take a decade to change. We were four hundred thousand strong at the time, so even bringing in a few experienced professional hires from the outside couldn't change the deeply rooted culture. But as John Kotter said bluntly, we had no choice: "You need to *change* the people, or change *the people!*"

Diagnosing the Current and Needed Culture

During the late '90s and the first decade of the new century, IBM decided to focus on improving our business unit strategies, which led to our launching the Strategic Leadership Forum at Harvard Business School and our work with Professors Tushman and O'Reilly. At that stage, we recognized that while there was an overall corporate culture, the cultures of the individual business units, whose roles were as diverse as developing semiconductors to performing high-level business consulting services, could be very different according to each one's strategy, the competitive climate, the tasks required for success, the leadership traditions, and even the geographic location. One way to diagnose a business unit's culture is to first start with the strategy as articulated by the new business model. That strategic business design—which customers, what differentiation, the approach to capturing and sustaining profit—drives the prioritized list of critical tasks as the first step of execution. The next step is to identify the *specific* attitudes, behaviors, and orientations that will help accomplish those critical tasks.

As we conducted our Leadership Forums, the professors counseled our teams to be very specific and not retreat to the platitudes of "best customer service, high quality, and flexibility." Our teams struggled to articulate what exactly creativity or innovation meant, what exactly we expected people to do regarding quality, what tradeoffs employees were expected to make, and how we would specifically articulate those desired behaviors in performance plans or as part of recognition rewards. A classic ambiguity was the inherent conflict between behavior and rewards for *team* performance versus *individual* performance.

Culture that Drives Innovation

During our leadership workshops, the teams built two lists of cultures, the existing attributes and the culture demanded by the new strategy. The desired culture had terms like *trust* and *openness, teamwork, client focus,* and *innovation.* We further dissected each of the broad banner terms into more specifics. For example, *innovation* has at least three components: creativity, implementation, and recognition. And each of those can be further detailed into observable behaviors. *Creativity* means showing support for risk taking and change, valuing others' ideas, being curious, challenging the status quo, being adaptive and experimental, having tolerance for risk taking, and accepting failures of a certain sort versus an expectation of flawless execution. Being safe, risk averse, and conservative is not OK. *Implementation* requires a higher level of teamwork, open communications, shared information, flexibility, and cooperation. It also requires speed and urgency, personal autonomy, wide latitude for employees to work, and clear objectives. And *recognition* means celebration of success, rewards for innovation, having fun, and strong commitment and encouragement from the top.

Trust: A Core Element of Culture

Stephen Covey's book *The Speed of Trust* presents a compelling argument that there's one fundamental factor that impacts our relationships with ourselves and everyone else, be they employees, family, shareholders, or society. That core element really determines our effectiveness as a leader, and it can be developed. Of course, that one thing is *trust*. In Covey's words:

> *There is one thing common to every individual, relationship, team, family, organization, nation, economy and civilization throughout the world. One thing that if removed will destroy the most powerful government, the most successful business, the most thriving economy, the most influential leadership, the greatest friendship, the strongest character, the deepest love. On the other hand, if developed and leveraged, the one thing has the potential to create unparalleled success and prosperity in every dimension of life. Yet it is the least understood, most neglected and most underestimated possibility of our time.*

The statistics are alarming and show that we have a crisis of trust. Harris poll data shows that only 27 percent of Americans trust government (for Congress it's been as low as 9 percent in 2008), 22 percent trust the media, 8 percent trust political parties, and only 12 percent trust big companies. Inside the corporation, data shows that only 51 percent of employees have trust and confidence in their senior management. Of course, in this increasingly connected global economy, this is not just a U.S. problem. A Halpern study in the UK concluded that while only 34 percent of Americans believe other people can be trusted, in the UK it's even lower at 29 percent, in Latin America 23 percent, and in Africa 18 percent.

Covey's suggested fix is that each of us navigates forward through five waves of trust, creating a ripple effect and making trust as actionable as any other developmental effort. The five waves begin with self-trust, the confidence in core credibility, our character, and ourselves. Secondly, we should build relationship trust, increasing our trust accounts with others. The third wave is organizational trust, creating the synergistic structures, systems, and symbols of trust inside the firm and enjoying the intangible dividends that trust produces for companies. The fourth wave is about market trust and reputation, the promise of the brand. Finally, societal trust encompasses corporate responsibility and the contribution to society. This connects directly with the results of this year's global CEO study and the increased emphasis on corporate responsibility.

In the third wave, you can see the clear contrast between companies that trust their employees enough to fully empower them and those firms that still rely on rigid and confining control mechanisms due to a lack of trust. The contrast between behaviors in a low-trust company and a high-trust one are stark. In one, people manipulate or distort facts, withhold and hoard information, engage in the blame game, resist new ideas, spin the truth, and over-promise and under-deliver, and the energy level is low. In the other, information is widely shared; mistakes are tolerated; people are loyal to those who are absent, share credit, and are candid and authentic; there is high accountability; and you can feel the positive energy and vitality.

Assessing Today's Culture

After determining the behaviors required for future success (based on the strategy, mission, markets, history, and current leadership), the next step is to candidly assess the way things currently happen, the existing norms. What are the half dozen or so current norms, what behaviors get recognized in a positive sense and rewarded, and conversely, which ones are avoided? These are not the espoused or desired values, but are what actually happens every day. Once the list is developed, certain characteristics can be asterisked as being especially strong. Some examples of norms, neither good nor bad, are: people don't come to work on weekends; taking initiative on your own is expected and encouraged; "ask forgiveness not permission"; we don't resolve conflict with heated debates in public forums; we are very respectful and resolve conflict one-on-one in private; never bring more than one staff member with you to a high-level meeting; and the principal always leads the discussion; every meeting needs a written agenda and objectives; and we always start meetings on time, it's respectful.

Not surprisingly, in the view of the various teams at our forum, the list of current cultural attributes included items like *analytical, bureaucratic, risk averse, hierarchical, individualistic, dedication, hard work, inward focus, conflict avoidance,* and *turf-protecting.* As we discovered in our workshops—with the entire intact team in the room, including the unit's general manager or top leader—this can be a very sensitive exercise, especially if the group's leader isn't open to criticism and the need for change. We tried to preempt this potential problem by laying out ground rules at the outset calling for equal voices, candor, honesty, and straight talk.

In one of our forums, the senior team of our new consulting organization attended. As they diagnosed the current culture, they concluded that in assembling the team from several of the top-tier firms in the industry and even acquiring some firms intact, they did not have a well-defined current culture. The new business unit was an aggregation of experts and strong personalities from very different environments. The cultural action plan required that they develop a new culture from scratch.

Naturally, the gap between each of the desired behaviors and what exists today is the focus for cultural change. The technique we used was to try to uncover the root cause for each gap. What was it: a lack of skills; motivation; leadership role modeling; lack of top leadership belief in the new value, a new strategy, and a different set of required cultures; inappropriate rewards or incentives; or simply a time lag in developing the new norms that had been articulated?

Dominant Culture: Four Major Styles

Most firms don't have just one culture, but they do have a dominant corporate culture, even if local units or specific functions have different ones. And as the leader goes to shape a dominant culture, it would be useful to know which culture is most appropriate for the strategy of the firm, its stage of maturity, and its values. Geoffrey Moore, building on the prior work of William Schneider, David McClelland, and Abraham Maslow, concludes that there are four dominant corporate cultures, each proposing a different route to business success. The *competence culture* reinforces individual accomplishment and is focused on beating competitors by knowing the "best way" and then outperforming competitors using objective data and measures. The *control culture* follows well-articulated plans, objective measurements, and a high degree of accountability. Firms with this culture follow the credo of "plan the work and work the plan." The *collaboration culture* uses the power of teamwork, accomplishing company goals by working together, even beyond the barriers of the firm. Finally, the *cultivation culture* appeals to the motivation of self-actualization and to the creative expression of individuals.

Organizing the four dominant cultures into a two-dimensional landscape helps to illustrate the contrasts and choices available.

Figure 23.
Four Cultures Model

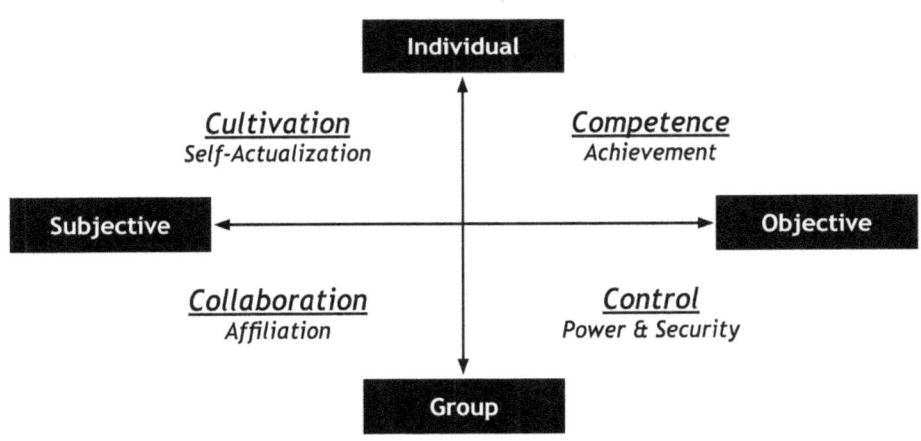

SOURCE: GEOFFREY MOORE

As the model demonstrates, each of these choices leans toward a bias in favor of individuals or groups on the y-axis, and on the x-axis, toward the left and right brains of subjective insights (the humanities) and objective data (the sciences). They present four different paths to success.

To go a level deeper, the competence culture is motivated by the drive for achievement, and the leaders of this culture demonstrate expertise and the proven ability to execute. The work environment is driven by high standards and a strong work ethic, the forced ranking of employees, high competitiveness, an intense pace, big bonuses for the stars, and firings for those who can't keep up.

By contrast, the control culture is motivated by power and security; the leader leads by authority and uses the formal hierarchical structure of the firm. In this environment, missions, goals, job descriptions, and tasks are all well defined with sufficient clarity so that people know what's expected of them. The downside can be rigidity and bureaucracy, especially risky in a dynamic environment. In many ways, this was the IBM of old.

In the collaboration culture, people make an effort to really know the others they work with. Data is not as important as the relationships among people, so interpersonal skills are valued highly, as is trust. The leadership role is not granted by authority but shifts to fit each situation. Rather than focus on individual performance, team performance and incentives are key.

The cultivation culture produces breakthrough innovations, with focus on individuals versus the team. Its strength lies in the ability of individual, charismatic, and visionary leaders to anticipate and react to the changes in the market. At the center of many venture start-ups are brilliant entrepreneurs who foster this culture. The structure is often undefined, loose, and adaptive. The major downside is the potential for arrogance and egotism. But it is the perfect culture for the emerging market.

So, the cultivation culture is ideal for the discontinuous innovation that Silicon Valley start-ups require. The competence culture is appropriate for sustained product performance, win-at-any-cost competitiveness. The control culture, with its focus on planning, discipline, and operational excellence, is ideal for sustained, reliable execution. Finally, the collaboration culture is ideal for those strategies that emphasize customer intimacy and the shaping of value nets of partners. Having the wrong dominant culture for a specific strategy, stage of company development, structure, or skill mix can ultimately lead to business failure.

A Prototypical Cultivation Culture: Google

The undisputed market leader in "Web-search" is Google, with 65 percent share, well ahead of Yahoo at 21 percent. The unique algorithm that provided the seed of their inspiration was ranking Web searches by the number of links to other Web pages. This is based on Metcalfe's Law, one of the fundamentals of network economics: value is proportional to the number of network nodes or users. Started in 1998, Google still maintains a small-company feel even though Googlers now number over twelve thousand. *Fortune* magazine ranks it as the best place in the United States to work, and it may be the only major firm to have a "chief culture officer," whose mission is to retain their unique company character. Of the four styles, it's clearly a cultivation culture, creating a fertile innovation environment.

Google's culture starts with their hiring policy, favoring ability and attitude over experience, hiring people who share an obsessive commitment to create "search perfection" and have a great time doing it. They recruit to hire people who are flexible, adaptable, and a good cultural fit, and not focused on titles and hierarchy.

The widely known and distinctive elements that define their workspace include:

- *Lobby décor*: piano, lava lamps, and live projection of current search queries from around the world.

- *Hallway décor:* bicycles and large rubber exercise balls on the floors, press clippings from around the world posted on bulletin boards everywhere.
- *Work space:* high-density clusters with three or four staffers sharing space with couches and dogs; it's fully pet friendly.
- *Equipment:* Googlers have high-powered Linux workstations on their desks. In its early days, desks were wooden doors mounted on two sawhorses; some are still in use within the engineering group.
- *Recreation facilities:* workout room with weights and rowing machine, locker rooms, washers and dryers, massage room, assorted video games, foosball, pool table, Ping-Pong, roller hockey twice a week in the parking lot.
- *Google café:* at the Googleplex headquarters, everyone eats in the Google café, which provides healthy, free lunches, plus dinner and breakfast; Google's most popular perk.
- *Snack rooms:* bins packed with cereals, gummy bears, M&Ms, cashew nuts, yogurt, carrots, fresh fruit, plus fresh juice, and make-your-own cappuccino.
- *TGIF:* weekly, company-wide get-togethers to welcome new employees, present recent Google news, and offer question-and-answer sessions hosted by top leaders.

Other creative perks include ski trips for team-building; a work-from-home policy via conference calling paid for by Google; a strong paternity-leave policy for dads, including family meals for the first few weeks; and reimbursement of up to $5,000 for hybrid or electric cars.

Of course, when companies are experiencing extraordinary market success, it's easy to be generous with perks, but the culture Google is developing is unique and entails much more than giveaways. Their core competitive advantage is not over-the-top perks; rather, it's Google's continuous adaptability. The culture supports it through its ultra-thin hierarchy, strong lateral communications, huge rewards for huge results, always putting users first, and small self-managed teams. For the software developers, a specific example is their "70-20-10" formula, which expects that roughly 70 percent of their time will be allocated to enhancing the base business, 20 percent to extending that core, and 10 percent to unbounded fringe ideas. This provides clear freedom for engineers to pursue their passions. Through relentless experimentation, their goal is to release ten to twelve new service offerings every quarter to remain the market leader.

Shaping and Nurturing a New Culture

After assessing the current culture and defining the new required one, the leader's final step is to lay out the specific actions to change the culture. As I said at the outset, culture is the most intangible, elusive, and perhaps most critical element of company success. There is clearly no "one-size-fits-all" since the approach that works is highly dependent on the existing culture in the firm and its intensity, the prowess of the leadership, the challenges of a new strategy, the mix and background of the employees, and the felt need for change; how serious is our current situation, and is it really worth the upheaval of our fundamental culture? There is no one way or formula to develop a new culture, but here are some ideas to consider:

1. Senior executive commitment and communications: Almost every large company has some vehicle or forum for the CEO to articulate issues of broad concern relating perhaps to company values, appropriate interpersonal behavior, dress codes, customer interaction, teamwork, or quality. It's often done via an internal TV network, a regular company publication, or a special executive briefing document. Writing about a firm's current culture and the need for change is a logical first step in clarifying the specific desired change and the rationale for it. While this communiqué may be necessary to remove any ambiguity, it is usually insufficient without many of the following supporting actions.

2. Using influencers and role models: Culture can be changed top-down, bottom-up, and from within. One approach is to explicitly identify the most influential people in the firm, with either positional or informal power. Use them as "apostles of change," reinforcing the need and rationale for change. Encourage them to recognize and publicize employees and accomplishments that highlight the desired new culture and behaviors. Using ceremonies and speeches to single out the new norm is very effective and appeals to our natural competitiveness. As an example, in IBM we created an annual Chairman's Award given to the entire sales team who achieved the most balanced performance, turned around a major customer in a hotly contested competitive environment, and sold them a full complement of IBM's most strategic hardware, software, and services—a triple play. That award often reinforced a dozen desired positive cultural attributes.

3. Symbolic actions: It's amazing how word of mouth spreads rapidly throughout a company, whether the grapevine is still centered around the analog water cooler or has been replaced with digital e-mail, speeding information flow much faster and further. IBM prided itself on its organic growth and internal hiring policies; unfortunately, that led to an inbred culture and a high degree of commonality and insularity. When Lou Gerstner arrived, he immediately hired a new team of senior executives to head the Finance, Human Resources, Communications, Marketing, and Legal functions, all with absolutely no IBM experience. This was like a cultural A-bomb and shook the very foundations of IBM's "promote-from-within" tradition. Immediately, every organization throughout the company began to assess their mix of "heritage IBMers" and new outside hires; the message was so strong.

Not long after, Gerstner held his first business unit review. IBM culture demanded that every meeting be supported with a graphics presentation, in those days with what we called "overhead foils" and later Freelance or PowerPoint. The value of a well-crafted chart was that it could be pitched in several ways depending on the speaker's emphasis and read of the audience. It was a crutch and fostered ambiguity. In the very first review, Gerstner stood up, turned off the projector, and said, "Let's just talk about your business and the challenges and opportunities you see." You could hear a pin drop. A major IBM tradition that had existed for decades was shattered forever, and without even convening a task force! He also reacted violently to every report or presentation that had unexplained acronyms or technical jargon, obfuscating the real message.

His other immediate actions became the stuff of legends as they spread like wildfire throughout the firm: business casual dress, not white shirts; alcohol served at customer education centers and IBM events; a new appraisal system; new leadership competencies; open offices versus walls even at CHQ; a new futuristic all-digital headquarters; and the list goes on—powerful cultural changes introduced early in his administration, each with an underlying and reinforcing message.

And it wasn't just that one IBM CEO who did it. As I was preparing to retire from IBM, the current CEO and chairman, Sam Palmisano, decided to visit a number of key IBM locations around the country and the world. As he, I, and a small entourage of corporate and group executives flew into our first location aboard one of the company planes, the largest stretch limo I've ever seen drove out onto the tarmac to meet us. It was gleaming white, just washed, and conjured up memories of prom night. But Sam wasn't amused. He had just issued a tough edict on the need for stricter expense controls, and this was clearly sending the wrong message. What made things worse was that at the Texas location we were visiting, nearly a thousand employees stood outside the main entrance to greet us and saw how the new CEO traveled: not a good symbol for expense consciousness.

At the next site visit in Boston a week later, three old unwashed SUVs were sent to meet us at the airport. The message had gotten out. Unfortunately, the employees weren't lining the sidewalk to greet us and witness our humble arrival, but they heard about it nonetheless.

4. Rewards, both intrinsic and extrinsic: In many firms, the reward system is a powerful lever for behavioral change. As Jack Welch once said, "a flat reward system is a big anchor to incrementalism. We want to give big rewards to those who do things, but without going after the scalp of those who reach for the big win but fail. Punishing failure ensures no one dares." Rather than give every manager a bonus in the 10–15 percent range, why not increase bonuses to 30–40 percent and give them to fewer people. Add group awards for team efforts and find creative ways to reward those who try to innovate, pursue new ideas, and experiment, even if they fail in their first market incursions. Find incentives to reward autonomy and independence and find the local heroes who are taking action that is compatible with the strategy.

Summary

Gary Hamel, this era's preeminent strategy consultant, captures the essence of this powerful ingredient of culture and its potential for corporate success. He asks future leaders to ponder, "How can we create work environments that inspire individuals to give their very best of themselves—that truly inspire human beings? In today's creative economy, value creation depends on the willingness of employees to bring their initiative, creativity and passion to work each day—human capabilities that are, quite literally, gifts."

SECTION IV:

Market Results and Reality

CHAPTER 12:

Market Results: A Strong Dose of Reality

*It is an immutable law in business that words are words,
explanations are explanations, promises are promises, but only
performance is reality.*
– Harold S. Geneen

*Measurement is the first step that leads to control and eventually
to improvement. If you can't measure something, you can't
understand it. If you can't understand it, you can't control it.
If you can't control it, you can't improve it.*
– H. James Harrington

No one likes to read critical reviews of themselves, their company, or their performance. It's especially frustrating for CEOs who believe they are boldly transforming their organizations as fast as is humanly possible, only to be criticized for being too slow or too timid. Fortunately, in this age of narrowcasting, we can easily find security analysts, pundits, and journalists who understand our point of view and report positively on it. There's always a core group of loyal customers and partners who, perhaps for self-interest, almost always support our strategy and programs. And, of course, there's an endless supply of employees who can spin the most dismal news and serve as a filter or smoke screen on reality. But in this self-deception lay the seeds of destruction.

Jim Collins suggests in his book *Good to Great* that confronting market reality, even the harshly bad news, can be an effective way to develop company strength. "In confronting the brutal facts, the good-to-great companies left themselves stronger and more resilient, not weaker and more dispirited. There is a sense of exhilaration that comes in facing head-on the hard truths and saying, 'we will never give up. We will never capitulate. It might take a long time, but we will find a way to prevail.'"

Crisis: The Catalyst for Change

Why does it always take a crisis to drive deep organizational change? In world politics, it was a few years ago that surging oil prices, deepening concern about carbon pollution, and worries about Russia's reliability as a gas supplier stimulated huge support and growth for Europe's nuclear and renewable energy industries. A similar phenomenon happened in the United States when gasoline prices topped $4 a gallon in 2008, finally making energy strategy a top national priority. In business, it's usually when a company is facing huge write-downs, massive layoffs, and plunging market values that the need for transformational change is suddenly triggered. Conversely, if, in the minds of employees, the firm faces no crisis, no threat of survival, then why should they make the strenuous effort to change? In fact, it's an accepted premise of change management that people have to want to change.

> *Why does it always take a crisis to drive deep organizational change?*

Successful firms don't wait for a crisis to occur. Their leaders find a way to proactively create the sense of crisis in advance by looking at presenting symptoms of future problems. They ask, "If left unchecked, what impact would today's business problems have on future company performance?" This is what we call "opportunity gaps," a topic we'll get to later in this chapter.

The second thing that successful firms do is measure against market results, not just period financials, or even financial trends. The insidious thing about focusing just on financials is that most standard financial measures and ratios are generated using internally generated data and look at how well the firm is performing against plan, often with little regard to how competitors and the market is performing. They also tend to look backward not forward, at lagging not leading indicators of performance. The CFO's team, who prepares the monthly, quarterly, and annual financial reports, often creates tons of data, rarely putting it in market context, unless asked. Comparing this month's revenues or profits with the plan or against last month's, last quarter's, or last year's may be useful data, but is grossly insufficient. That type of "internal comparison" thinking contributed to IBM nearly going out of business. Some argue that market share measures, for example, lack a level of integrity because the denominator, which defines the size of the market, can be manipulated to show higher or lower market share. But if top management puts the rigor into defining consistent market envelopes, maybe even sizing market data in a separate department, market-based measuring can be accurate, auditable, and enormously valuable.

This chapter occurs near the end of this book because we logically think of measuring the results of a strategy after it has been implemented. But in strategy formulation, confronting market reality is actually one of the early steps in the overall process because it can direct the team's focus to

> *Confronting market reality is actually one of the early steps in the overall process because it can direct a team's focus to the specifics of what needs changing.*

the specifics of what needs changing. As we create the strategy itself with its accompanying strategic intent, business model, and goals, we need to do an honest appraisal of how we're doing against them today, using external market comparisons. This is the cold dose of reality. As FDR once said, "We need the ability to face facts, even unpleasant ones, bravely." In business, that means ensuring we're monitoring the *right* market-based measurements, those that best indicate the viability of our strategy, and that's not just the revenue and expense numbers.

Before discussing performance and opportunity gaps, let's review some of the most successful techniques that are used to monitor market performance and that balance the strategic with the tactical.

The Balanced Scorecard

In the early 1990s, the quality-, customer-, and market-driven movements surged worldwide and the business world began to create strategic performance measurement systems beyond just traditional financial ones. One of the most widely used techniques for monitoring strategic goals was the *balanced scorecard*, originated by Drs. Robert Kaplan of the Harvard Business School and David Norton. It was a performance measurement framework designed to give company leaders a more "balanced" view of organizational performance. Even more than that, it was intended as a way to get firms to be more strategy focused. Kaplan and Norton describe it as follows:

> *The balanced scorecard retains traditional financial measures, which tell the story of past events, an adequate story for industrial age companies. These financial measures are*

*inadequate, however, for guiding and evaluating the jour-
ney that information age companies must make to create
future value through investment in customers, suppliers,
employees, processes, technology, and innovation.*

The balanced scorecard provides clarity on what top management believes are the company's top priorities, those worthy
of measurement on a par with the financials. Companies using
the balanced scorecard say it helps to clarify and reinforce the
strategy, make strategy more operational, link budget with strategy, and broaden the enterprise view to the importance of more
strategic measures.

The framework that Kaplan and Norton created portrays the
organization from four strategic perspectives: 1) learning, 2) internal business processes, 3) the customer, and 4) financials, and
develops metrics based on each of these categories. Naturally, every company is different and should develop a scorecard in a se-
quenced priority that aligns with its strategy, but here's what they
suggest.

The Learning and Growth Perspective

This area focuses on the intangible assets of an organization, mainly the internal skills and capabilities. This dimension
is concerned with jobs (human capital), systems (information
capital), and climate or culture (organization capital). It also
reflects the transition of firms becoming "knowledge based," requiring employees to be in continuous learning mode. As such, it
encompasses employee training, cultural attitudes related to self-
improvement, tutoring, mentoring, employee productivity, and
information sharing. Metrics can be put into place to guide managers to focus training funds where they can have the most impact.
It also includes technological tools, what the Baldrige criteria call

"high performance work systems." Structured well, these metrics can be a leading indicator of "brain drain." Like any other strategic action, an improvement in the learning and growth perspective requires spending that decreases short-term financial results, while contributing to long-term success.

The Business Process Perspective

This view monitors the internal processes that create and deliver customer value and help managers know how well their businesses are running. It focuses on the key processes and activities required for a company to excel at providing the value expected by the customers, delivering offerings that meet customer needs. Typically, they include operations management (by improving asset utilization, supply chain management, etc.), customer management (by expanding and deepening relations), innovation (by new products and services), and regulatory and social issues (by establishing good relations with external stakeholders). These can include both short-term and long-term objectives.

The Customer Perspective

Customer-perceived satisfaction, value, and loyalty are all leading indicators of performance. Poor performance from this perspective is a leading indicator of future decline, even though the current financial picture may look good. The metrics selected should measure both the value that is delivered to the customer, which may involve time, quality, performance, service, and cost, and the outcomes that result from this value proposition, such as customer satisfaction, market share, and loyalty. The value proposition can be centered on one of the three: operational excellence, customer intimacy, or product leadership, while maintaining threshold levels in the other two. So, if your primary source of differentiation is customer intimacy, then you might want to put the customer view at the top of your scorecard.

The Financial Perspective

This final area monitors whether the execution of a company's strategy is contributing to the bottom line. It represents the long-term strategic objectives of the organization, and thus it incorporates the tangible outcomes of the strategy in traditional financial terms. Obviously, what's measured depends on what stage of strategy a firm is in: rapid growth, sustain, or harvest. Financial measures for the growth stage will tend to focus on increased sales volumes, acquisition of new customers, and growth in revenue. The sustain stage, on the other hand, will be characterized by measures that evaluate how well the firm is managing its operations and costs, return on investment, and return on capital employed. Finally, the harvest stage will likely be based on cash flow analysis with measures of payback periods and revenue volume.

The Dashboard

When the balanced scorecard concept took hold in the mid-nineties, most enterprises weren't that digital. A decade later, nearly every employee had a PC on his or her desk and full access to the company intranet, and increasingly could view large screen monitors in conference rooms or public meeting spaces. Translating the one-page scorecard into an attractive, real-time, easy-to-understand digital graphic became the next logical step. The metaphor to a car or plane's dashboard was obvious. The main questions firms faced were: what do we measure, who should own each metric, who should be allowed to see it, and how do you cram so much information onto the small real estate of a computer screen and still provide enough information to be of value? One trend that began to unfold was different dashboards for different purposes. Following are examples.

An *executive dashboard* might be appropriate for a high-level or CEO view of everything you need to know about business performance on a single digital page. The format can be arranged in the order of the corporate goals or address the key perspective for each major stakeholder: shareholders, employees, customers, and partners. Or the format could simply display the balanced scorecard, with metrics for the customer, operations, organizational development, and finance perspectives. This view might be updated monthly or weekly.

A *sales dashboard* can be designed for the sales and marketing functions with performance indicators showing key sales trends such as sales for each major customer set, geography, or product line. It could feature key issues like competitive wins, customer returns, tie-in sales, or special promotions. This data could be refreshed weekly, daily, or in real time, depending on the data feeds.

A *production dashboard* can be invaluable for every manufacturing manager. It could incorporate all production-related metrics such as production costs, inventory levels, product movements, throughput, productivity, production employees, safety, deliveries, quality, and essentially everything you need to control and manage your production successfully. This could be updated in real time, hourly, daily, or by shift so that management remains constantly informed.

A *quality dashboard* can include a quality scorecard with standard metrics for each key Six Sigma or TQM measure and for each production site.

Measuring New Ventures

As we discussed in the chapter on innovation, internal ventures require a management system and discipline; it's just different than those required for mature businesses. When we launched our EBO effort in IBM, we decided that each Horizon 3 general manager needed to create and maintain a one-page summary report of the most important metrics and milestones for his or her business. To understand progress, we asked them to answer five questions:

1. *Have we assembled a strong core team?* (Staffing with strong leaders, core employees, key partners inside and out…)
2. *Are we making progress toward a clear strategy?* (Addressed a portfolio of initiatives, crafted well-defined strategies/plans, proposed new business model[s]…)
3. *Are we executing according to plan?* (Key milestones on market trials, key development milestones, partner commitments, customer acceptances, product launches…)
4. *Are we making progress in the marketplace?* (Mindshare, image, recognition as market leader, ahead or behind competition…)
5. *Are we achieving our business results?* (Customer reference accounts, expenses, and revenues…)

For one venture, Life Sciences, we were entering into a new business domain of biotech, genome research, and pharmacology, markets that most people had no idea we were in. As we sought to attract partners, customers, and resources to this exciting new team, we concluded that at the outset the two most important measures were to track the building of the core leadership team and to track the traction we were getting in the mainstream media regarding mindshare in this new business extension. The key metric: how many positive, negative, and neutral articles were being written about IBM's Life Sciences business in major publications. This was correlated with mindshare surveys that tracked our increasing awareness.

Another new venture was Pervasive Computing (PvC), and as the name suggests, it's about everywhere, or ubiquitous, computing. PvC encompasses very tiny—even invisible—devices, embedded in almost any type of object imaginable, including handheld devices, cars, tools, home appliances, clothing, and virtually any consumer good, all communicating through increasingly interconnected networks. Here our milestones were quite different. We had already developed the core technologies, but the Pervasive Computing solutions had to support much more than just the devices and the embedded technology. Our strategy was to promote open-source solutions and focus on three markets: software providers, services providers, and device manufacturers, with a specific strategy for each. End-user enterprises didn't buy the devices as stand-alones. They were embedded in other offerings. Our key actions included: 1) incorporating PvC support into IBM middleware like the Websphere Everyplace Suite; 2) partnering with at least four leading application providers; 3) gaining the support of the major telecom equipment manufacturers such as the top three cell phone manufacturers; 4) selling the core software platform to device manufacturers; and 5) creating a worldwide team of 150 sales support/product specialists. Each of these had clear metrics, target dates, and assigned owners, so the measurements were clear.

A Balanced Scorecard Dashboard for Ventures

In a consulting engagement for the federal government, our firm created a digital dashboard summarizing business performance and the key business indicators. The project was divided into five major phases, from business planning through business expansion, and the dashboard was tailored for each specific phase reflecting key tasks for that phase. For example, in Phase II, which was the business building phase, the most important tasks were associated with solicitations or RFPs for attracting business partners in three different areas, the overall staffing of the unit, and initial customer research.

In designing the dashboard, we created major sections reflecting each of those key project tasks and milestones. As figure 24 illustrates with sample data, at the center of the dashboard were the critical path timelines for partner solicitation. Tied directly to our project management system, they were color-coded in red, yellow, or green to highlight progress and where deadlines were being made or missed. At the top, we showed the staffing status compared to the plan: trend graphs showing how many acceptances and on-boards and a summary of the morale index. Another section began to build the customer view with the status of initial market research actions, followed by brand awareness trends, customer acceptances, and customer satisfaction at target bases and overall. In the financials section, we tracked expense burn rate, along with revenues and profits of a legacy business being superseded by this project, all against plan. And finally, the last section of the dashboard was devoted to major unresolved issues, the status, and actions planned.

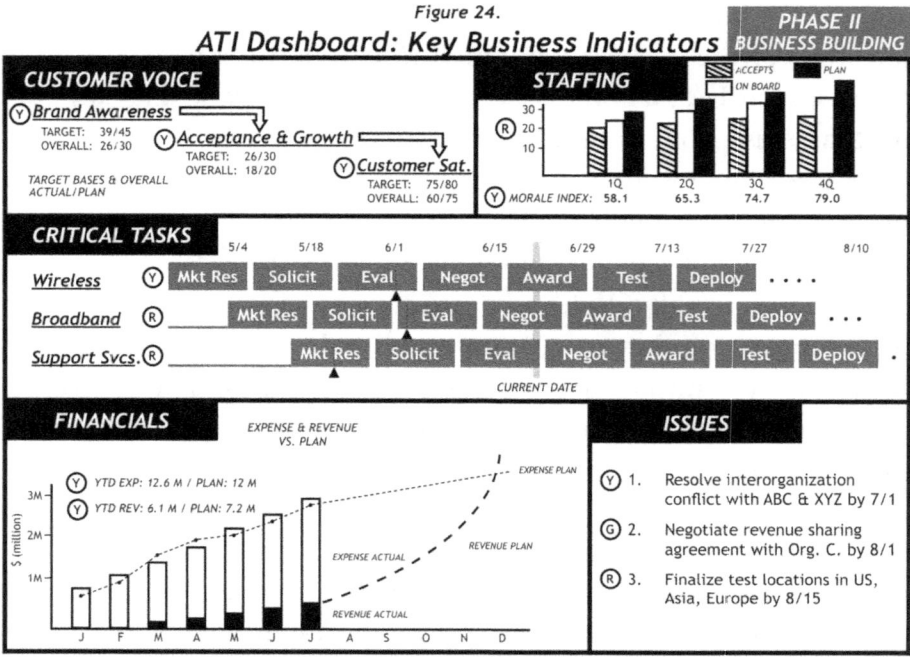

Figure 24.
ATI Dashboard: Key Business Indicators

While it sounds complicated, the visual was easy to understand and gave a snapshot of progress. It was displayed on each employee's desktop and in the team's war room, and was updated weekly or biweekly by data fed by each section's owner. Further details were available for all five sections of the dashboard for those who wanted to drill down deeper into the details.

Dashboard Benefits

Designed well, a digital dashboard can bring the benefits of forward-looking balanced strategic measurement systems to a business population that is used to seeing only lagging financials. Specific benefits include:

1. <u>Visibility</u>: All employees can view the dashboard to see what is important in their departments and the overall organization. It can also cast a spotlight on company-wide successes, challenges, and problems.
2. <u>Alignment</u>: It tracks projects to easily analyze information and gain a universal view of performance, aligning energy behind key objectives.
3. <u>Communication</u>: It gives visibility to company-wide emphasis programs—status of annual and strategic plans, physical readiness, customer satisfaction ratings, and any program areas that need highlighting.
4. <u>Decision support</u>: Quickly delivers real-time, detailed performance information to decision makers in key areas without the need for multiple meetings to identify issues.
5. <u>Integration</u>: It links performance measurement and strategic planning into an integrated management tool.

Performance Gaps

Market performance provides the brutal reality of an organization's current performance. By comparing actual performance against expected performance, we gain clarity and agreement among the leader team about what's off target. Performance gaps might include loss of market share, inability to launch new replacement products, declining customer satisfaction or increased churn, major quality issues, shrinking profit margins, defection of key partners to competitors, or loss of highly visible executives or key employees. These performance gaps are issues that are specifically within the purview of this organizational team or business unit and its leaders; we're not raising someone else's issues.

After developing a list of the most important issues perceived by management, the next step in the process is to zero in on the most critical one to be solved. It's not worth debating for a long time among the top two or three issues, because they're usually interrelated. Declining customer satisfaction levels, poor quality products, and spiraling warranty costs may all be directly related. The next step is to diagnose the root cause creating that specific shortfall in performance. For example, is the strategy flawed or unrealistic? Have market factors changed in some way because of competitor actions or industry forces? Has there been some other market shift unforeseen by the company? Or are the four execution factors out of alignment? For the specific tasks, is our structure causing or contributing to the problem, or our skill base or our culture? Again, the person leading the diagnosis must own the "gap"; it's his or her responsibility.

Opportunity Gaps

For most organizations, finding a major performance gap isn't too hard; in fact, there are usually so many that the challenge is deciding which one to focus on. But for some highly effective firms, current performance may be meeting or exceeding expectations or plans. To focus attention on needed changes, strategic leaders need to define opportunity gaps, missed opportunities in adjacent markets,

> *Strategic leaders need to define opportunity gaps, missed opportunities in adjacent markets, future markets to be created, or predictions of future problems.*

future markets to be created, or predictions of future problems as competitors strengthen or market fundamentals erode. One way to create the potential of a future problem is to artificially raise performance standards to address potential future market forces and then create a model to see what might happen to future revenues and profits. Scenario planning can play a role here in visioning alternative future states, some of which will adversely affect the success of the firm.

In IBM's case, we were constantly creating large opportunities for other firms in areas such as equipment leasing and financing, application software, and later computer services. Each of these grew to be enormous industries in their own right and very profitable opportunities. Missing the opportunity to shape, lead, or even participate in these were missed opportunity gaps.

Success can breed conservative behavior and risk avoidance, and that can lead to stagnation in a comfort zone. To break the cycle of inertia, strategic leaders need to define a pending opportunity gap with passion and with sufficient compelling evidence that it motivates the organization into action. One graphic that can help illustrate the opportunity gap is the market map. When the entire market is sized, including all the surrounding segments—distribution, services, financing, ancillary products/accessories, maintenance services, application, content, sales to other customer segments, etc.—an entirely different picture of market share will be portrayed. Dominance in one segment may be overshadowed by the miniscule share of the entire market. All the other unoccupied spaces or competitively occupied spaces are opportunity gaps.

As with performance gaps, identify opportunity gaps that are logically part of the mission or a logical extension of the mission of your unit or team.

Figure 25.

Market Reality

Performance Gap	Opportunity Gap
• Current Business Problems • Actual current performance against expected or desired performance	• Future business problems • Projected business performance against long-term expectations or strategic goals
Examples - Loss of market share - Declining profits - Customer dissatisfaction/churn - Quality or defect issues - Defection of key partners - Key people losses	*Examples* - Missed market opportunities - Future revenue & profit shortfalls - Declining competitive position - Major business risks due to market forces - Eroding business fundamentals

SOURCE: TUSHMAN & O'REILLY

A Classic Leadership Example

In 2001, Janet Perna was general manager of the four-thousand-person Data Management team, one of IBM's highest-ranking female executives and very well respected. She and her core leaders attended one of our first Strategic Leadership Forums. On the first evening breakout session, they agreed to define their most critical business problem and, like many other teams, called it a future "opportunity gap." The sense we had was that teams did so because they didn't want to admit they had immediate performance gaps. The next morning, Janet stood up to give the team readout in front of seven other business units and her peers. She surprised us all with her candor in admitting, "We've been kidding ourselves. We called this an 'opportunity gap,' but it's really a 'performance gap' that we've been trying to solve for a long time. We let ourselves get distracted and haven't solved it, and that's my fault as the team's leader." Janet gave the best demonstration of straight talk, accountability, and leadership! For the rest of the session, her team focused honestly and intensely on solving that performance gap, calling it what it was.

Summary

Defining the most critical performance or opportunity gap, through the reality of powerful market forces, can focus the attention of the entire leadership team. It is the starting point for mobilizing for strategic action. The more discomfort a team feels and the better understanding they have of how fleeting success can be, the more motivated they will become to confront strategic challenges and overcome the resistance to change. In the chapter ahead, we will discuss specifically how to apply the leadership model.

CHAPTER 13:

Applying the Leadership Model in the Real World

The dogmas of the quiet past are inadequate to the stormy present. The occasion is piled high with difficulty, and we must rise with the occasion. As our case is new, so we must think anew and act anew.
— **Abraham Lincoln**

Knowing is not enough; we must apply. Willing is not enough; we must do.
— **Johann Goethe**

Like any long-term improvement program, developing strategic competence is a challenging task. For operational executives who are working sixty to seventy hours a week putting out tactical fires, it just isn't realistic to think they'll want to spend time thinking about future challenges or crafting long-term preemptive market moves or learning new theories of strategy. In traditional leadership development, businesses often sent a lone executive to a one-week executive seminar, either in-house or to a university. Of course, half the time, the student would be on the phone calling back to the office trying to handle crises remotely. Another typical complaint is that most strategy conferences and classes just aren't that relevant to the specific current challenges facing the leader in his or her business. And even if the course is relevant and the entire experience is *"life altering,"* the one executive would come back on fire for change, enlightened about the power of strategic thinking, only to find his or her peers still trapped in the old paradigm, a frustrating experience. Driving organizational change through this approach is virtually impossible.

The solution to this dilemma was obvious to us. Send the entire intact team and their key support partners off together to work on a relevant strategic issue affecting their specific business unit. It's not strategic theory; it's really group problem solving and group growth. In the process, individual development occurs, but also the entire team works together, grows together, and reinforces each other as they return to work. A real sense of team commitment is developed. And by having multiple teams attend the same program together, better learning and a sense of peer competitiveness adds to the experience.

Strategic Leadership Forum: An Intensive Work Session

We can develop strategic mind-sets and processes in one of two ways: impassively teaching it from the front of a classroom or engaging the key players in an intensive workshop experience. Naturally, we chose the latter, and while the exact format may vary according to the needs of your specific firm, the format that follows was very effective for over a hundred of our business teams. We even used it for research scientists, our legal team, and several corporate staffs, a diverse set of workgroups.

The objective of the Strategic Leadership Forum (SLF) was to provide executive teams with an intense learning experience that would help them develop and apply skills in strategic leadership at the business unit level. We used creative approaches to stimulate better strategic insight and nurture innovation, techniques to mobilize their organizations for strategic execution, and focused on the practical application of these concepts to their existing business.

The forum was conducted off-site at Harvard Business School to reinforce the learning environment and to minimize office distractions. We devoted three or four very full days to the forum, minimizing time away from the business but still providing a full learning experience. That meant prework, evening work sessions, overnights, and no golf, recreation, or sightseeing! This was not a recognition event. We typically invited about seven or eight teams of ten to twelve executives each, so a full forum comprised eighty to one hundred participants. Each business unit comprised the general manager as leader of his or her team, the six or eight core leaders who were usually direct reports, and two or three leaders outside the organization but integral to the business mission. We insisted that every one of our most senior corporate officers, including the CEO, attend at least one forum so they could share in the learning experience and weigh in, when appropriate.

We typically conducted the program Sunday night through Thursday noon, so about forty hours of working and learning together. We emphasized at the outset that this was the start of a new leadership journey and a continued application of learnings after the forum was required for ultimate success.

The Format

The prework was pretty simple. We told each team member to come prepared to articulate an initial business issue that was impacting his or her business unit. We also asked participants to read a Stanford University case study that highlights the challenges and dynamics of organizational change.

To demonstrate the level of intensity of this program at the outset, the arrival evening program lasted two and a half hours after dinner. We began with an overview of the format, the objectives of the forum, and what was expected of each team.

A "Harvard B School" professor used the case study format to focus on the "Challenge of Change." The initial discussion was designed to discomfort the participants in order to help them understand the challenge of strategic leadership. We highlighted how fragile and fleeting success can be in competitive markets and how a history of previous success in no way guarantees the future.

The case study introduced the topics of innovation, leadership, and change, and stimulated class discussion about the sources of organizational inertia. Where does resistance come from, why, and how relevant is it to your firm today? We introduced the leadership model and then asked teams to move off into breakout sessions to discuss and gain initial agreement of the performance gap or opportunity gap needing to be closed.

Although it was late, we gave everyone a reading assignment to prepare for the Day 1 speaker and discussion the next morning.

Day 1 began with a strategy "wakeup-call" to shake teams out of their comfort zones, to awaken them to the critical need for revolutionary thinking and bolder moves. We retained one of a few world-class strategy facilitators, such as Gary Hamel or Clayton Christensen, to challenge the teams to think about bold revolutionary strategies in a nonlinear world. Where does wealth creation come from? Why does incremental thinking no longer work? How can we challenge the industry orthodoxies that are embedded in our business? We examined and discussed many examples of innovative business designs.

In the evening work session, each team defined their current business design—which customer, what unique value proposition, what scope, how they captured value and sustained it, etc.—and then developed four or five breakthrough ideas on how to radicalize that business design. Then we asked the teams to apply those ideas to the performance or opportunity gap identified. Finally, they were to prepare to present to the entire forum on Day 2. That gets competitive juices flowing.

Day 2 began with the readout from each team on their previous night's assignment. We then set the strategy aside for the moment and switched into execution mode, introducing the congruence model; the four critical elements of tasks, skills, culture, and structure; and how to perform an organizational diagnosis. Professors Tushman and O'Reilly used case studies and breakout sessions so that each team could begin the diagnosis of their unit's strategy execution and perform root cause analyses.

Because culture is so often misunderstood, we spent considerable time exploring how culture can be a powerful social control system within a business unit and how it is a critical source of either advantage or disadvantage in adapting to discontinuous markets. How can leaders actively shape their cultures to enhance execution and facilitate design of ambidextrous organizations? In case studies and breakout sessions, each team reached closure on a diagnosis and root cause analysis of their culture.

Day 3 zeroed in on how to manage the dynamics of organizational innovation. How can leaders design organizations that are not trapped by disruptive technologies or market forces; how do leaders really design an ambidextrous organization that pursues incremental and radical innovation simultaneously? Using more case studies and then breakout work sessions, each team revisited their new business model designs and tied the strategic and execution halves together. They then developed an action or solution plan.

Day 4 featured the final presentation of each of the seven or eight teams' solutions to their performance or opportunity gaps, from root cause analysis through radical new business designs. A closing wrap-up session reinforced the team commitments and our planned follow-up with them to monitor progress.

Many of the teams that attended our Strategic Leadership Forums were the two dozen Horizon 3 start-ups. As they presented their synergistic implementation plans, we began to see common elements, even though the venture business models were quite different. As the following figure, "Driving Emerging Growth", illustrates, the key tasks were related to market trials, segment managers, and engaging potential partners. The actions required in the culture and organization areas emphasized entrepreneurship and portfolio disciplines. And the skills area focused on breakthrough thinking and market insight.

Figure 26.

Driving Emerging Growth

- Assemble core team: Critical skills/leadership/segment managers
- Focus skills: Domain expertise, strategy, marketing, business development, technology
- Competencies: Breakthrough thinking, market insight

People & Skills

Critical Tasks

Organization Structure

Culture

- Create core offering
- Complete market map
- Select target segments/ focus areas
- Identify range of market trials to test market uncertainties
- Assign segment managers
- Launch market trials, adapt/ terminate trials
- Develop core partnerships
- Engage VC's

- Create entrepreneurial environment
- Engage external players early & aggressively
- Tie incentives to effective portfolio management, investment milestones
- Manage failure constructively

- Create standalone business unit
- Create market advisory board
- Develop internal management system
- Adopt portfolio management disciplines

SOURCE: IBM STRATEGIC LEADERSHIP FORUM

Benefits

The benefits of the Strategic Leadership Forums cannot be overstated and bear repeating. In our view, although it was both an individual and team development experience, we achieved greater individual learning because of the team context. There was immediate application of content to very relevant business needs. The shared learning experience created a fast start in mobilizing for strategic execution and kicked off a shared journey to apply learnings over time. And all got to practice and strengthen their individual leadership skills of listening, collaborating, thinking, creating, and deciding. Our strat-

> *The shared learning experience created a fast start in mobilizing for strategic execution and kicked off a shared strategic leadership journey to apply learnings over time.*

egy executives in each unit said they often gained newfound respect; they were no longer regarded as irrelevant "blue-sky thinkers" in a sea of tacticians.

Obviously, the model can really be applied in several ways, as a group workshop along with other peer organizations as we discussed, as the format for a stand-alone strategic planning work session for one unit, or as an instant strategic assessment of an organization as discussed below.

Instant Diagnosis of Strategic Health

In one of my first consulting engagements, I visited a very large organization with fifty thousand employees, one you could barely get your arms around. In a series of interviews with a half dozen corporate execs, I used the strategic model as a simple interview guide and asked the following open questions.

1. Tell me about your firm's vision for the future or your strategic intent. How is it communicated; where can employees find it? Has it changed or been updated recently? How do you know if employees support it?

2. How do you determine what's happening in the marketplace? Do you use online or in-person surveys with customers? With prospects? How often do you do this? How much primary versus secondary market research do you do? How do you know what competitors are doing in your key markets?

3. How does innovation happen here? Is there a specifically defined process? Is it centralized, dispersed, or a combination of both? Does it work well? How do you measure its impact?

4. How would you describe the core business model? Are specific customer markets segmented and targeted? What do you do differently or better than others in this space? What are the profit trends over the past three or four years?

5. How do you monitor and ensure that critical actions or tasks get done? Who does the monitoring, and how rigorous is it? What are the ramifications of missing deadlines?

6. How are you organized? How well is the current structure working? What conflicts occur?

7. How strong are the people skills compared to your industry and key competitors? How do you know? How do you attract new people with required skills?

8. How would you describe the culture here, the way things get done? Does the current culture contribute or hinder successful performance of the firm?

9. What are the principal ways you measure the firm's performance both short and long term? And how is the firm performing short and long term?

The Assessment

The honest direct answers to these questions can be truly insightful. In the client engagement I referenced, we determined the following in just a day or two:

1. The company vision was well crafted, conveyed motivational purpose, was clearly articulated and widely communicated, and resonated well with employees. It appeared on posters and in-house company publications. A subset of it was on signage outside corporate HQ. We scored it a (+).

2. The approach to gathering market insights was very inadequate. A mainstream survey was done by an outside research organization every other year or so. It captured data about current business performance as perceived by current frequent customers, with no view to future or unmet needs. It did compare some data to competitors. But overall, customer perception analysis had been outsourced. We rated this area a (-).

3. There was no innovation system of any kind. Innovation, like efficiency and quality, was encouraged by management, but there was no explicit program, measurements, or processes in place to drive innovation. A strategic programs directorate at corporate was developing a few new venture businesses, but without success to date. To their credit, a failed attempt at innovation was recognized in a positive way. Overall, we rated this area a (-).

4. The business model for the firm was not clearly defined, although it could be easily derived from the current business operations. The major issue was the firm's inability to sustain differentiation, revenues, and profits over the long term. The strategic control point concept was not being deployed. Rated (-).

5. Multiple rigorous task-monitoring procedures were in place to track major company initiatives. A color-coded grading scheme was widely used so that projects falling behind schedule could be immediately identified. The protective culture of the firm, however, did not strictly enforce missed deadlines with consequences, so major projects were often late, costing millions in lost revenue or savings. Rated (-).

6. The structure of the core business was well defined and effective; a lightweight structure for new internal ventures was just

being developed. Reliance on outside partners was commonplace and well controlled. Rated (+).

7. Overall company skills assessment or focus on core competencies was nonexistent. The firm did almost no hiring of external professionals or executives, so the company tended to be inbred. Rated (-).

8. The culture of the enterprise could be characterized as strong, proud, patriotic, disciplined, paternalistic, inflexible, risk averse, slow, short-term oriented, and insular. But those were impressions gained from interviews, unsupported by specific employee opinion survey data or other research. Rated (-).

9. Regarding performance and opportunity gaps, the firm focused almost exclusively on current year performance. Although the current performance was on track to meet the annual financial plan, those plans were set at conservative levels with little growth due to recent weak performance. The company was in a long downhill decline in terms of revenue, profits, and resources. No mainstream process existed to identify opportunity areas for growth. Rated performance gap (+); opportunity gap (-).

That assessment was sufficient to recommend a broad-based initiative to become a more strategically focused enterprise for the CEO to develop and launch.

Developing Strategic Competence in Leaders

The focus of this book is on developing strategic competence in enterprises, with the hope that the leaders executing the process will enhance their SQ, or strategy quotient, along the way. However, a more proactive leadership development approach might be warranted, explicitly adding it to executive development plans, performance plans, and incentive plans. Techniques worth considering include a rotation program for line executives through corporate strategy or executive exchange programs with another enterprise with strong strategy competence.

As you assess your own strategic competence and those of other leaders you are developing, consider the following questions, using the strategic framework as a template:

1. Strategic competence: Overall, are you striving to master *strategic competence?* As a leader, are you helping to make your company or department more strategy-focused, balancing short-term tactics with long-term strategies? Are you encouraging employees to invest time and energy to achieve future organizational success? Have you put strategy education activities and strategy work sessions in place? Is your focus on creative strategic *thinking*, not analytical strategic *planning?*

2. Strategic intent: Do you lead through inspiration? Have you inspired a shared vision or strategic intent, a motivational view of the ideal future for your department, business unit, or company? Do you know what your firm, its leaders, and its employees feel truly passionate about, enough for them to take the initiative and work to the best of their abilities? Beyond articulating a strategic intent, are you actively demonstrating it and reinforcing it in everyday behaviors?

3. Market insights: Are market insights the inherent driving force behind your team's actions? Since the ultimate purpose of any business is to create customer value, have you put a continuous scanning and feedback process in place to monitor shifts in customer value and market trends? Are you sensing change ahead of competitors, and are you preempting them? Do you understand where profits are migrating to in your industry and where competitors are repositioning themselves?

4. Innovation: Innovation is about finding new and better ways to create and deliver customer value, both evolutionary continuous improvement *and* bold revolutionary change. Are you creating and actively supporting a firmwide commitment to innovation? Have you put innovation processes, investments, measurements, and incentives in place? Are you empowering everyone to play a role in innovation and encouraging dissenting voices for breakthrough thinking?

5. Business design: Business models are the new competitive battleground. Are you helping to create and clarify a unique business design that specifically articulates which customer sets have been selected, your unique value proposition, and the scope, value capture, and strategic control approaches of your business? Have you explicitly defined the *digital* business design, leveraging information and the Internet? Is your business model dynamic, a living strategy that constantly explores and tests alternative designs in the market? Are you making effective strategic choices to lead, play in, or exit a market using fact-based data and an effective decision-making process?

6. Critical tasks: Are the most important tasks explicitly tied to the strategy and business design you're executing? Are you executing strategy with urgency, intensity, and synergy? Is there a process that focuses your organization on the very few, top priority strategic tasks? Is there clarity on accountability and firm deadlines, even as you adapt and experiment in the market? Is strategy execution being reinforced by pursuing tasks, skills, culture, and structure synergistically? Given the rapid pace of the new economy, is your execution timing effective, and are you executing with market speed?

7. Structure: Structure encompasses a lot more than the organization chart. It entails the processes, linkages across functions and companies, the management system, rewards, and the informal organization. Have you created the best structure inside your area of the business to execute the new strategy and best respond to market forces? Is your structure appropriate for the new empowered, fast, and innovative cultures required for success? Is it flat, fluid, and networked or predominantly hierarchal? Are all the key elements of structure including measurements and linkages aligned?

8. Skills: Are you continuously attracting, developing, deploying, motivating, and retaining top talent to execute your strategy? Have you developed a realistic assessment of your firm's recognized strengths, skills, and core competencies as perceived by your customers? Are you leading from those strengths? Are you attracting fresh talent like the Millennials, using recruitment 2.0 approaches and the Web? Are you managing the diversity of your workforce, recognizing different motivations that exist? Are you empowering your team, investing in their growth, and treating them as your most valuable asset?

9. Culture: Are you shaping and reinforcing a high-performance culture? Have you assessed the gap between current culture and what's necessary for success? Have you selected and developed an overall culture appropriate for the firm's stage of maturity and new strategy: control, competence, collaboration, or cultivation? Are the attributes of the new culture explicit, such as *empowered, fast, innovative, collaborative, customer centric,* and *continuously adaptive*? Is trust a core element of your culture? Are you taking specific actions to develop and reinforce culture, such as incentives, role models, hiring guidelines, and symbols?

10. Measurements: Are the performance gaps and opportunity gaps clearly defined, the subject of shared focus, and widely known inside your organization? Are market-based measurement systems in place and used to guide performance? Does the measurement system encompass more than short-term financials? Is it balanced with measures of strategic progress including market share, customer value, employee measures, and longer-term strategic milestones? Does it adequately compare your progress with industry trends and key competitors?

Summary

As current and future leaders develop their fundamental business skills, these strategic competencies will be most valuable over the course of their careers, regardless of the responsibilities they are given or the ultimate level to which they rise. *Strategic thinking* and *strategic competence* will distinguish the high-performance leaders of the new economy in this world of unpredictable chaos. Whether the organization is a complex global enterprise, a small local non-profit or a major division of government, the parallels are clear. Power has become democratized, steadily dispersed to the end points, extending all the way to the customer. As leaders, the only strategy that makes sense is one that is innovative, collaborative, and responsive to the challenges of the market. We need to create a strategy and culture that enables:

- *adaptability* through continuous market insight, flexible business design, and a fluid supporting structure,
- synergy among all the component pieces of strategy and execution, and
- *market reality* focused on customer-perceived value to monitor true progress and enduring success.

We also need to leverage the continuing advancements in information and network technology to help us achieve the agility, synergy and strengthened linkages to the market. And finally, as strategic leaders, we need to continually demonstrate and reinforce our most positive values: inspiring, encouraging, and enabling others with a culture that especially embraces trust. As the great English poet Alexander Pope reminded us, "*Act well your part, there all the honor lies.*"

Acknowledgments

As anyone who's written a book knows well, it is rarely a one-person task, more often the collective effort of dozens of people. I want to express my deep appreciation to all who helped me through this creative process. The concept for the book was formed in my mind years before I wrote it. My wife, Susanne, encouraged me to take the plunge and finally commit it to paper, and above all others, she deserves my deepest gratitude. She was a terrific source of insight and encouragement, and suffered through the reading of multiple drafts, making valuable suggestions at every stage. Her decades at IBM as an eyewitness to many of the major events, and her role in IBM Leadership Development added a perspective few others have. And, by paving the way with her own successful book, she guided me through the intricacies of the publishing process.

In IBM Corporate Strategy, I was surrounded by a terrific team of bright, energetic, and creative people. The strategy team was a blend of handpicked "high-potentials" from IBM's business units, rotational assignees from around the world and external hires from top-tier consulting firms and leading high-tech companies. Collectively, they had the intellectual savvy, passion, and determination to challenge IBM's deeply held traditions, explore radical new ideas, and enable the historic transformation. Joel Cawley, Dan McGrath, and Florence Hudson were some of the core members of that team, employees who Lou Gerstner called "the unsung heroes." Many of the most valuable insights in this book came from this group, who built on each other's ideas, engaged with strategy experts within and beyond IBM, and advanced our breakthrough thinking. Mike Giersch, my longtime colleague and IBM's current VP of Strategy, was especially helpful as a personal adviser and editor. He made countless suggestions for improvement and updated many IBM facts. Another of my strategic collaborators, Steve Haeckel, former Director of IBM Strategic Studies, helped stretch my thinking with his vision of the *adaptive enterprise*, the title of his best-selling book. Steve has been a persuasive advocate of the "sense and respond" model of management, a good friend and adviser in this project.

During my long career, I was also fortunate to have a succession of exceptional managers and teachers, who modeled key elements of strategic leadership. My boss during the last phase of my career, Bruce Harreld, was especially supportive as coach and colleague. He empowered our strategy team to pursue the most creative solution to every issue we confronted and helped us to architect the strategic leadership model.

After creating the first draft of *THINK Before You Leap*, I circulated it among a group of business colleagues at our consulting firm American Telemanagement Solutions. Many are seasoned executives who've lived through their own experiences in global companies striving to remain competitive, firms like Coca-Cola, Allied Signal, and AT&T. John Gammino and Rich Kusmer invested countless hours reading the manuscript and providing invaluable feedback. Another longtime associate, Joe Pine, prolific author of *The Experience Economy, Mass Customization,* and *Authenticity* made numerous insightful suggestions.

To all, please accept my most heartfelt thanks and appreciation.

Douglas Sweeny

Bibliography

Ackoff, R. L. *The Democratic Corporation: A Radical Prescription for Recreating Corporate America and Rediscovering Success.* New York: Oxford University Press, 1994.

Arthur, B. *Increasing Returns and Path Dependence in the Economy.* Ann Arbor: University of Michigan Press, 1994.

Baghai, M., S. Coley, and D. White. *The Alchemy of Growth: Practical Insights for Building the Enduring Enterprise.* London: Orion Business, 1999.

Barabba, V. P. *Meeting of the Minds.* Boston: Harvard Business School Press, 1995.

Barker, J. A. *Discovering the Future: The Business of Paradigms.* Lake Elmo, Minnesota: ILI Press, 1988.

Bartlett, C.A., and S. Ghoshal. *Managing Across Borders: The Transnational Solution.* Boston: Harvard Business School Press, 1991.

Block, Z., and I. C. MacMillan. *Corporate Venturing: Creating New Businesses within the Firm.* Boston: Harvard Business School Press, 1993.

Burgleman, R. A., and A. Grove. "Strategic Dissonance." *California Management Review* 38, 2 (Winter): 8–28.

Christensen, C. M. *The Innovator's Dilemma: When New Technologies Cause Great Firms to Fail.* Boston: Harvard Business School Press, 1997.

Collins J. *Good to Great: Why Some Companies Make the Leap, Others Don't.* New York: Harper Collins Publishers, 2001.

Covey, S. M. R. *The Speed of Trust: The One Thing that Changes Everything.* New York: Free Press, 2006.

Covey, S. R., and J. Colosimo. *The Four Disciplines of Execution*. New York: Simon and Shuster, 2004.

Drucker, P. E. *Managing in Turbulent Times*. New York: Harper & Row Publishers, 1980.

Fingar, C.T. *National Intelligence Council, Global Trends 2025: A Transformed World*. U.S. Government Printing Office, 2008.

Friedman, T.L. *Flat, Hot, and Crowded: Why We Need a Green Revolution - and How It Can Renew America*. New York: Farrar, Straus and Giroux, 2008.

————. *The Lexus and the Olive Tree: Understanding Globalization*. New York: Farrar, Straus and Giroux, 1999.

Garvin, D. A., and L.C. Levesque. "Meeting the Challenge of Corporate Entrepreneurship." *Harvard Business Review* (October 2006).

Gerstner, L. V. Jr. *Who Says Elephants Can't Dance? Inside IBM's Historic Turnaround*. New York: HarperBusiness, 2002.

Haeckel, S. H. *Adaptive Enterprise: Creating and Leading Sense-And-Respond Organizations*. Boston: Harvard Business School Press, 1995.

Hamel, G. *Leading the Revolution*. Boston: Harvard Business School Press, 2000.

————. *The Future of Management*. Boston: Harvard Business School Press, 2007.

Hamel, G., and C. K. Prahalad. *Competing for the Future*. Boston: Harvard Business School Press, 1994.

Harreld, J. B., C. A. O'Reilly, and M. L. Tushman. *Dynamic Capabilities at IBM: Driving Strategy into Action*. California Management Review, University of California Berkley, 2007.

Kotter, J. P., and J. L. Heskill. *Corporate Culture and Performance*. Boston: Harvard Business School Press, 1992.

Liker, J. K. *The Toyota Way: 14 Management Principles from the World's Greatest Manufacturer*. New York: McGraw-Hill, 2005.

Maxwell, J. C. *Leadership Gold: Lessons I've Learned from a Lifetime of Leading.* Thomas Nelson, 2008.

McGrath, R. G., and I. M. McMillan. *The Entrepreneurial Mindset.* Boston: Harvard Business School Press, 2000.

Moore, G. A. *Crossing the Chasm: Marketing and Selling Technology Products to Mainstream Customers.* New York: HarperBusiness, 1991.

————. *Living on the Fault Line: Managing for Shareholder Value in the Age of the Internet.* New York: HarperCollins, 2000.

Negroponte, N. *Being Digital.* New York: Alfred A. Knopf, 1995.

Pine, B. J. II, and J. H. Gilmore. *The Experience Economy: Work Is Theatre and Every Business a Stage.* Boston: Harvard Business School Press, 1999.

Porter, M. E. *Competitive Advantage: Creating and Sustaining Superior Performance.* New York: The Free Press, 1985.

————. "What Is Strategy?" *Harvard Business Review* (Nov–Dec 1996).

Prusak, L., and E. Matson. *Knowledge Management and Organizational Learning: A Reader.* Oxford Management Readers, 2006.

Prusak, L., and D. H. Davenport. *Working Knowledge: How Organizations Manage What They Know.* Boston: Harvard Business School Press, 1998, 2000.

Senge, P. *The Fifth Discipline: The Art and Practice of the Learning Organization.* New York: Currency Doubleday, 1990.

Sherman, S., and N. M. Tichy. *Control Your Destiny or Someone Else Will.* New York: Doubleday, 1995.

Slywotsky, A. J., and D. J. Morrison. *The Profit Zone.* New York: Random House, 1997.

————. *Profit Patterns.* New York: Random House, 1999.

————. *How Digital Is Your Business?* New York: Crown Business, 2000.

Tapscott, D. *The Digital Economy: Promise and Peril in the Age of Networked Intelligence.* New York: McGraw-Hill, 1995.

Tapscott, D., D. Ticoll and A. Lowy. *Digital Capital, Harnessing the Power of Business Webs.* Boston: Harvard Business School Press, 2000.

Tushman, M. L., and C. A. O'Reilly III. *Winning Through Innovation: Leading Organizational Change and Renewal.* Boston: Harvard Business School Press, 1997.

Zakaria, F. *The Post-American World.* New York: W.W. Norton & Company, 2008.

www.ingramcontent.com/pod-product-compliance
Lightning Source LLC
Chambersburg PA
CBHW071402170526
45165CB00001B/154